Oxford Studies in European Law

General Editors: Paul Craig and Gráinne de Búrca

THE ENFORCEMENT OF EU LAW

This book is dedicated to my parents, Ellen and Peter.

It could not have been written without the support and supervision of Gráinne de Búrca and Christian Joerges, whom I greatly admire.

Many other friends and colleagues helped me, including Tommi Ralli, Cormac Mac Amhlaigh, Andrew Glencross, Robert Schütze, Paul Nemitz, Flemming Reislev, Kenn Skau Fischer, Niels Fenger, Bruno de Witte, Jacques Ziller, Joanne Scott, Deirdre Curtin, Aitor Erce, Tom Daly, Pontus Rendahl, Ben Johnston, Ann-Marie Enggard, Elisabeth Day, and Marsha Green.

I am grateful to my husband Martin and our daughter Elisabeth for their patience and encouragement.

The Enforcement of EU Law

The Role of the European Commission

STINE ANDERSEN

OXFORD
UNIVERSITY PRESS

OXFORD
UNIVERSITY PRESS

Great Clarendon Street, Oxford OX2 6DP
United Kingdom

Oxford University Press is a department of the University of Oxford. It furthers the University's objective of excellence in research, scholarship, and education by publishing worldwide. Oxford is a registered trade mark of Oxford University Press in the UK and in certain other countries

First Edition published in 2012
Reprinted 2014

Published in the United States of America by Oxford University Press
198 Madison Avenue, New York, NY 10016, United States of America

British Library Cataloguing in Publication Data
Data available

Library of Congress Cataloging in Publication Data
Data available

ISBN 978-0-19-964544-2

CONTENTS

GENERAL EDITORS' PREFACE

This book tackles the familiar subject of the European Commission's role in enforcing compliance with EU law.

Although it begins with a thorough and up-to-date treatment of the public enforcement procedure under Articles 258–260 TFEU, including the operation of the pecuniary penalty payment, the book then moves beyond conventional dimensions of the subject. Exploring a little-known aspect of the Commission's attempts to expand its power in this respect, the author examines how the Commission tried unsuccessfully to strengthen its powers of enforcement by means of secondary legislation in fields such as fisheries and internal market policy.

Having concluded for reasons of institutional balance and constitutional principle that the Commission's direct enforcement powers can only be expanded through treaty amendment, the author moves on to consider the relationship between the Commission's role in enforcing compliance with EU law and its role in executing, implementing, and guiding the interpretation of EU norms. In a series of interesting chapters, Andersen probes the notions of 'implementation' through the exercise of executive power, and the 'management of compliance' through what she describes as 'auxiliary enforcement procedures' devised and used by the Commission. These include the establishment of expert groups on the implementation of particular EU laws and directives, and the use of peer review to monitor implementation.

This is an original work which functions both as a study of the Commission's use and adaptation of its powers as an institutional actor within the EU framework, and as an exploration of the nuances of the meaning of compliance and enforcement in the context of EU law. The book usefully combines careful legal analysis and interesting case studies with insights and questions drawn from political and regulatory theory.

It should be of considerable interest to students and scholars of EU law, as well as to political scientist students and scholars interested in questions of compliance and enforcement.

Paul Craig
Gráinne de Búrca

TABLE OF CASES

The Court of Justice of the European Union

TABLES OF LEGISLATION

Annual reports and related reports

Communications

Decisions

Directives

Opinions

Press releases

Proposals

Protocol

Regulations

Report

Resolutions

Written questions (European Parliament)

Other

Introduction

1. Introduction to the Book and its Central Themes

This book undertakes a comprehensive analysis of the Commission's general role in supervising member state compliance with EU law.[1] The Commission works within the legal framework set under the general EU infringement procedure stipulated in Articles 258 and 260 of the Treaty on the Functioning of the European Union (TFEU). On several occasions the Commission has proposed that its enforcement powers against the EU member states should be amended either through a comprehensive treaty amendment or on an ad hoc basis.[2] Against this background, this book describes the Commission's general powers of enforcement and investigates how the Commission manages its role in promoting compliance with EU law. The enquiries driving this book are of pressing importance given that the Commission has voiced criticism of the general infringement procedure's viability in a European Union of 27 member states covering numerous and substantially different policy areas.

This introductory chapter outlines the arguments made throughout the book and fleshes out their major implications for the understanding of the Commission's role in ensuring member state compliance with EU law. In addition, it explains in more detail the research methodologies applied in the book and how the work is situated within literature on international law and international relations, governance, and constitutional law.

Chapter one provides a general introduction to EU enforcement. It discusses the political dimension of EU enforcement and the member states' call for flexibility, which is reflected in the design of the general infringement procedure. The chapter proceeds to set out some of the particular challenges

[1] Article 17(1) TEU. [2] See chapter four.

EU legal tools such as directives and regulations pose from an enforcement point of view. Albeit to various degrees, most types of binding regulatory instruments leave margins of discretion to the member states. This leeway reflects basic political choices made at treaty level. The degree of regulatory detail and, in turn, member state discretion is a result of concrete political compromise between the Commission and the 'EU legislators', ie, the Council and the European Parliament.[3] At the same time, differences in the member states' legal and administrative systems may also necessitate procedural and/or substantive leeway in the transposition phase. As a consequence, compliance can often materialize in different ways. These aspects are important in order to fully appreciate the specific enforcement powers granted to the Commission. These are examined in chapters two and three. Likewise, they are central to the analysis of this book's other central themes. Chapter four: the Commission's proposals that it should be empowered with supplementary enforcement powers on an ad hoc basis. Chapter five: the functional overlap between implementation tools and enforcement tools, and, finally, chapter six on the piecemeal emergence of non-binding, auxiliary enforcement powers. Even though they are non-binding they have significant policy implications.

The arguments made throughout this book have five major implications for the understanding of the Commission's role in ensuring member state compliance with EU law.

First, whereas the Commission pleads that its enforcement powers should be invigorated using arguments of effectiveness, chapter one maintains that the EU as well as the general infringement procedure is shaped by political conditions underpinning the EU polity more broadly. In this regard, effectiveness is a deceptive notion. Specifically, it tends to obscure the very central point that EU enforcement is a dialectical exercise in which the Commission and the Court of Justice help refine and flesh out EU law. The notion of responsive enforcement allows for further discussion of whether it is viable to establish stronger Commission powers of enforcement at this point in time. Moreover, it helps explaining how such powers would change the dynamics in the relationship between the member states and the Commission and ultimately between the member states and the EU. Finally, the

[3] With the ratification of the Lisbon Treaty the Council and the European Parliament became co-legislators in most policy areas. The Commission also plays a central role given its legislative monopoly according to the ordinary legislative procedure (Art 294 TFEU) and given that where the Council acts on a proposal from the Commission, it may with certain exceptions only amend the proposal by acting unanimously (Art 293 TFEU).

notion of responsive enforcement helps unpack the policy implications of the burgeoning non-binding enforcement measures in the EU.

Second, with the ratification of the Lisbon Treaty the Commission obtained general powers to supervise compliance with EU law and not merely EC law. Moreover, the Lisbon Treaty invigorates the Commission's tools against repetitive infringements and provides the Commission more easily employable tools against failure to transpose directives. Chapters two and three take stock of the general EU infringement procedure established under Articles 258 and 260 TFEU. Chapter three provides an analysis of the sanctioning mechanism established by the Maastricht Treaty in view of pertinent case law. Moreover, it analyses the amendments of the general EU infringement procedure made in the Lisbon Treaty, including their practical implications and extra-legal significance. The aims of the chapters are two-fold. They account for the procedural steps involved and appraise the procedures against contemporary international law and international relations enforcement theory. It is demonstrated that the general EU infringement procedure is primarily based on non-coercive problem-solving. Nonetheless, it proposes a durable procedural framework for awarding pecuniary sanctions. Specifically, it is argued, Article 260 TFEU remedies some of the drawbacks that characterize sanctions against states according to international lawyers. Thus, the Commission has been granted a tool to put sustained pressure on defaulting member states while maintaining them in a process towards compliance and this in a manner which does not undermine the treaty regime's legitimacy.

Third, this book examines the Commission's quest for ad hoc enforcement powers in secondary legislation. Neither lawyers nor political scientists have addressed this issue in a comprehensive manner. The case studies undertaken in chapter four demonstrate how the principle of attributed powers has indeed served as a constitutional safeguard barring the Commission from obtaining direct enforcement powers. More generally, the case studies illustrate that although the fundamental distribution of powers and competences is established in the Treaty on European Union (TEU) and the TFEU, significant struggles for influence between the national level and the EU level are negotiated between the Council and the Commission. The analysis in chapter four frames the legal question of ad hoc infringement procedures as a matter of institutional balance. It argues that the Commission's proposals examined in the chapter have broader implications not only for the horizontal, but also for the vertical division of EU powers. Moreover, it is maintained, because the Commission's current tools of enforcement mirror basic constitutional choices any question pertaining to the Commission's enforcement powers against member states should be decided upon in primary legislation, ie, in the EU Treaties. The analysis and the arguments made in chapter four, as well as the appraisal of the general EU infringement procedure in chapters two and three, add to an understanding as to why the Commission retreats to other instruments available to it, such as non-binding, auxiliary enforcement mechanisms and implementation measures. The difficulties in amending the treaty basis have been discussed thoroughly by political scientists. This book provides concrete examples of the strategies the Commission can employ in order to make up for the unsuccessful attempts to gain stronger enforcement powers in secondary legislation.

Fourth, this book addresses the functional overlap of enforcement tools and implementation tools and the broad range of instruments available to the Commission in ensuring member state compliance despite not being part of its enforcement powers *sensu stricto*. It argues that notwithstanding the doctrinal distinction between enforcement and implementing measures, there are effective points of functional overlap between enforcement powers and certain types of implementing tools, which are lawful in that they serve other aims and purposes than enforcement. Since the Commission employs these measures in conjunction with the general infringement procedure or as an alternative with the less discernible aim of ensuring compliance, a comprehensive EU enforcement analysis must take note of them. Potential legal constraints on the Commission in employing these instruments, such as the proportionality principle, are among the questions raised in chapter five. In addition, the chapter explores how any perceived misuse may have ramifications for the Commission's ability to have certain implementation powers established in secondary law.

Against this backdrop, chapter six proceeds to describe and analyse a range of tools available to the Commission other than the general infringement procedure. Article 70 TFEU establishes a mechanism whereby the Council may, on a proposal from the Commission, adopt peer-review arrangements. Thus, the member states can conduct 'objective and impartial evaluation of member state implementation' in collaboration with the Commission. The legal basis to establish ad hoc procedures is aimed at policies concerning an area of freedom, security, and justice, in particular in order to facilitate the full application of the principle of mutual recognition. The mechanism displays potential to install and strengthen mutual confidence in the respective member state systems. This trust may indeed be a prerequisite for effective implementation and enforcement of the very sensitive obligations established within an area of freedom, security, and justice. However, non-binding peer-review also creates a potential slippage of competences and accidental institutional empowerment. Particularly, the procedure may bring about a degree of *de facto* interpretation of EU law as well as normative adaptation. Article 70 TFEU mirrors a more general turn to less formalized means of enforcement in the EU. They supplement the Commission's general and binding enforcement powers. Significantly, they provide more easily employable ways of ensuring compliance and of gathering information on whether and how EU law is being applied. The described turn is illustrated by the themes described and analysed in chapter six on: 'The Emergence of Non-Binding, Auxiliary Enforcement Procedures: Expert Management of Compliance with Directives'. In addition, the Commission has established a comprehensive system of cooperation between the Commission and national authorities with a view to facilitating practical solutions to compliance problems. The fifth contribution this book makes to existing literature on centralized enforcement is to account for these turns and to assess the implications they have for the overall understanding of the Commission's role in ensuring compliance with EU law and how it executes its task as guardian.

Chapter seven ties together the themes of the various chapters. It argues that the enforcement stage shares many features with earlier steps in the legislative process. These include flexibility and deliberation. Finally, it places the Commission's enforcement function in the broader context of the EU policy process.

2. Research Methodologies

Enforcement of EU law has received considerable academic attention in recent years by lawyers and political scientists alike. Early legal literature includes Audretsch's monograph *Supervision in European Community Law* first published in 1978.[4] Since then, a number of journal articles and monographs have examined the general EU infringement procedure or specific procedural aspects thereof.[5] Recent publications by Borzsák,

[4] HAH Audretsch, *Supervision in European Community Law* (Elsevier Science Publishers BV, 1986).

[5] A Barav, 'Failure of Member States to Fulfil their Obligations under Community Law' (1975) *Common Market Law Review* 12, 369–83; A Evans, 'The Enforcement Procedure of Article 169 EC: Commission Discretion' (1979) *European Law Review* 4:6, 442–56; A Dashwood and

Hedemann-Robinson, and Wennerås look closer at enforcement of EU environmental law.[6] Rawlings, Harlow, and Smith have raised pertinent questions pertaining to good governance, transparency, and legitimacy in relation to the general infringement procedure and the Commission's exercise of powers.[7] More recently, lawyers and political scientists alike interested in enforcement of EU law have also drawn on the work of international law scholars Chayes and Chayes.[8]

R White, 'Enforcement Actions under Articles 169 and 170 EEC' (1989) *European Law Review* 14, 388–412; G Tesauro, 'Remedies for Infringement of Community Law by Member States' in W van Gerwen and M Zuleeg (eds.), *Sanktionen als Mittel zur Durchsetzung des Gemeinschaftsrechts* (Bundesanzeiger, 1996); M Mendrinou, 'Non-Compliance and the European Commission's Role in Integration' (1996) *Journal of European Public Policy* 3:1, 1–22: AJG Ibáñez, 'A Deeper Insight into Article 169' *Harvard Jean Monnet Working Paper* 11/98; AJG Ibáñez, *The Administrative Supervision and Enforcement of EC Law* (Hart, 1999); M Zürn and C Joerges (eds.), *Law and Governance in Postnational Europe, Compliance Beyond the Nation-State* (Cambridge University Press, 2004); R Rawlings, 'Engaged Elites: Citizen Action and Institutional Attitudes in Commission Enforcement' in C Kilpatrick, T Novitz, and P Skidmore (eds.), *The Future of Remedies in Europe* (Hart Publishing, 2000); MA Theodossiou, 'An Analysis of the recent response of the Community to non-compliance with Court of Justice judgments: Article 228(2) E.C.' (2002) *European Law Review* 27, 25–46; P Wennerås, 'A New Dawn for Commission Enforcement under Articles 226 and 228 EC: General and Persistent (GAP) Infringements, Lump Sums and Penalty Payments' (2006) *Common Market Law Review* 43, 31–62; I Kilbey, 'Financial Penalties under Article 228(2) EC: Excessive Complexity?' (2007) *Common Market Law Review* 44, 743–59; Stine Andersen, 'Procedural Overview and Substantive Comments on Articles 226 and 228 EC' (2008) *Yearbook of European Law* 27, 121–66; L Prete and B Smuders, 'The Coming of Age of Infringement Proceedings' (2010) *Common Market Law Review* 47, 9–61; M Smith, 'Inter-institutional Dialogue and the Establishment of Enforcement Norms: A Decade of Financial Penalties under Article 228 EC (now Article 260 TFEU)' (2010) *European Public Law* 16, 547–70; and I Kilbey, 'The interpretation of Article 260 TFEU (ex 228 EC)' (2010) *European Law Review* 35, 370–86.

[6] L Borzsák, *The Impact of Environmental Concerns on the Public Enforcement Mechanism under EU* (Wolters Kluwer, 2011); P Wennerås, *The Enforcement of EC Environmental Law* (Oxford University Press, 2007); M Hedemann-Robinson, *Enforcement of European Union Environmental Law: Legal Issues and Challenges* (Routledge-Cavendish, 2006); and M Hedemann-Robinson, 'Article 228(2) EC and the Enforcement of EC Environmental Law: A Case of Environmental Justice Delayed and Denied? An Analysis of Recent Legal Developments' (2006) *European Environmental Law Review* 15:11, 312–42.

[7] R Rawlings and C Harlow, 'Accountability and Law Enforcement: the Centralised EU Infringement Procedure' (2006) *European Law Review* 31, 447–75; M Smith, *Centralised Enforcement, Legitimacy and Good Governance in the EU* (Routledge Cavendish, 2009); and M Smith, 'Enforcement, Monitoring, Verification, Outsourcing: the Decline and Decline of the Infringement Process' (2008) *European Law Review* 33, 777–802.

[8] A Chayes and AH Chayes, *The New Sovereignty: Compliance with International Regulatory Agreements* (Harvard University Press, 1995). See not least L Borzsák, *The Impact of Environmental Concerns on the Public Enforcement Mechanism under EU* (Wolters Kluwer, 2011). For a literature survey see, eg, WC Bradford, 'International Legal Compliance: Surveying the Discipline'

2.1 *Procedural law, governance, and constitutional theory*

Chapters two and three provide descriptive procedural accounts of Articles 258 and 260 TFEU. The analyses will inevitably touch upon some of the same elements that the general literature on the infringement procedure addresses. However, chapters two and three also contain comments on legitimacy and efficiency. The main theoretical emphases in those chapters are on EU constitutional law and governance theory. In chapter five it is argued, among other things, that there are points of functional overlap between enforcement and certain EU implementing measures. This type of argument, as well as the arguments made in the chapter on the legality of establishing infringement procedures in secondary law, touch upon the distribution of powers to (and between) the EU institutions as well as the legality of delegation of power, ie, two central issues in EU constitutional law. These questions have not hitherto been addressed comprehensively in EU enforcement literature. The legal questions ultimately concern the institutional structure of the EU polity. Because the analyses touch upon the distribution of powers, the case studies in turn become illustrative of the interplay between law and politics in practice. Another theme of this book is that of non-binding multilateral enforcement mechanisms established on an ad hoc basis. This type of enforcement method raises some of the same questions often addressed in new governance literature. For instance, who sets the agenda, which actors shape the policy outcomes, and are the policy outcomes *de facto* binding or norm-setting?

2.2 *Political science, international relations, and international law theory*

The legal foundations of the EU are 'instruments of international law'.[9] Moreover, the EU has been conceptualized within the terms of various frameworks including that of public international law. Still, significant differences persist in terms of organization and authority and the EU is most often referred to as a third and *sui generis* entity. It is the special features of supranationalism such as the institutionalization of autonomous legislative, judicial, and executive powers which set apart the EU from

ExpressO Preprint Series Working Paper 2004/331. For a survey and analysis see H Koh, 'Why Do Nations Obey International Law?' (1997) *Yale Law Journal* 106, 2599–659.

[9] AA Levasseur and RE Scott, *The Law of the European Union—A New Constitutional Order* (Carolina Academic Press, 2001), 341.

existing international and regional organizations. Moreover, the EU enforcement regime has departed from classical international law principles of reciprocity and the treaty signatories cannot legitimately resort to retaliation as a means of enforcement.[10] However, one of the general problems of enforcement of international law is a lack of ultimate authority and this is also a constraint on EU enforcement. A *real*-political account of compliance within the EU would stress the lack of ultimate means of enforcement in situations of irreconcilable conflicts of interest, the member states' right of secession and the, if not legal, *de facto* option of retaliation.[11] None of these arguments explain in full the relationship between the EU and the member states and the various and interrelated factors, which may be decisive for (non-)compliance. These include the degree of normalization of the *acquis*, perceptions among member states that EU membership is critical (or not) to their economic and security situation, and short-term and long-term self-interests. Such factors are politically and legally speaking complex and have potential both to cement and challenge the EU's claim of supremacy and thus authority. They are, however, not unique to the EU, but at varying degrees apply to other treaty regimes.

Lawyers and students of international relations concerned with enforcement of supranational and international law have considered a range of themes pertinent also to enforcement of EU law, including deterrence, norm internalization, persuasion, the significance of long-term and short-

[10] Advocate General Léger notes in his opinion in C-5/94 *Hedley Lomas* [1996] ECR I-2553, point 27: 'Nothing is more alien to Community law than the idea of a measure of retaliation or reciprocity proper to classical public international law.' See also joined cases C-90 and C-91/63 *Commission v Luxembourg and Belgium* [1964] ECR 625, at 631; case 325/82 *Commission v Germany* [1984] ECR 777, para 11; and case 232/78 *Commission v France* [1979] ECR 2729, para 9.

[11] Some scholars argue that the member states have recourse to retaliation based on principles of general international law if another member state consistently refuses to comply. HAH Audretsch, *Supervision in European Community Law* (Elsevier Science Publishers BV, 1986), 139. B de Witte notes that notwithstanding the amendment of Art 260 TFEU which now encompasses sanctions, 'there may even today remain room for residual recourse to general international law remedies in the context of the application of the EC Treaty'. B de Witte, 'Rules of Change in International Law: How Special is the European Community?' in LANM Barnhoorn and KC Wellens (eds.), *Diversity in Secondary Rules and the Unity of International Rules* (Martijn Nijhoff Publishers, 2005), 301, with reference to C Tomuschat, 'Völkerrechtliche Schadensersatzansprüche vor dem EuGH' in JF Baur, P-C Müller-Graff, and M Zuleeg (eds.), *Europarecht—Energierecht—Wirtschaftsrecht. Festschrift für Bodo Börner zum 70 Geburtstag* (Heymanns, 1992), 441–58. G Bebr contends that the European Community (now the EU) is instead governed by a 'principle of solidarity'. G Bebr, 'Agreements Concluded by the Community and their Possible Direct Effect: From International Fruit Company to Kupferberg' (1983) *Common Market Law Review* 20, 35–73.

time interests, the extent to which federal experiences can be relied upon, and the difficulties in assembling and maintaining the support necessary for sanctions to work. One condition in particular underpins international law in general as well as the EU. That is the lack of a definitive central authority, or an identifiable sovereign, to back legal commands by force vis-à-vis sovereign states.[12] Therefore, this book and especially chapters two and three concerning Articles 258 and 260 TFEU draw on important literature on international law and international relations. In addition, it draws on a number of studies published by political scientists on enforcement of EU law and the closely related question of compliance. Indeed, some of the most instructive literature available on these topics comes from political science and also international relations theory.[13] For instance, hypotheses on state behaviour and compliance help explain the function of the legal procedures, which govern dispute settlements and their method of conciliation. Likewise, understanding the political underpinnings of the procedures and consequently how they shape outcomes constitute useful background knowledge for an appraisal of alternative and auxiliary methods of enforcement.

Based on different premises, compliance schools offer different explanations to why states comply with international obligations. Rationalists ascribe compliance to national benefits. States will thus comply if it optimizes their self-interests. Followers of the 'process school' argue that compliance is

[12] See discussion by C Joerges in M Zürn and C Joerges (eds.), *Law and Governance in Postnational Europe. Compliance Beyond the Nation-State* (Cambridge University Press, 2005), 262–6. See also R Fisher, *Improving Compliance with International Law* (University Press of Virginia, 1981), 11–12.

[13] See, eg, PM Haas, 'Compliance with EU Directives: Insights from International Relations and Comparative Politics' (1998) *Journal of European Policy* 5:1, 17–37; T Börzel, 'Non-compliance in the European Union: Pathology or Statistical Artifact?' (2001) *Journal of European Public Policy* 8:5, 803–24; J Tallberg, 'Paths to Compliance: Enforcement, Management, and the European Union' (2002) *International Organization* 56:3, 609–43; T Börzel, 'Guarding the Treaty. The Compliance Strategies of the Commission' in T Börzel and R Cichowski (eds.), *State of the European Union Volume 6: Law Politics and Society* (Oxford University Press, 2003); J Tallberg, *European Governance and Supranational Institutions—Making States Comply* (Routledge, 2003); D Beach, 'Why Governments Comply: An Integrative Compliance Model that Bridges the Gap between Instrumental and Normative Models of Compliance' (2005) *Journal of European Public Policy* 12, 113–42; G Falkner, O Treib, M Hartlapp, and S Leiber, *Complying with Europe: EU Harmonisation and Soft Law in the Member States* (Cambridge University Press, 2005); R Thomson, R Torenvlied, and J Arregui, 'The Paradox of Compliance: Infringements and Delays in Transposing European Union Directives' (2007) *British Journal of Political Science* 37:4, 685–709; and R Thomson, 'Opposition through the back door in the transposition of EU directives' (2010) *European Union Politics* 11:4, 577–96.

the result of continuous communication among the treaty parties, etc.[14] The dominant strands within the compliance theory, namely enforcement and managerial approaches, find their roots in rationalist and constructivist theories, respectively.[15] Of late, and increasingly so, scholars concerned with enforcement seem to acknowledge that the theoretical frameworks can indeed complement each other.[16] Clearly, both schools of thought face theoretical difficulties per se. For instance, we do not know all the elements a state includes in its compliance calculus (if it has one) and the relative value it attaches to them and at what time. The basic difficulties in assessing the right parameters for understanding how a rational state conceives its own interests constitutes another difficulty in rationalism and with that its strict belief in deterrence and punishment. This is exacerbated by the fact that states and not least EU member states participate in treaty regimes that deal with many different policy matters that are directly and indirectly connected. Moreover, as pointed out by Müller,[17] moral discourse constitutes an observable characteristic of much negotiation. However, it is difficult to account for in a rationalist conceptualization, which assumes that all actors pursue self-interested optimization applying means-end rationality. The managerial approach explains regime participation and compliance with interdependency arguments. Thus it starts from the idea that the mere ability to exercise sovereign rights (or to form ad hoc coalitions) constitute inadequate means to achieve national policy objectives such as economic growth and national security. Consequently, the significance of maintaining a good relationship with the other treaty parties, and thus avoiding loss of status through loss of reputation, constitutes an impetus for compliance.[18]

[14] For an overview of major theoretical compliance theories see H Koh, 'Why Do Nations Obey International Law?' (1997) *Yale Law Journal* 106, 2599–659.

[15] J Tallberg, 'Paths to Compliance: Enforcement, Management, and the European Union' (2002) *International Organization* 56:3, 609–43, with references. This is a rough classification. Subtler distinctions differentiate between realism, enforcement theory, rational choice, managerial theory, and constructivism, etc. See WC Bradford, 'In the Minds of Men: A Theory of Compliance with the Laws of War' *ExpressO Preprint Series Working Paper* 2004/290, 2.

[16] J Tallberg, 'Paths to Compliance: Enforcement, Management, and the European Union' (2002) *International Organization* 56:3, 609–43 with references.

[17] H Müller, 'Arguing, Bargaining and All That: Communicative Action, Rationalist Theory and the Logic of Appropriateness in International Relations' (2004) *European Journal of International Relations* 10:3, 395–435, 401. See also O Young, *Compliance and Public Authority: A Theory with International Implications* (Johns Hopkins University Press, 1979).

[18] A Chayes and AH Chayes, *The New Sovereignty: Compliance with International Regulatory Agreements* (Harvard University Press, 1995), 123.

The compliance models each comprise elements that cannot categorically be referred to as one of the two and it is difficult to obtain full empirical support for either of the theoretical strands and their practical significance. The managerial model appears to consider communicative action a central method to obtain compliance. Yet, it cannot be considered strictly within a constructivist framework. According to Chayes and Chayes, states have an incentive to comply in order not to be excluded from international regulatory regimes. The argument can be rephrased in rationalist terms and fear of exclusion or loss of good standing thus conceived as an infringement deterrent. Their enforcement model itself suggests when cost/benefit calculations would make a state not comply. For example, in treaty regimes characterized by a significant degree of integration, a minor infringement or infringements in areas of low politics is unlikely to entail significant consequences for a state; even more so when it comes to undetected infringements.[19]

Generally and specifically in the EU context, conflicts can be legitimate confrontations of legal and political viewpoints. Even in the enforcement phase it is difficult for a regime to address such disputes in a coercive manner without putting its own legitimacy at risk. Significantly, within the limits of law the member states can and will represent and advocate national interests during all policy phases and also in relation to enforcement and before the Court of Justice. Interestingly, Chayes and Chayes recognize the significance of state preferences although they consider managerial problems a main reason of non-compliance. The answer they propose in the former case is negotiation, but also persuasion. As will be discussed in more detail, the Commission surely applies strategies in attempts to convince member states to change behaviour throughout infringement proceedings and, where relevant, prior to launching proceedings. This type of means of exerting influence and affecting a state may be coined persuasion.[20] However, such action is not a one-dimensional exercise in which the Commission can insist on correct behaviour. This is for two reasons. Often non-compliance can be remedied in numerous ways, which the member state itself defines. Moreover, where non-compliance is rooted in a dispute over the law, the Commission has no authoritative

[19] See also GW Downs, D Rocke, and PN Barsoom 'Is the Good News about Compliance Good News for Cooperation?' (1996) *International Organization* 50:3, 379–406.

[20] JT Checkel, with reference to Habermas, discusses strategies and attempts to convince as elements of persuasion as opposed to arguing in 'Why Comply? Constructivism, Social Norms and the Study of International Institutions' *ARENA Working Paper* 99/24.a

power of interpretation. These aspects of enforcement of EU law are discussed in chapter one.

The analyses made throughout the book chapters explore different aspects of the Commission's powers to ensure member state compliance with EU law under the general EU infringement procedure and through other and supplementary mechanisms. The concluding chapter ties together the arguments as well as the insights generated by the different theoretical approaches and it discusses more generally the role of the Commission when it comes to enforcement of EU law.

1

The Commission's General Powers of Enforcement

1. Introduction

According to Article 4 TEU, the member states shall take any appropriate measure, general or particular, to ensure fulfilment of the obligations arising out of the Treaties or resulting from the acts of the institutions of the Union. That is to say, the member states have the primary responsibility of giving effect to EU law.[1] The Commission in turn ensures the application of the Treaties and of the pursuant measures adopted by the institutions. This is one of its core tasks according to Article 17(1) TEU. In many international law regimes, non-compliance is a matter to be addressed and settled between treaty-signatories. One of the distinct features of the EU treaties system by contrast is thus the existence and function of the Commission with autonomous powers to monitor member state compliance and to engage judicially binding sanctions. The Commission's general enforcement powers stipulated in Articles 258 and 260 TFEU are analysed in more detail in chapters two and three. These procedures contain a number of successive administrative and judicial phases and the Commission has to observe rather extensive procedural guarantees in favour of the member states. The procedures are protracted. A system with an autonomous supervisor was already established in the Treaty establishing the European Coal and Steel Community (the ECSC Treaty) signed in

[1] See, eg, answer given by Commissioner Fischler on behalf of the Commission to European Parliament Question P-1052/2000. J Ziller, 'Separation of Powers in the European Union's Intertwined System of Government—A Treaty Based Analysis for the Use of Political Scientists and Constitutional Lawyers' (2008) *Il Politico*, Vol LXXIII, No 3, 133–79. Available at SSRN: http://ssrn.com/abstract=1398902.

Paris in 1951.[2] In comparison with the current procedure, the ECSC Treaty provided the High Authority with more easily employable enforcement powers. Significantly, after hearing a member state the High Authority could itself record an infringement. The member state in turn had recourse to the Court to challenge the decision within two months of the decision's notification. Whereas the High Authority was entrusted with extensive enforcement powers, not to mention obligations,[3] and was authorized to exert command-based enforcement, the Commission's relatively weaker powers according to Article 258 TFEU have altered its bargaining powers and require it to be more responsive towards the member states. At the same time, the Commission enjoys a wide margin of discretion under the general EU infringement procedure. This enables the Commission to establish enforcement priorities and to engage in a widespread practice of reaching friendly settlements with member states.

This chapter provides a general introduction to the general EU infringement procedure and discusses the political conditions underpinning it. It proceeds as follows. First, it outlines Article 88 ECSC. It then proceeds to discuss the in practice important tradition of friendly settlements according to Article 258 TFEU. Significantly, the Commission can employ its general enforcement powers as a tool to pursue policy objectives more broadly. The penultimate section examines the political conditions underpinning the general infringement procedure's modus operandi. It is argued that the relatively weak powers of the Commission and the drawn-out procedure reflects member state governments' call for flexibility in the implementation phase and hence in the enforcement phase. At the same time, the weaker powers of the Commission are offset by its wide margin of discretion. The Commission shall exercise this discretion with political tact. Significantly, its task is to ensure the delicate balance between supervising compliance, on the one hand, and sustaining diplomatic relations with the individual member states, on the other. Both dimensions are important per se and for the EU policy process more widely. The Commission is thus handling a complex, semi-political, semi-legal task. This is reflected in the notion of effectiveness discussed in the final section.

[2] The treaty expired on 23 July 2002.

[3] As a consequence of the binding nature of reasoned opinions under Art 88 ECSC, proceedings could be initiated against the High Authority for failure to act. See, eg, joined cases 7/54 and 9/54 *Groupement des Industries Sidérurgiques Luxembourgeoises v High Authority* [1954–1956] ECR 175.

2. Infringement Procedures in the ECSC, the (E)EC, and the EU—From Binding to Investigatory Powers of Enforcement

One of the significant institutional inventions of the ECSC Treaty was the High Authority composed of nine members designated for six years and chosen for their general competence. Notably, the members should exercise their functions in complete independence. The High Authority had, among other things, responsibility for assuring the fulfilment of the purposes stated in the ECSC Treaty under the terms thereof.[4] According to Article 88 ECSC, the High Authority was empowered to make a decision concerning a member state failure to comply after the state had been offered an opportunity to present its views. The member state could then appeal the decision to the Court's plenary jurisdiction within a period of two months from the notification thereof. Although subject to judicial review, the procedure thus granted the High Authority potent enforcement powers against the member states. This part of the procedure was complemented by a three-step semi-political, semi-judicial phase whereby the High Authority could intensify the pressure on defaulting member states. Specifically, if the member state failed to take steps for the fulfilment of its obligation within the period fixed by the High Authority, or if its appeal had been rejected, the High Authority could, with the concurrence of the Council acting by a two-thirds majority: (a) suspend the payment of sums which the High Authority may owe to the state in question under the present Treaty; (b) adopt measures or authorize the other member states to adopt measures so as to correct the effects of the delinquency in question. There is, however, no case of sanctions having actually been imposed according to Article 88 TFEU.[5] In principle, an appeal to the Court's plenary jurisdiction could be brought against the decisions taken in application of paragraphs (a) and (b) within two months following their notification. Finally, if these measures should prove inoperative, the High Authority would lay the matter before the Council. The procedure was, in the wording of the Court of Justice, '. . . a procedure far exceeding the

[4] Article 9 ECSC.

[5] J Usher, *EC Institutions and Legislation* (Longman, 1998), 50; and T Hartley, 'Constitutional and Institutional Aspects of the Maastricht Agreement' (1993) *The International Quarterly* 42:2, 213–37, 228.

rules heretofore recognized in classical international law to ensure that obligations of States are fulfilled'.[6]

The European Commission was originally modelled upon the High Authority. The Commission's general enforcement powers stipulated under the EEC Treaty (one of the Treaties of Rome from 1957) were, however, rather different and consisted of two separate procedures addressing member state failure to fulfil an obligation under the EEC Treaty (and later the EC Treaty) and failure to comply with a judgment of the Court of Justice respectively. Both procedures consisted of a two-stage administrative phase and a judicial phase. Under those procedures, the power to determine member state rights and duties and to appraise member state conduct rests with the Court of Justice exclusively.[7] Thus, whereas the High Authority had powers to declare infringements, the Commission was—and still is—best described as an institution with investigatory powers.[8] Moreover, the procedure established under the ECC Treaty with subsequent amendments does not contain a mechanism that can correct the effects of non-compliance comparable to that under the general ECSC infringement procedure.[9]

The Maastricht Treaty in force from 1993 amended the general (E)EC infringement procedure for the first time.[10] The two procedures stipulated in Articles 258 and 260 TFEU had so far been largely identical. Now the Commission was empowered to request the Court of Justice to impose a lump sum or a penalty payment on a member state in addition to a declaration that the member state has failed to comply with a ruling under Article 258 TFEU.[11] The Lisbon Treaty amended the general

[6] Case 20/59 *Italian Government v High Authority* [1960] ECR 325.

[7] Article 19 TEU and C-393/98 *Ministério Público, António Gomes Valente v Fazenda Pública* [2001] ECR I-1327, para 18.

[8] The Commission, however, does not have general powers to make investigations within the member states and it is thus dependent on the replies and cooperation of the member states when investigating cases. This limitation is to some extent remedied by the fact that member states are required to cooperate in good faith with the enquiries of the Commission pursuant to Art 258 TFEU and to provide the Commission with all the information requested for that purpose. See, eg, C-82/03 *Commission v Italy* [2004] ECR I-6635, para 15; and C-221/08 *Commission v Ireland* [2010] ECR I-1669, para 60. This obligation has been established with reference to the member states' duty of loyalty stipulated in Art 10 EC (now repealed and replaced, in substance, by Art 4(3) TEU).

[9] Article 88 ECSC.

[10] [1992] OJ C 224 (consolidated version 1992).

[11] A lump sum is a 'single sum of money that serves as complete payment'. See *The American Heritage Dictionary of the English Language* (4th edn, Houghton Mifflin, 2004). Penalty payments

infringement procedure for the second time since the original Treaty establishing the European Economic Community first entered into force.[12] It did so in three respects. First, the Commission is no longer obliged to issue a reasoned opinion under Article 260 TFEU before bringing a member state before the Court of Justice for failure to take the measures required to comply with a ruling under Article 258 TFEU. Second, the Commission may request that the Court of Justice awards a pecuniary penalty already during the procedure stipulated in Article 258 TFEU for failure to fulfil an obligation to notify measures transposing a directive adopted under a legislative procedure. Third, in doing so, the Court of Justice's discretion in deciding on the amount of pecuniary penalties has been restricted. Thus, in line with the Lisbon Treaty's desire to enhance the efficiency of the European Union,[13] the Commission can employ sanctions against non-compliant member states more rapidly. In addition, the procedure, from being restricted to the Community *acquis*, is applicable to certain policy areas previously regulated in the so-called third EU Treaty pillar concerning police and judicial cooperation in criminal matters.[14]

3. The Political Conditions of the Commission's Enforcement Powers

3.1 *The Commission's discretion and the practice of friendly settlements*

The Commission is not generally 'empowered to determine conclusively, by opinions formulated pursuant to Article 169 of the EC Treaty [Article 258 TFEU] or by other statements of its attitude under that procedure, the rights and duties of a Member State'.[15] The infringement procedure,

are sums of money to be paid periodically from the date the Court of Justice awards them until the member state breach has been brought to an end. It is established case law that the Commission can request both a lump sum and a penalty payment. See generally chapter three.

[12] Treaty of Lisbon amending the Treaty on European Union and the Treaty establishing the European Community, signed in Lisbon, on 13 December 2007 [2007] OJ C 306.

[13] Treaty of Lisbon amending the Treaty on European Union and the Treaty establishing the European Community [2007] OJ C306/1.

[14] See also House of Commons Library, 'The EU Reform Treaty: Amendments to the Treaty on European Union' *Research Paper 07/80*.

[15] Joined cases 142 and 143/80 *Amministrazione delle Finanze dello Stato v Essevi SpA and Carlo Salengo* [1980] ECR 1413, para 18.

however, leaves room for friendly settlements between the Commission and a member state about the manner in which the member state shall fulfil its EU obligations, or rather, how it can arrange itself in a manner acceptable to the Commission. This is a consequence of the Commission's broad margin of discretion described in more detail in chapter two. The vast majority of infringement cases are closed this way.[16]

With the establishment of the doctrines of direct effect,[17] supremacy,[18] and, more recently, of member state liability,[19] the Court of Justice has developed a constitutional framework in which citizens monitor member state compliance. National courts are obliged to give full effect to EU law[20] and they have come to play an important role in enforcing member state compliance within their domestic jurisdictions.[21] For the same reason, the Commission has actively campaigned to raise citizen awareness of the possibility of challenging member states before national courts and to bring actions for state liability.[22] In addition to the gains decentralized enforcement yields per se in terms of general compliance, it also adds to the bargaining position of the Commission during the administrative phase of Article 258 TFEU. A member state which acts in accordance with a friendly agreement is not necessarily *sensu stricto* substantively complying. Thus, the fact that member states may be held liable before national courts constitutes an important impetus for genuine, substantive compliance and ensures that friendly settlements do not effectively amount to a member state haven.

In the context of infringement proceedings under Article 258 TFEU, the Commission exercises the powers conferred on it by Article 17 TEU in the general EU interest.[23] The notion of 'the general EU interest' is inherently political and requires the Commission to make policy choices.

[16] Commission '*28th annual report on monitoring the application of EU law*', COM/2011/588, 5; and Statistical Annexes I to III, SEC(2011)1094—Volume1.

[17] Case 26/62 *van Gend en Loos* [1963] ECR 1.

[18] Case 6/64 *Costa v ENEL* [1964] ECR 585.

[19] In that case, the Court of Justice established that liability is 'inherent in the system of the [EC] Treaty'. Joined cases C-6/90 and C-9/90 [1991] ECR I-5357, para 35.

[20] Case 14/83 *von Colson* [1984] ECR 1891, para 26.

[21] The national courts may seek interpretive guidance from the Court of Justice of the European Union according to Art 267 TFEU.

[22] See A Slaughter, AS Sweet, and JHH Weiler (eds.), *The European Court and National Courts—Doctrine and Jurisprudence: Legal Change in its Social* Context (Hart Publishing, 1998) on the significance of decentralized enforcement; and further A Burley and W Mattli, 'Europe before the Court: A Political Theory of Legal Integration' (1993) *International Organization* 47:1, 41–76.

[23] See, eg, case 167/73 *Commission v France* [1974] ECR 359, para 15; and C-191/95 *Commission v Germany* [1998] ECR I-5449, para 35.

Far from pursuing all cases of non-compliance the Commission has enforcement priorities. The Commission continuously reviews its enforcement actions under Article 258 TFEU. In its White Paper on Governance, the Commission established priority criteria.[24] These have been adjusted over time, however, and by and large concern: (i) infringements that undermine the foundations of the rule of law; (ii) infringements that undermine the smooth functioning of the EU legal system; and finally (iii) infringements consisting in the failure to transpose or the incorrect transposal of directives.[25] In 2006 '[p]riority was given to the non-communication of national measures transposing directives, failures to implement the Court of Justice's judgments (Article 258 TFEU) and complaints denouncing structural problems in MS'.[26] Among the selected types of infringements are those that raise issues of principle or have particularly far-reaching negative impact for citizens. According to the Commission these types of cases need to be identified on a sectorial basis; however, they all concern the application of Treaty principles and key elements of framework regulations and directives.[27] Moreover, having established an array of supplementary methods to manage non-compliance the Commission relies on different enforcement strategies. In addition to infringement proceedings the Commission has, for instance, developed informal and non-binding methods to remedy specific cases of non-compliance such as EU Pilot[28] and

[24] Commission Communication *'European Governance—A White Paper'*, COM/2001/428, 26.

[25] Commission Communication *'Better Monitoring of the Application of Community Law'*, COM/2002/725, 11–12. The categories are further explained by way of examples.

[26] Commission Staff Working Document, annex to the 24th annual report from the Commission on monitoring the application of community law (2006), 'Situation in the different sectors', COM/2007/398 final, para 1.3. In addition, there may be policy specific priorities. See, eg, Commission Staff Working Document *'Situation in Different Sectors'* accompanying document to the report from the Commission 27th Annual Report on Monitoring the Application of EU Law (2009), SEC/2010/1143 final, 20–1, concerning enterprise and industry and a range of other examples.

[27] Commission Communication *'A Europe of Results—Applying Community Law'*, COM/2007/502 final.

[28] EU Pilot was introduced by the Commission in its Communication *'A Europe of Results—Applying Community Law'*, COM/2007/502 final, section 2.2 *'Improving working methods'*, 8. It aims at correcting infringements of EU law at an early stage without initiating infringement proceedings. The procedure is discussed in more detail in chapter two. According to the Commission's EU pilot evaluation report COM/2010/70 final, as of beginning of February 2010, 723 files had been submitted to EU Pilot. Of these, 424 files have passed all the way through the EU Pilot process. See also Commission Staff Working document *'Facts on the functioning of the system up to beginning of February 2010'* accompanying document to the Commission's EU pilot evaluation report, SEC(2010) 182; and Commission report *'Second Evaluation*

SOLVIT[29] concerning the internal market and services area. According to the Commission the latter supplementary procedures are particularly apt for 'nonpriority cases and non-structural issues' that call for pragmatic solution.[30]

The discretion enjoyed by the Commission enables and arguably requires it to employ its enforcement powers with a view to pursuing policy objectives and for reasons of effectiveness. There are many examples of this, direct taxation being one. Here, the rule of unanimity has significantly stalled the Commission's attempts to harmonize direct taxation. According to settled case law, while this politically sensitive policy area falls within the competence of the member states, they must nonetheless exercise that competence consistently with EU law.[31] This has enabled the Commission to shrewdly employ the general infringement procedure as a policy tool to bring greater alignment between member state tax regulation and EU law.[32]

Another instructive case concerns bilateral air transport agreements between several member states and the USA, the so-called 'Open Skies' agreements. On several occasions the Commission requested a mandate from the Council to conclude a single air transport agreement between the EU and the USA. Thus concerned that bilateral agreements were imbalanced and could only be remedied by concerted action, the Commission initiated infringement proceedings in parallel with the negotiations with the Council. Notably, it challenged the legality of the bilateral agreements

Report on EU Pilot', COM/2011/930 final. Whereas EU Pilot establishes contact between individual member states and the Commission SOLVIT establishes contact between member states. Commission Staff Working Document '*Facts on the functioning of the system up to beginning of February 2010*' accompanying document to the Commission's EU pilot evaluation report, SEC/2010/182, 6.

[29] SOLVIT is a network established with a view to solving problems that arise for individual citizens and businesses from the misapplication of internal market law. All member states have created SOLVIT centres, which cooperate directly via an on-line database to solve problems submitted by citizens and businesses in a rapid and pragmatic fashion. See, eg, Commission Staff Working Document '*SOLVIT 2006 Report—Development and Performance of the SOLVIT network in 2006*', SEC(2007) 585; and Commission communication '*Effective Problem Solving in the Internal Market ("SOLVIT")*', COM/2001/702. The Commission's SOLVIT webpage can be accessed at http://ec.europa.eu/solvit/site/index_en.htm.

[30] Commission Staff Working Document '*Situation in different sectors*' accompanying document to the report from the Commission '*27th annual report on monitoring the application of EU law*', COM/2010/538, 266.

[31] See, eg, case C-10/10, *Commission v Austria* [2011] not yet published in the ECR, para 23.

[32] See in this regard '*24th annual report on monitoring the application of EU law*', COM/2007/398, 23.

maintaining that they were contrary to the principles governing the division of external powers between the EU and the member states and that there were elements of the agreements that were in breach of the right of establishment. First, the Commission threatened a majority of the member states with infringement proceedings and later, they were referred to the Court of Justice.[33] What was particularly noteworthy was that the Commission was frank about its bargaining tactics.[34] Prete and Smulders comment on the 'Open Skies' cases that '... it should not come as a surprise that the Commission has, at times, used infringement proceedings as one of the means to encourage and stimulate a progressive evolution of Community laws and policies in certain areas'.[35]

The possibility for the Commission to employ infringement proceedings for cross-functional purposes was made possible owing to the wide discretionary powers attributed to it. Indeed, as Schmidt points out, by 'using its competencies as a guardian of the Treaty... the Commission may manipulate either the Council's default condition of decision making or the preferences of some of its members'.[36] Steunenberg finds support that the Commission is selective in its enforcement actions and initiates infringement proceedings to sustain its own policy preferences.[37] More generally, some scholars have expressed doubts whether the role as policy-maker is compatible with that of guardian.[38] In the 'Open Skies' cases the Belgian, Luxembourg, and German Governments submitted that the actions should be declared inadmissible on the ground of misuse of procedure because their true purpose was to put pressure on the Council to authorize the opening of EU negotiations with the United States with a view to the

[33] The Commission brought actions before the Court of Justice against the United Kingdom, Denmark, Sweden, Finland, Belgium, Luxembourg, Austria, and Germany in cases C-466/98–C-476/98.

[34] Interview with former Commissioner de Palacio, Florence, 21 April 2005. See also C Woll, 'Transatlantic Relations as a Catalyst to European Integration: European Commission Activism in International aviation' *AICGS Policy Paper*, from 2003.

[35] L Prete and B Smulders, 'The Coming of Age of Infringement Proceedings' (2010) *Common Market Law Review* 47, 9–61, 14. Prete and Smulders' journal article provides a thorough analysis of the general EU infringement procedure and related case law.

[36] SK Schmidt, 'Only an Agenda Setter? The European Commission's Power over the Council of Ministers' (2000) *European Union Politics* 1:1, 37–61, 38.

[37] Bernard Steunenberg, 'Implementation of EU directives. Is big brother watching? Commission oversight of the national' (2010) *European Union Politics* 11:3, 359–80.

[38] See, eg, R Macrory, *Regulation, Enforcement and Governance in Environmental Law* (Cameron May Ltd, 2008), 721; and P Wennerås, *The Enforcement of EC Environmental* Law (Oxford University Press, 2007), 294.

conclusion of an agreement on air services.[39] However, the Court of Justice rejected the plea thereby reaffirming that the Commission alone is competent to decide whether it is appropriate to bring infringement proceedings against a member state, and on account of which conduct or omission attributable to the member state concerned those proceedings should be brought.[40] According to the Court of Justice, in the context of the balance of powers between the institutions, it is not for the Court to consider what objectives are pursued in an action brought under Article 258 TFEU.[41] The Court of Justice thus maintains an absolute distinction between the powers and investigatory discretion attributed to the Commission in its role as guardian of the Treaty and the Court of Justice's own judicial discretion to decide whether or not the member state in question has failed to fulfil its obligations as alleged.

Infringement proceedings are often coupled with interpretative communications. Typically they contain summaries of jurisprudence and sometimes explain how the Commission further interprets EU law and case law. Thus, they serve a purpose of unification; however, to the extent they have legally and politically contentious elements they appear closer to policy instruments. Although such communications are non-binding they may have *de facto* significance on the way in which member states interpret EU law.[42] Thus, the Commission can exert individual pressure on the member states through the bilateral infringement procedure under Articles 258 and 260 TFEU, but also via interpretive communications and other channels in which it promotes its interpretations. Notably, the Commission has managed to turn the general infringement procedure into a powerful policy tool enabling it to pursue policy objectives and to exert influence on EU policies.

This begs the question whether the Commission has, in legal or political terms, advanced its powers beyond those attributed to it in the Treaties. In relation to the Court of Justice of the European Union, this type of question

[39] See joined opinion of Advocate General Tizzano in cases C-466/98–C-476/98, *Commission v UK and others* [2002] ECR I-9427, points 29–30.

[40] C-471/98 *Commission v Belgium* [2002] ECR I-9681, para 24; C-472/98 *Commission v Luxembourg* [2002] ECR I-9741, para 37; and C-476/98 *Commission v Germany* [2002] ECR I-9855, para 38.

[41] C-415/85 *Commission v Ireland* [1988] ECR 3097.

[42] See in this regard Case T-258/06 *Germany v Commission* [2010] ECR II-2027 (the case is discussed in more detail in chapter six); and J Scott, 'In Legal Limbo: Post-Legislative Guidance as a Challenge for European Administrative Law' (2011) *Common Market Law Review* 48:2, 329–56; and AJG Ibáñez, *The Administrative Supervision and Enforcement of EC Law* (Hart, 1999), 205–7.

has been discussed in terms of judicial activism.[43] However, the roles of the two institutions are fundamentally different. The Court of Justice of the European Union shall ensure that in the interpretation and application of the Treaties the law is observed.[44] The Commission by contrast is a semi-political branch of government and has been so since the establishment of the ECSC Treaty, both generally and when executing its supervisory functions. This was already the case in the ECSC. According to Article 86 ECSC the member states bound themselves to take all general and specific measures which would assure the execution of their obligations under the decisions and recommendations of the institutions of the EU, and facilitate the accomplishment of the EU's purposes.[45] As Henry Mason notes in his monograph on the ECSC from 1955, this general clause was 'phrased in such way as to give the HA the widest possible leeway in its interpretation of delinquency'.[46] Especially the last part concerning the facilitation of the accomplishment of the then Community's purposes, he further noted, might '... even lend itself to develop an "implied powers" doctrine in the Community. This would enable the HA to extend its jurisdiction beyond problems relating to coal and steel'.[47] In his conclusions on the legal structure of the ECSC Mason comments on the governmental character of the High Authority. It has, he maintains, an undeniable governmental or political character and this is at 'the crux of the CSC experiment. Legally at least, the EU's organs are sufficiently independent and enjoy adequate powers to constitute the first governmental-like structure on an international level'.[48] Similarly, the governmental character of the Commission finds many expressions in the Treaties' provisions concerning the Commission's composition and independence, voting rules etc, and most notably in its overall role in promoting the general interest of the Union.[49] This is not

[43] H Koch, K Hagel-Sørensen, U Haltern, and JHH Weiler (eds.), *Europe: The New Legal Realism: Essays in Honour of Hjalte Rasmussen* (3rd edn, Djøf, 2011).

[44] Article 19 TEU.

[45] According to Art 4(3) TEU the member states shall 'facilitate the achievement of the Union's tasks and refrain from any measure which could jeopardise the attainment of the Union's objectives'.

[46] H Mason, *The European Coal and Steel Community. Experiment in Supranationalism* (Martinus Nijhoff, 1955), 39.

[47] H Mason, *The European Coal and Steel Community. Experiment in Supranationalism* (Martinus Nijhoff, 1955), 40.

[48] H Mason, *The European Coal and Steel Community. Experiment in Supranationalism* (Martinus Nijhoff, 1955), 74.

[49] Article 17 TEU and Arts 244–250 TFEU.

to say that there are no constraints on the Commission. In its capacity as co-legislator, the Council can of course attempt to pre-empt the Commission's powers *ex ante* by construing detailed legislation or even by refraining to legislate further. The Commission may, in addition, be held politically accountable *ex post* by the Council, which proposes to the European Parliament a candidate for President of the Commission and adopts the list of the other persons whom it proposes for appointment as members of the Commission.[50]

Member state governments have not seriously challenged the legitimacy of the Commission's use of enforcement powers or sanctioned its behaviour *ex post* at the intergovernmental conferences (IGCs) when amending the Treaties. Admittedly, it would be difficult to obtain the support required to amend the Commission's treaty-based enforcement powers.[51] However and tellingly, rather than maintaining status quo the member states have indeed continued to strengthen and broaden the scope of the Commission's enforcement powers. This suggests that member state governments generally consider the Commission capable of exercising its enforcement powers in a politically acceptable manner. Alternatively, or at the same time, they consider the Commission's exercise of discretion to be an indispensable quid pro quo when delegating competences to the EU.[52]

3.2 *The semi-political role of the Commission*

In their compliance study, Falkner et al observe that the Commission 'appears far from willing, or able, to pursue all (or at least all major) violations'.[53] This restraint has prompted private stakeholders to criticize

[50] Article 17 TEU. This is the case generally speaking. Whether the Council is indeed concerned about enforcement in this regard is outside the scope of this book.

[51] F Scharpf, 'The Joint Decision Trap: Lessons from German Federalism and European Integration' (1988) *Public Administration* 66, 239–78. See also G Falkner (ed.), *The EU's Decision Traps: Comparing Policies* (Oxford University Press, 2011).

[52] Compare the arguments made concerning the Court of Justice by P Biering in 'Has the Court of Justice Ever Taken Integration Too Far?' in H Koch, K Hagel-Sørensen, U Haltern, and JHH Weiler (eds.), *Europe: The New Legal Realism: Essays in Honour of Hjalte Rasmussen* (3rd edn, Djøf, 2011).

[53] G Falkner, O Treib, M Hartlapp, and S Leiber, *Complying with Europe: EU Harmonisation and Soft Law in the Member States* (Cambridge University Press, 2005), 204. See also RO Keohane, A Moravcsik, and A Slaughter, 'Legalized Dispute Resolution: Interstate and Transnational' (2000) *International Organization* 54, 457–88, 473. The authors maintain that the Commission 'was initially—and to an extent, remains—reluctant to sue member states, due to its fear of retaliation and need to establish its own policy legitimacy'.

the Commission, for instance, in relation to the internal market. Their viewpoint is that the Commission is too lenient towards member states, both when initiating investigations and during negotiations with the member states.[54] Commission officials have likewise maintained that 'political horse-trading' within the College of Commissioners hinders vigorous enforcement policy.[55] A related and at times overlapping question concerns whether the Commission manages to work in the interest of the EU and maintain its independence from partisan politics.[56] Börzel plays down the practical significance of the phenomenon. The Commission's 'identity as a truly supranational body makes it inappropriate for Commissioners . . . to block legal action against their own member state'.[57] The above-mentioned concerns share a common worry that the Commission is not vigorous enough in its enforcement of EU law. However, the critiques may not be fully justified. This is especially due to the fact that the Commission is a semi-political player and that the infringement proceedings can form part of a much broader policy dialogue. It is a dialogue which may be tied with wider legal, economic, and political considerations and which requires priorities.

This leads to the question of the semi-political role of the Commission. Both generally and in the specific context of enforcement the Commission can usefully be thought of as comprising two decision-making levels. One is that of officials and the other is that of political actors. Within these levels, political, cultural, and personal diversity will of course be present. Although senior officials and in particular the Director Generals in the organizational hierarchy of the Commission may possess some political authority, they ultimately refer to the authority of a commissioner and ultimately the Commission College. When contrasting the two types of levels, their traits are those of administration and politics, respectively. The Commission executes its powers under Articles 258 and 260 TFEU in its capacity as an autonomous institution. Decisions to issue a reasoned

[54] Final Report of the Committee of Wise Men (the Lamfalussy Committee) on the regulation of the European securities markets, 15 February 2001, 40.

[55] European Voice, Brussels, 2 May 1996 (EDC 33, 2:19).

[56] In the area of environmental law, P Wennerås, *The Enforcement of EC Environmental Law* (Oxford University Press, 2007), 294–5, points out the fact that a significant number of personnel are on secondment from EU member state administrations.

[57] T Börzel, 'Guarding the Treaty. The Compliance Strategies of the Commission' in T Börzel, and R Cichowski (eds.), *State of the European Union Volume 6: Law Politics and Society* (Oxford University Press, 2003), 212.

opinion and to bring an action for a declaration of failure to fulfil obligations must be the subject of collective deliberation by the College of Commissioners.[58] Moreover, and importantly, all the members of the College of Commissioners should bear collective responsibility at political level for the decisions.[59]

The Commission's relationship with and approach to the member states touch upon the more general question of the Commission's overall role. One perception is that of the Commission as a 'super-government'. In this depiction, the Commission acts primarily as a political and autonomous branch of government. Underlying this interpretation is a suggestion of the Commission being 'the others'. Among the Commissioners, the dominant perception of the institution appears to be that of a facilitator above all.[60] The underlying premise is that isolating a member state is dangerous. As a consequence, member states should always be given a chance to find a compromise.[61] Where non-compliance is of a political rather than interpretative nature, the Commission exerts a moral type of pressure on the member state by emphasizing what is appropriate behaviour. Clearly, the notion of appropriate behaviour is ambiguous and has political undertones. As will be discussed in more detail in chapter seven, the Commission engages in a process of arguing where clarification is required, as well as bargaining when the margin for political leniency is being stretched. At the level of officials, a technical leaning to make full use of the legal remedies available may well surpass more subtle understandings of the legal and political dimension of enforcement. Indeed, it is a key feature of the institutional design of Articles 258 and 260 TFEU that the Commission College bears responsibility for infringement cases at political level.

58 C-191/95 *Commission v Germany* [1998] ECR I-5449, para 48. According to the judgment, the College is not, however, obliged to frame the actual wording of the acts which give effect to those decisions and put them in final form. See in that regard C-198/97 *Commission v Germany* [1999] ECR I-3257, para 20. For a description of the internal working procedure, including how infringement cases are prepared and by whom in practice, see M Smith, *Centralised Enforcement, Legitimacy and Good Governance in the EU* (Routledge Cavendish, 2009).

59 C-191/95 *Commission v Germany* [1998] ECR I-5449, para 39. According to Rules of Procedure of the Commission (2000) OJ L 308/26, meetings of the Commission shall not be public. Discussions are confidential.

60 Interview with former Commissioner de Palacio, Florence, 21 April 2005.

61 Interview with former Commissioner de Palacio, Florence, 21 April 2005.

3.3 *The member state governments' call for flexible enforcement*

The special enforcement procedure that applies to the Stability and Growth Pact provides an example of a 'high politics' area where the governments have emphasized the political dimension of enforcement.[62] The Commission plays a central role of early warning under the Excessive Deficit Procedure.[63] However, its procedural prerogatives are limited compared to those under Articles 258 and 260 TFEU and the responsibility of enforcement essentially lies with the Council.[64] In a 2004 judgment, the Court of Justice dismissed the Commission's claim that it should annul a Council failure to adopt a decision to notify France and Germany that they had failed to take adequate measures to reduce their budgetary deficits.[65] The dispute between the Commission and the EcoFin Council had implications beyond that of procedural clarification. For the Commission it was a matter of sustaining 'credibility in the rule-based framework for budgetary surveillance' and with that the 'process of multilateral surveillance'.[66] For the Council members it appeared to be a question of necessary flexibility and political pragmatism.

The actions before the Court of Justice may be explained by the Commission's apparent institutional self-interest in having its role in the procedure substantiated. However, the case also aimed at securing one of the foundational principles underpinning the EU, namely that compliance is not a matter of the relative size or power of the regime participants. Did the way the Council proceedings progressed suggest that although the EU

[62] The Stability and Growth Pact consists of the Resolution of the European Council of 17 June 1997 [1997] OJ C 236/1; Council Regulation (EC) No 1466/97 of 7 July 1997 on the strengthening of the surveillance of budgetary positions and the surveillance and coordination of economic policies [1997] OJ L 209/1); and Council Regulation (EC) No 1467/97 of 7 July 1997 on speeding up and clarifying the implementation of the excessive deficit procedure [1997] OJ L 209/6. These regulations were amended by Council Regulation (EC) No 1055/2005 and Council Regulation (EC) No 1056/2005 of 27 June 2005 respectively [2005] OJ 2005 L 174/1 and 5. Regulation (EU) No 1173/2011 of the European Parliament and of the Council on the effective enforcement of budgetary surveillance in the euro area [2011] OJ L 306/1 further amends Regulations No 1466/97 and (EC) No 1467/97.

[63] Article 126 TFEU. See also Protocol (No 12) on the excessive deficit procedure annexed to the Treaty on European Union.

[64] Article 126 TFEU; and C-27/04 *Commission v Council* [2004] ECR I-6649, para 76.

[65] C-27/04 *Commission v Council* [2004] ECR I-6649.

[66] Answer by Commissioner Mira on behalf of the Commission to European Parliament Question E-474/02.

member states are equally restricted by their legal obligations, enforcement is contingent upon considerations that essentially relate back to power politics? For the Commission, which had successfully required steps to be taken against Portugal, the episode was considered particularly grave in bringing to light the fact that member states are not equal in political terms.[67] The German/French disregard for their budgetary commitments and the Council's refusal to go along with the Commission's insistence on a strict 3 per cent maximum deficit gap brought about a discussion on flexibility. However, this debate was not really a new topic on the policy agenda. Rather, it reflected the political conditions underpinning enforcement in the EU and, in particular, that the member state governments require some degree of flexibility during enforcement.[68]

The EU treaty regime and its members are vulnerable to confrontations. Even in a polity by some considered close to a federation or a confederation in the making (or even accomplished) enforcement carries a risk of triggering a sense of antagonism before that of fostering compliance. A member state which contemplates direct infringement proceedings will have to carefully consider the potential direct or indirect negative costs it may entail. Diplomatic considerations may in part explain EU member states' reluctance to initiate direct infringement proceedings under Article 259 TFEU. The Commission as a non-state and perhaps less contentious actor has inherent advantages in its approach vis-à-vis the member states. Some shortcomings may be suggested too. Whereas states may be too lenient enforcers, EU institutions or individual actors within these institutions may not be sufficiently responsive to domestic conditions, which the member states would consider politically legitimate barriers to immediate or absolute enforcement. These are circumstances that can be overcome gradually and over time. To meet this political dimension of enforcement in a Union based upon the rule of law, the member states have granted the Commission powers to ensure compliance. However, the very particular institutional

[67] Interview with former Commissioner de Palacio, Florence, 21 April 2005.

[68] The enforcement mechanisms concerning the Stability and Growth Pact are beyond the scope of this book. However, in the light of the above comments on flexibility it should be mentioned that enforcement has been strengthened more recently. Specifically, a new set of financial sanctions have been introduced for euro-area member states. These tools (including a non-interest-bearing deposit amounting to 0.2 per cent of GDP would) now apply much earlier in the process according to a graduated approach. Regulation (EU) No 1173/2011 of the European Parliament and of the Council on the effective enforcement of budgetary surveillance in the euro area [2011] OJ L 306/1.

architecture of the general infringement procedure requires it to act responsively. Notably, some degree of flexibility inevitably takes place between the member states and the Commission under Articles 258 and 260 TFEU. This can usefully be thought of as procedural responsiveness.

Whereas the High Authority was empowered to make a decision concerning a member state's failure to comply the Commission possesses relatively weaker enforcement powers.[69] The Commission has merely been provided with a 'warning procedure'.[70] Compared to the enforcement procedure in the ECSC Treaty the Commission therefore has a greater incentive to genuinely engage in dialogue with non-complying member states. The Maastricht Treaty introduced economic sanctions and the Lisbon Treaty reinforced the Commission's powers against repetitive infringements and late transposition notices. These amendments do carry a political message, namely that long-term inertia is detrimental and unacceptable. However, the actual role attributed to sanctions should be seen in view of the time which elapses from the moment when the Commission first becomes aware of a potential infringement and initiates proceedings under Article 258 TFEU and the actual imposition of sanctions awarded by the Court of Justice in the final phase of Article 260 TFEU. Similarly, the fast-track sanctioning mechanism stipulated in Article 260(3) TFEU is of limited general significance since it merely concerns failure to notify the Commission about measures transposing a directive. Economic coercion has not become a primary, general tool against infringements.

There are exceptions in primary legislation where the Commission has been permitted more potent enforcement powers, competition law including state aid being one. It has been suggested that these powers reflect a perception that considerable delegation would be necessary to ensure compliance within a particular policy area.[71] Alternatively, it may also be

[69] According to Article 88 ECSC the member state was however offered an opportunity to present its views.

[70] Joined cases 2/62 and 3/62 *Commission v Luxembourg and Belgium* [1962] ECR 793.

[71] F McGowan, 'Competition Policy' in H Wallace and W Wallace (eds.), *Policy-Making in the European Union* (4th edn, Oxford University press, 2000), 120, and G Garrett, 'Competition Policy' in H Wallace and W Wallace (eds.), Policy-Making in the European Union (4th edn, Oxford University Press, 2000). See also *Rapport des Chefs de Delégations aux Ministres des Affaires Etrangères* (Secretariat of the Intergovernmental Conference, Brussels, 21 April, 1956) in which it was stressed that producers' legal interests could not ultimately hinge on *'la voie complexe des relations et des organisations intergouvernementales'*. Cited and commented in P Kapteyn,

the case that the member states misjudged the reach of the powers and also the manner in which the Commission would exercise them.[72] Similarly, the Commission's relatively weak investigatory powers may reflect that the member states do not trust that the Commission can exercise stronger powers in a politically acceptable manner. It may however also signify a belief that pursuing such a procedural avenue will not entail greater compliance, ie, that the general EU infringement procedure is sufficiently solid for ensuring compliance. The following sections will offer a third proposition supplementing those outlined right above. It maintains that the powers available to the Commission should be understood in the light of the EU's, in effect, weak claim of supremacy. Moreover, the EU legislative style requires responsive enforcement responses. These elements apply in addition to the member states' demand for flexible enforcement discussed above.

3.4 *EU law's dependency on a dual source of authority*

Up until the Lisbon Treaty it was generally assumed that the signatory states ultimately possess the, if not legal, political option of secession although the Treaty itself was silent on the matter.[73] Article 50 TEU now stipulates that any member state may decide to withdraw from the Union in accordance with its own constitutional requirements.

At the same time, with the establishment of the doctrine of supremacy the Court of Justice clarified that EU law does not depend upon member state enactment. It is per se 'an integral part of the legal systems of the Member States'.[74] The member states have accepted, in the wording of the Court of Justice, 'a permanent limitation of their sovereign rights'[75] by signing up to

L Gormley, and P van Themaat Verloren, *Introduction to the Law of the European Communities after the Coming into Force of the Single European Act* (Kluwer Law International, 1989), 14.

[72] F McGowan, 'Competition Policy' in H Wallace and W Wallace (eds.), *Policy-Making in the European Union* (4th edn, Oxford University Press, 2000); and P Pierson, 'The Path to European Integration: A Historical Institutionalist Analysis' (1996) *Comparative Political Studies* 29:2, 123–63.

[73] S Weatherill, *Law and Integration in the European Union* (Oxford University Press, 1995), 14, considered it a prevalent view point. Compare Draft Treaty establishing a Constitution for Europe [2003] OJ C 169/1, Art I-59. For a discussion of whether this accordingly implies a 'loss of sovereignty on the part of the Member States' see the analysis by G de Búrca, 'Sovereignty and the Supremacy Doctrine' in Neil Walker (ed.), *Sovereignty in Transition* (Hart, 2003).

[74] Case 6/64 *Costa v ENEL* [1964] ECR 585.

[75] Case 6/64 *Costa v ENEL* [1964] ECR 585.

the (E)EC Treaty. Thus the fundamental idea of an autonomous legal order, so dear to the EU, is in legal terms, contingent on a single source of authority, namely the member state entering into the Treaty. In actual, ie, political, terms one may however speak about a dual source of authority. One source is the EU's claim of authority through the Treaties. The other source is actual observance by the member states. This dual source of authority requires some day-to-day recognition. The interaction between national courts and the Court of Justice of the European Union in relation to preliminary rulings under Article 267 TFEU is illustrative thereof. The Court of Justice of the European Union and the national courts are in principle organized heterarchically,[76] and their relationship is usually considered to be frictionless.[77] In spite of the heterarchically organized relationship there are features which may bring about some degree of hierarchical norm generation.[78] These include, not least, the supremacy of EU norms and the binding nature of preliminary rulings.[79] Or so it seems. In an attempt to explain what appears to be near-absolute acceptance by national courts, Maduro looks for explanations beyond that of uncritical implementation of the Court of Justice's jurisprudence. The author holds that legitimacy and integrationist considerations have necessitated a jurisprudence of an essentially negotiated nature in dialogue with, in particular, national courts, which in turn facilitates the interpretative claims via implementation.[80] This is not just abstract theorizing. A number of member

[76] H Rasmussen, *EU-Ret i Kontekst* (Gad Jura, 1995), 491. See also H Schermers and D Waelbroeck, *Judicial protection in the European Communities* (5th edn, Kluwer, 1992), para 689, on the cooperative nature of the procedure.

[77] C-224/01 *Gerhard Köbler v Österreich* [2003] ECR I-10239, in which the Court of Justice established that a member state may be held liable for infringements attributable to a last instance national court, may be considered a slight dent in a relationship normally characterized by trust and cooperativeness.

[78] For an analysis of the policy impact in different sectors of prejudicial references beyond that of the referring court see L Conant, *Justice Contained: Law and Politics in the European Union* (Cornell University Press, 2002).

[79] Case 52/76 *Benedetti v Munari* [1977] ECR 163, paras 24–7; and G Bebr, *Judicial Control of the European Communities* (Stevens & Sons, 1962), 366, on the functional division of jurisdiction between national courts and the Court of Justice.

[80] M Maduro, 'Contrapunctual Law: Europe's Constitutional Pluralism in Action' in N Walker (ed.), *Sovereignty in Transition* (Hart, 2003), 512. In her book *Establishing the Supremacy of European Law* (Oxford University Press, 2001), K Alter examines what she calls a 'process of negotiation between the ECJ, national governments, and national courts, through which the relationship between European law and national law is continually defined, redefined and nuanced'. In this regard, see also K Alter, Memorandum, *The UK Parliament House of Lords*, Select Committee on European Union, 26 November 2003. The author is concerned with the

states actively recognize proceedings before the Court of Justice in prejudicial references as a deliberative, discursive forum, in which they can exert influence by acting as repeat players.[81] According to the Court of Justice, 'the system of references for a preliminary ruling is based on a dialogue between one court and another'.[82] Likewise, the Commission contends that it is through Court of Justice decisions in 'dialogue with national courts ... that the common policies have been encouraged, that the Community's identity has been affirmed, and that discriminatory and nationalistic temptations have been resisted'.[83] Maduro's interpretation elucidates two intertwined features of post-decisional EU law, namely, its conditionality upon acceptance and enactment by a wide range of actors and its discursive nature. The author argues that non-adversarial, discursive interaction between the Court of Justice and national courts strengthens the claims officially made by the former through national enforcement by the latter. It thus constitutes an important enforcement mechanism. Significantly, the problem-solving approach implied in 'dialogue rather than dictation'[84] shows how cooperative and participatory processes can be capable of generating pressure for compliance.

The discursive, heterarchical nature of judicial interaction between the national courts and the Court of Justice is a significant characteristic of indirect enforcement, ie, enforcement before domestic courts. However, the argument made by Maduro, namely that the Court of Justice is in an interdependent relationship with national courts, is instructive for the analysis of other relationships between the member states and the EU institutions, including the Commission. The Court of Justice and the referring national court are merely two out of many 'government voices' that articulate EU and national interests respectively and which engage in a process of negotiated dialogue. This is a type of dialogue that recognizes

constitutional dimension of supremacy claims by the Court of Justice on behalf of the EU. See also E Iankova and P Katzenstein, 'European Enlargement and Institutional Hypocrisy' in T Börzel and Rachel A Cichowski (eds.), *State of the European Union Volume 6: Law Politics and Society* (Oxford University Press, 2003), 277.

[81] MP Granger, (2004) 'When Governments go to Luxembourg: the influence of governments on the Court of Justice' *European Law Review* 29:1, 3–31.

[82] Case C-210/06 *Cartesio* [2008] ECR I-9641, para 91.

[83] Commission *'Report on the Operation of the Treaty on European Union, Brussels'*, 10 May 1995 SEC(95) 731, final, 25.

[84] M Maduro, 'Contrapunctual Law: Europe's Constitutional Pluralism in Action' in N Walker (ed.), *Sovereignty in Transition* (Hart, 2003), 513.

diversity within the member states. Moreover, it resonates with the 'substantive flexibility'[85] allowed for to some degree in the implementation phase in line with the principle of proportionality.[86] The less recognized *Prinzip des Interventionsminimums*, which focuses on the 'encroachment upon the national legal systems as such',[87] might in fact be more accurate for the present discussion.

3.5 *Particularities of the EU normative framework*

That EU law effectively relies upon a dual source of authority is not merely reflected in the procedural frameworks that govern communicative action between the EU institutions and the member states. It also finds expression in substantive EU law and some characteristics are particularly useful to keep in mind when considering centralized enforcement.

Zürn has developed a theoretical framework for legal regimes beyond the nation-state that display a high degree of compliance. Taking the European Union as a successful government construction, he acknowledges the significance of traditional Principal-Agent enforcement means such as 'effective monitoring mechanisms and sanctions'.[88] However, an additional and central element is that of legalization. This is, on the one hand, juridification and, on the other, legal and civil internalization. The latter refers to supremacy and direct effect. These processes are seen to be in a dynamic cycle.[89] Clearly, supremacy and direct effect constitute central

[85] On substantive and procedural flexibility in the implementation phase see J Scott, 'Flexibility in the Implementation of EC Environmental Law' *Yearbook of European Environmental Law* (Oxford University Press, 2000), 36–60. The author draws attention to the significance that choice of legal basis and choice of policy instrument at the EU level have for the 'scope of Member State autonomy'.

[86] Whether a measure is proportional is tested on the background of a two-fold test concerning effectiveness and efficiency. The employed means should be suitable for the purpose of achieving the desired objective and not go beyond what is necessary to achieve it C-426/93 *Germany v Council* [1995] ECR I-3723, para 42. In some cases, the principle is defined as a requirement that a measure is appropriate and necessary and that the least onerous measure must be chosen if more available. See joined cases C-184/02 and C-223/02 *Spain and Finland v EP and Council of the European Union* [2004] ECR I-7789, para 57.

[87] R Lauwaars, *Lawfulness and Legal Force of Community Decisions* (A W Sijthoff, 1973), 232.

[88] M Zürn, 'Introduction: Law and Compliance at Different Levels' in M Zürn and C Joerges (eds.), *Law and Governance in Postnational Europe, Compliance beyond the Nation-State* (Cambridge University Press, 2004), intro.

[89] M Zürn, 'Introduction: Law and Compliance at Different Levels' in M Zürn and C Joerges (eds.), *Law and Governance in Postnational Europe, Compliance beyond the Nation-State* (Cambridge University Press, 2004), 24–5.

elements of the aggregate enforcement picture and they do to a significant degree explain the level of compliance displayed by the EU. Juridification however is closer to the central theme of this section; it concerns rule requirements such as 'clarity, pertinence, stringency, adaptability and a high degree of consistency, both within themselves and in relation to other laws'[90] as well as delegation of authority. Falling back on Abbott et al, the concept of juridification is taken to cover legal obligation, rule precision, and third party delegation of implementing, supervisory, and adjudicative power.[91] Abbott et al argue that the EU generally displays a high degree of obligation, precision, and delegation. In their terminology a 'precise rule specifies clearly and unambiguously what is expected by a state... (in terms of both the intended objective and the means to achieve it)'.[92] Often, but not necessarily, such precise rules set out the conditions of application in detail.[93] Zürn draws a link between both precision and delegation and the question of ambiguity.[94] The central point is that a high degree of autonomy and power conferred to authorities in order to undertake interpretation and adjudication, but also fact-finding and implementation, corresponds to the higher degree of juridification.[95]

The member state commitments covered by Articles 258 and 260 TFEU are binding hard law and clearly impose constraints on member state behaviour thus hinting at some stringency. The corresponding enforcement procedure relies primarily on friendly settlement. However, it is ultimately characterized by a high degree of delegation in that the Court of Justice of the European Union is empowered to hand down binding

[90] M Zürn, 'Introduction: Law and Compliance at Different Levels' in M Zürn and C Joerges (eds.), *Law and Governance in Postnational Europe, Compliance beyond the Nation-State* (Cambridge University Press, 2004), 23.

[91] K Abbott, R Keohane, A Moravcsik, A Slaughter, and D Snidal, 'The Concept of Legalization' (2000) *International Organization* 54:3, 401–19.

[92] K Abbott, R Keohane, A Moravcsik, A Slaughter, and D Snidal, 'The Concept of Legalization' (2000) *International Organization* 54:3, 401–19, 412.

[93] K Abbott, R Keohane, A Moravcsik, A Slaughter, and D Snidal, 'The Concept of Legalization' (2000) *International Organization* 54:3, 401–19, 413.

[94] M Zürn, 'Introduction: Law and Compliance at Different Levels' in M Zürn and C Joerges (eds.), *Law and Governance in Postnational Europe, Compliance beyond the Nation-State* (Cambridge University Press, 2004), 23.

[95] M Zürn, 'Introduction: Law and Compliance at Different Levels' in M Zürn and C Joerges (eds.), *Law and Governance in Postnational Europe, Compliance beyond the Nation-State* (Cambridge University Press, 2004), 24.

judgments.[96] Nevertheless, the criteria of rule precision and also the type of powers delegated to the Commission and the Court of Justice merit further consideration in the specific EU context.

One sort of ambiguity is characteristic of most international treaties as well as EU law, reflecting the fact that obligations have been negotiated in a diplomatic setting. This ambiguity may perhaps amount to a tacit condition for the member states' increasing loss of regulatory autonomy. Even if one understands the notion of compliance in a neutral fashion as 'a state of conformity between an actor's [state's] behaviour and a specified rule',[97] compliance can often take numerous forms. That is to say, there is a margin for interpretation and absolute specificity is rare. This is a matter of substantive flexibility.[98] Even when a law is backed by a sovereign, or when law claims sovereignty, some interpretation is required.[99]

Much EU law is inherently responsive to differences in the member states' legal and administrative systems. The most common legislative form within the EU is that of (framework) directives, with a more or less narrowly defined objective. It is, however, up to the member state legislators to incorporate it into the domestic legal order, if not already observed, and to give effect to it.[100] This is a less intrusive way to integrate supranational law into the national legal systems and a method that also has a political dimension to it. Whereas, in the words of Majone, 'total harmonization reflects a federalist vision of the integration process' and with that a 'federal preemption',[101] the EU body of law is to a large degree based upon optional and minimum harmonization, the principle of mutual recognition,[102] a range of soft-law measures, and framework directives. Even in

[96] See generally K Abbott, R Keohane, A Moravcsik, A Slaughter, and D Snidal, 'The Concept of Legalization' (2000) *International Organization* 54:3, 401–19.

[97] K Raustiale and A Slaughter, 'International Law, International Relations and Compliance' in W Carlsnaes, T Risse, and B Simmons (eds.), *Handbook of International Relations* (SAGE, 2002), 539.

[98] See C Joerges, 'Compliance Research in Legal Perspectives' in M Zürn and C Joerges (eds.), *Law and Governance in Postnational Europe, Compliance beyond the Nation-State* (Cambridge University Press, 2004), on legal indeterminacy.

[99] See F Kratochwil, *Rules, Norms, and Decisions: On the Conditions of Practical and Legal Reasoning in International Relations and Domestic Affairs* (Cambridge University Press, 1989) on legal realism.

[100] Article 288 TFEU.

[101] G Majone, *Dilemmas of European Integration: The Ambiguities and Pitfalls of Integration by Stealth* (Oxford University Press, 2005), 70.

[102] G Majone, *Dilemmas of European Integration: The Ambiguities and Pitfalls of Integration by Stealth* (Oxford University Press, 2005), 71.

areas of exclusive EU competence member states often retain a significant margin for meeting their obligations. Thus, the degree of obligation is incontestably high within the EU. Yet, the element of precision is more subtle. That is to say, the objectives of law can have a significant degree of precision and still leave a broad margin of discretion concerning how to give law effect. In the specific EU context this flexibility amounts to a constitutional virtue, namely the doctrine of proportionality. This type of flexibility has a procedural dimension under EU enforcement. Significantly, the corresponding powers of the Commission as well as the Court of Justice and the procedural design of the infringement procedure acknowledge the mentioned degree of flexibility as to the manner in which EU law is given effect.

In its structure, the general EU infringement procedure resembles to some degree the 'gradual turning the screw' variant of coercive diplomacy[103] and also Brunée's theory of a 'persuasive continuum', in which the measures range from facilitation to punishment.[104] Audretsch, a Community law scholar, has explained Articles 258 and 260 TFEU in terms of an enforcement ladder, which allows for intensifying the pressure on a member state.[105] Somewhat similarly, Tallberg has analysed Article 258 TFEU as a process of both managerial and enforcement types of interaction.[106] He argues that the twinning of the measures constitute the optimal enforcement mechanism and draws a parallel with responsive regulation theory. Notably, Tallberg points out, there is an inverse relation between the potency of the supervisors' control mechanisms and their actual use.[107] This is certainly true. At the same time, even though the EU is characterized by unprecedented autonomous powers, there are few examples of powers that can be employed without a high degree of appreciation of the member states either directly or indirectly, including in the enforcement phase. Audretsch, for instance, notes that it 'is to be regarded

[103] On this type of enforcement, see A George, *Forceful Persuasion: Coercive Diplomacy as an Alternative to War* (United States Institute of Peace Press, 1991), 9.

[104] J Brunée, 'Fine Balance: Facilitation and Enforcement in the Design of a Compliance Regime for the Kyoto Protocol' (2000) *Tulane Environmental Law Journal* 13, 223–70.

[105] HAH Audretsch, *Supervision in European Community Law* (Elsevier Science Publishers BV, 1986).

[106] J Tallberg, *European Governance and Supranational Institutions—Making States Comply* (Routledge, 2003), 7.

[107] J Tallberg, *European Governance and Supranational Institutions—Making States Comply* (Routledge, 2003), 7.

as a consequence of its supervisory task that the Commission . . . indicates to the best of its ability how an infringement can be terminated'.[108] It is implicitly understood that the Commission cannot give compliance instructions.[109] The Court of Justice is the single authority of legal interpretation and ability to appraise member state conduct.[110] Even in this definitive instance the manner in which law is applied is not an EU matter, as long as the member states give effect to it. Significantly, the Court of Justice hands down judgments of a declaratory nature[111] and it is not assumed to possess powers to specify the measures to be taken by a member state.[112] When the Court of Justice has established the failure to comply, the member state determines the action it will take to comply.[113] Things may be different with what Audretsch denotes 'arrêts educatifs', namely guidance as to 'how the law could be observed'.[114] This is a more open-ended and pragmatic form of communication, which leaves the member state with discretion, or flexibility, in the compliance phase ensuing the judgment. Even when sanctions are imposed neither the Commission nor the Court of Justice can prescribe how a state should comply.[115] The

[108] See HAH Audretsch, *Supervision in European Community Law* (Elsevier Science Publishers BV, 1986), 53. Another question is whether there is a legal obligation to do so as, eg, Advocate General Lagrange argues in his opinion in case 7/61 *Commission v Italy* [1961] ECR 317.

[109] According to settled case law the Commission cannot be required to indicate in the reasoned opinion or in the application submitted to the Court of Justice what steps should be taken to eliminate the impugned conduct. See, eg, C-247/89 *Commission v Portugal* [1991] ECR I-3659, para 22; and C-559/07 *Commission v Greece* [2009] ECR I-47, para 23. See also chapter three on the general infringement procedure stipulated in Art 258 TFEU.

[110] C-393/98 *Ministério Público and António Gomes Valente v Fazenda Pública* [2001] ECR I-1327; C-142 and 143/80 *Amministrazione delle Finanze dello Stato v Essevi SpA and Carlo Salengo* [1980] ECR, 1413.

[111] Advocate General Alber in C-260/98 *Commission v Greece* [2000] ECR I-6537, point 76, notes that: 'proceedings for failure to fulfil Treaty obligations seek a declaration of principle on the content of the rules of Community law.'

[112] HAH Audretsch, *Supervision in European Community Law* (Elsevier Science Publishers BV, 1986), 115. The author, however, maps out legal arguments modifying this strict doctrinal assumption. See also AJG Ibáñez, *The Administrative Supervision and Enforcement of EC Law* (Hart, 1999), 92–5.

[113] Opinion of Advocate General Mischo in C-78/00 *Commission v Italy* [2001] ECR I-8195, point 65.

[114] HAH Audretsch, *Supervision in European Community Law* (Elsevier Science Publishers BV, 1986), 116 and 119. The author falls back on a broad interpretation of Art 19 TFEU (ex Art 220 EC).

[115] Because a question concerning the measures required for the implementation of a judgment under Art 258 TFEU does not form part of the subject-matter of such a judgment, the Court of Justice has ruled, 'such a question cannot form the subject-matter of an application for

autonomy enjoyed by a member state to define the manner in which it will give effect to EU law thus remains intact. When considering the Commission's function it is significant that the absence of prescriptive powers is complemented by an obligation of mutual duty of cooperation.[116] The Commission's endeavours to exert influence are thus part of a dialectical dialogue and the context of this dialogue changes with each response of the member state and vice versa. To recap, a high degree of delegation to autonomous institutions occurs in respect of and in interaction with a nucleus of statal self-rule and management.

3.6 *Preliminary conclusions*

This section has examined a number of intertwined factors that are useful to keep in mind when discussing enforcement of EU law and the role of the Commission. They concern: (i) the discrepancy between the EU's legal and *de facto* authority; (ii) the nature of the normative framework; and (iii) the institutional design of the general EU infringement procedure.

First, it was argued that the EU *acquis* relies *de facto* on a dual source of authority. One stems from its formal adoption and thus qualification as EU law, whilst the other stems from substantiation through domestic implementation, application, and/or enforcement. The idea was explored with reference to Maduro's interpretation of inter-judicial dialogue between national courts and the Court of Justice under the preliminary reference procedure. The resulting type of dialogue was seen as a consequence of the symbiotic relationship between Member States and the EU and to be a general condition of EU negotiation. This dualism of autonomy and interdependence manifests itself in substantive and procedural flexibility. Specifically, it was argued, member states often enjoy considerable margin when implementing EU law. Moreover, the general EU infringement procedure requires the Commission to engage in dialogue. That is to say, the procedure is inherently cooperative and flexible.

interpretation of a judgment' according to Art 102 of the Rules of Procedure. C-503/04 *Commission v Germany* [2007] ECR I-6153, para 15. The consolidated version of Rules of Procedure of the Court of Justice of the European Communities can be accessed at the Court of Justice of the European Union's web-page www.curia.europa.eu.

[116] Ex Art 10 EC (now repealed and replaced, in substance, by Art 4(3) TEU).

4. The Notions of Enforcement, Compliance, and Effectiveness

4.1 *Enforcement*

The notions of enforcement, compliance, and effectiveness deserve brief consideration. In its literal meaning, enforcement is the process of increasing the strength of something, to compel observance or fulfilment of an obligation. Some authors employ enforcement in a more generic sense as 'the process of compliance-generation, independent of the means chosen'.[117] In this book, enforcement refers to all action undertaken by the Commission according to Articles 258 and 260 TFEU, irrespective of whether it is done in a cooperative, persuasive, or coercive fashion or in a combination thereof.

4.2 *Compliance*

Compliance refers to conduct in conformity with a specified rule.[118] Carter adds that the notion implies more than merely acting in accordance with a given norm. There is an additional indication of 'consensual conformity'.[119] The author thus suggests that norm-conforming behaviour which has been brought about by sheer coercion should not be included in the standard conception of compliance. This type of compliance constitutes a variety of 'conformity for instrumental reasons'.[120] Even when absolute compliance is not reached, law itself and also institutional designs may yield some

[117] M Zürn, 'Introduction: Law and Compliance at Different Levels' in M Zürn and C Joerges (eds.), *Law and Governance in Postnational Europe, Compliance beyond the Nation-State* (Cambridge University Press, 2004), 6.

[118] K Raustiale and A Slaughter, 'International Law, International Relations and Compliance' in W Carlsnaes, T Risse, and BA Simmons (eds.), *Handbook of International Relations* (SAGE, 2002), 539. R Fisher, *Improving Compliance with International Law* (University Press of Virginia, 1981), 20.

[119] K Carter, 'New Crimes against Peace? The Application of International Humanitarian Law Compliance and Enforcement' in Canadian Council on International Law and The Markland Group (eds.), *Treaty Compliance: Some Concerns and Remedies* (Kluwer Law International, 1998), 2.

[120] K Raustiale and A Slaughter, 'International Law, International Relations and Compliance' in W Carlsnaes, T Risse, and BA Simmons (eds.), *Handbook of International Relations* (SAGE, 2002), 539

behavioural change. Young maintains that non-compliance is 'when actual behaviour departs significantly from prescribed behaviour'.[121]

The administrative and judicial phases foreseen in Article 258 TFEU constitute a mechanism by which the Commission can intensify pressure on a member state to change its behaviour. Thus, persistence is anticipated with a gradual increase of the cost of violation.[122] The Commission publishes annual reports with statistical annexes on application of EU law.[123] It appears from these reports that the Commission closes the vast majority of infringement cases at the early stages of infringement proceedings.[124] Thus, parallel to the increase of the cost of violation there is an actual reduction of cases.[125] These inverse trends should be read with care.[126] Notably, the gradually decreasing number of pending cases merely reflects termination decisions adopted by the Commission. Moreover, the Commission enjoys a broad margin of discretion and the statistical reports do not reveal the Commission's motivations. Termination of infringement cases does not necessarily reflect a behavioural change. However, according to the Commission, friendly settlements are usually due to changes in national legislation.[127] Because the Commission is not obliged to pursue all cases of alleged non-compliance a pending caseload may reflect a particular set of compliance priorities.[128] Finite executive resources would anyway not allow the Commission to pursue strict top-down enforcement

[121] O Young, *Compliance and Public Authority: A Theory with International Implications* (Johns Hopkins University Press, 1979), 3.

[122] See, eg, HAH Audretsch, *Supervision in European Community Law* (Elsevier Science Publishers BV, 1986), 410–11.

[123] The reports from 1998–2010 can be accessed at the Commission's webpage. http://ec.europa.eu/eu_law/infringements/infringements_annual_report_en.htm.

[124] See generally Commission '*28th annual report on monitoring the application of EU law*', COM 2011/588, with annexes.

[125] See furthermore, R Rawlings, 'Engaged Elites: Citizen Action and Institutional Attitudes' in C Kilpatrick, T Novitz, and P Skidmore (eds.), *Commission Enforcement, The Future of Remedies in Europe* (Hart Publishing, 2000), 273.

[126] M Hartlapp and G Falkner, 'Problems of Operationalization and Data in EU Compliance Research' (2009) *European Union Politics* 10(2), 281–304, discuss several reasons why the Commission's statistics are unreliable as indicators of genuine levels of compliance.

[127] Single Market News, No 33, April 2004, 5.

[128] Temporary increases in cases brought before the Court of Justice in accordance with Art 258 TFEU is in part to be seen in the context of the substantive and geographical expansion of EU law. Report by the Working Party on the Future of the European Communities' Court System, 19 January 2000 (Due Report), 2. The enlargement however does not seem to have had a significant effect on the infringement statistics. See in this regard, M Smith, *Centralised Enforcement, Legitimacy and Good Governance in the EU* (Routledge Cavendish, 2009), 155.

and even less so absolute enforcement of EU legislation.[129] Like domestic and federal legal systems, international treaty regimes will inevitably display some non-compliance and there are scholars who maintain that there is no evidence that international[130] and European[131] levels of compliance are necessarily lower.

A study by Falkner et al systematically looks at compliance patterns at the state level concerning selected secondary law acts.[132] The authors examine the success and failure of implementation by looking at application and enforcement, in addition to formal transposition. Interestingly, their survey reveals remarkably low degrees of perfect compliance within the established time limits and considerable variations between the then 15 member states. In their explanatory analytical framework, the authors operate with 'different worlds of compliance' under the categories 'a world of law observance',[133] 'a world of domestic politics',[134] and 'a world of neglect'.[135] Notably, none of these worlds of compliance account for defection as a rational choice. Occasionally the Commission initiates sector-specific studies at the level of selected member states. One such survey concerned implementation of Article 15(2) of the EC Royalty and Interest Directive[136] and was conducted by the International Bureau of Fiscal

[129] Compare, eg, N Lebessis and J Paterson, 'Evolution in Governance: What Lesson for the Commission? A first Assessment', *European Commission, Forward Studies Unit Working Paper* 1997, 24. See also M Smith, *Centralised Enforcement, Legitimacy and Good Governance in the EU* (Routledge Cavendish, 2009), 97, on operational problems with the infringement mechanism.

[130] M Bulterman and M Kuijer (eds.), *Compliance with Judgments of International Courts* (Martinus Nijhoff Publishers, 1996), 39.

[131] M Zürn and C Joerges (eds.), *Law and Governance in Postnational Europe, Compliance beyond the Nation-State* (Cambridge University Press, 2004), 2, note that compliance records are in some respects higher than that of comparable enforcement of German federal law. See furthermore SM Schwebel, 'Commentary in the European Communities' in MK Bulterman and M Kuijer (eds.), *Compliance with Judgments of International Courts* (Martinus Nijhoff Publishers, 1996), 39.

[132] G Falkner, O Treib, M Hartlapp, S Leiber, *Complying with Europe: EU Harmonisation and Soft Law in the Member States* (Cambridge University Press, 2005). See also G Falkner, M Hartlapp, S Leiber, and O Treib, 'In Search of the Worlds of Compliance: Promises and Pitfalls of Quantitative Testing' *IHS Political Science Series* Paper No 113, July 2007. See also G Falkner and O Treib, 'Three Worlds of Compliance or Four? The EU-15 Compared to New Member States' (2008) *Journal of Common Market Studies* 46:2, 293–313.

[133] Finland, Sweden, and Denmark.

[134] Germany, UK, Austria, the Netherlands, Spain, and Belgium.

[135] Greece, Portugal, Luxembourg, France, Ireland, and Italy.

[136] Council Directive 2003/49/EC of 3 June 2003 on a common system of taxation applicable to interest and royalty payments made between associated companies of different member states [2003] OJ L157/49.

Documentation (IBFD).[137] Other studies again suggest that 'systemic variation across functional domains' occur too.[138] Both in domestic, federal, and international law regimes, a certain degree of failure is, and has to be, accepted.[139] Perhaps it is more useful to ask whether tolerable levels of law-deviance are maintained.[140]

4.3 *Effectiveness*

Effectiveness is another central notion in the Commission's rhetoric. In its most literal sense, effectiveness can be understood as making a law operative. The European Council has defined effectiveness as full implementation and enforcement by member states.[141] Some scholars emphasize the *sui generis* nature of the notion in its particular EU context.[142] More generally, Raustiala and Slaughter draw attention to the conceptual distinction between compliance and effectiveness in regime theory. They phrase effectiveness as, for instance, 'the degree to which a rule induces changes in behaviour that further the rule's goals; improves the state of the underlying problem; or achieves its policy objective'. Effectiveness is, thus, not automatically equal to a high level of compliance, although, as the authors acknowledge, 'more compliance is better'.[143] When a supranational obligation matches domestic law from the beginning, compliance does not per se reflect a particularly effective treaty regime.[144] Dehousse et al suggest that effectiveness can be read as more than a merely substantive or procedural

[137] Can be accessed at: http://ec.europa.eu/taxation_customs/resources/documents/common/publications/studies/survey_IR_dir.pdf.

[138] PM Haas, 'Compliance with EU Directives: Insights from International Relations and Comparative Politics' (1998) *Journal of European Policy* 5:1, 17–37.

[139] See, eg, R Fisher, *Improving Compliance with International Law* (University Press of Virginia, 1981).

[140] Compare A Chayes and AH Chayes, *The New Sovereignty: Compliance with International Regulatory Agreements* (Harvard University Press, 1995), 17.

[141] Statement of European Council, Bull EC 6–1990, 18–21, fn 4, concerning the area of environmental law.

[142] See AJG Ibáñez, *The Administrative Supervision and Enforcement of EC Law* (Hart, 1999), 12; F Snyder, 'The Effectiveness of European Community Law. Institutions, Processes, Tools and Techniques' (1993) *The Modern Law Review* 56:1, 19–54, and 24–7; and HAH Audretsch, *Supervision in European Community Law* (Elsevier Science Publishers BV, 1986), 350.

[143] K Raustiale and A Slaughter, 'International Law, International Relations and Compliance' in W Carlsnaes, T Risse, and BA Simmons (eds.), *Handbook of International Relations* (SAGE, 2002).

[144] LR Helfer and A-M Slaughter, 'Why States Create International Tribunals: A Response to Professors Posner and Yoo' (2005) *California Law Review* 93, 28.

notion, but as 'multi-directional processes of reaction and adaptation, potentially involving political and legal processes and changes in organizations'.[145] Snyder emphasizes that the notion of effectiveness also reflects power struggles, value choices, and strategy considerations. Consequently, it has implications of a political nature.[146] At first sight, there is incongruence between the Commission's general obligation to monitor member state compliance as foreseen in Article 17 TEU and the Commission's broad discretion whether to initiate and maintain infringement proceedings. However, the practice of negotiated settlements shows that the Commission may pursue objectives of effectiveness rather than of absolute compliance.

[145] R Dehousse, C Joerges, G Majone, and F Snyder, 'Europe after 1992, New Regulatory Strategies' *EUI Working Paper*, LAW No 92/31. See also F Snyder, 'The Effectiveness of European Community Law. Institutions, Processes, Tools and Techniques' (1993) *The Modern Law Review* 56:1, 19–54, 19.

[146] F Snyder, *New Directions in European Community Law* (Weidenfeld & Nicholson, 1990), 3, and 22–5.

2

Failure to Comply with EU Law: Article 258 TFEU

1. Introduction[1]

The general EU infringement procedure consists of two distinct procedures stipulated in Articles 258 and 260 TFEU, each with its own subject-matter. The procedure established under Article 258 TFEU is designed to obtain a declaration that the conduct of a member state is in breach of EU law and that the conduct will be terminated. The procedure provided for under Article 260 TFEU is designed to induce a defaulting member state to comply with a judgment establishing a breach of obligations, ie repetitive infringements, and it has a much narrower ambit than Article 258 TFEU.[2] The procedural construction thus distinguishes between compliance with treaty obligations, 'first order compliance', and compliance with judgments of the treaty regime's dispute settlement body, 'second order compliance'.[3] The two procedures however have the same purpose, that is to say, to ensure the effective application of EU law.[4]

[1] This chapter is based on my article entitled 'Procedural Overview and Substantive Comments on Articles 226 and 228 EC' published in 2009 in (2008) *Yearbook of European Law* 27, 121–66. It does not provide a description of the Commission's internal working procedures. More information on that can be found in, eg, M Smith, *Centralised Enforcement, Legitimacy and Good Governance in the EU* (Routledge, 2009). See the introductory chapter for a list of literature on the general EU infringement procedure.

[2] Joined cases C-514/07 P, C-528/07 P, and C-532/07 P *Sweden* v *API and Commission* [2010] ECR I-08533, para 119.

[3] See generally R Fisher, *Improving Compliance with International Law* (University Press of Virginia, 1981) for this distinction. Fisher is not concerned with EU law specifically. This distinction aside, nothing of the author's general theoretical framework is implied.

[4] Joined cases C-514/07 P, C-528/07 P, and C-532/07 *Sweden* v *API and Commission* [2010] ECR I-08533, para 118.

Prior to the Maastricht Treaty entering into force, the two procedures were largely identical despite tackling different types of non-compliance.[5] However, the Maastricht Treaty empowered the Commission to request the Court of Justice to award pecuniary sanctions against member states for failure to take the necessary measures to comply with a judgment of the Court of Justice. Moreover, the Lisbon Treaty amended Article 260 TFEU in important ways.[6] Among those amendments, the fast-track sanctioning mechanism stipulated in Article 260(3) targeting late transposition of directives has direct implications for the procedure stipulated in Article 258 TFEU. Article 260(3) TFEU and the other amendments are discussed in detail in chapter three.

This chapter takes stock of the general EU infringement procedure established under Article 258 TFEU concerning 'first order compliance'. It proceeds as follows. First, it describes the procedural stages involved and reviews relevant case law. Then it discusses questions pertaining to confidentiality and the Commission's discretion according to Article 258 TFEU. The final part of this chapter analyses the general EU infringement procedure in view of the international law compliance theory on managerialism. It does so in order to explain and better understand the purpose and function of the procedural stages and the role of the Commission, and to bring out the distinct features of the institutional designs and organizational rules which have made it a particularly robust enforcement mechanism.

2. Procedural Clarifications

Article 258 TFEU reads:

If the Commission considers that a Member State has failed to fulfil an obligation under the Treaties, it shall deliver a reasoned opinion on the matter after giving the State concerned the opportunity to submit its observations.

If the State concerned does not comply with the opinion within the period laid down by the Commission, the latter may bring the matter before the Court of Justice of the European Union.

[5] Treaty establishing the European Community (consolidated text) [2002] OJ C 325.

[6] Treaty on European Union and the Treaty on the Functioning of the European Union (consolidated text) [2010] OJ C 83.

Failure to fulfil an obligation under the Treaties can take many different forms. They include: (i) failure to apply and enforce primary law, as well as failure to cooperate loyally (see also the section on the principle of sincere cooperation); (ii) failure to transpose, apply, and enforce a directive; (iii) failure to achieve, in a specific case, the result intended by the directive; (iv) failure to notify, where required, measures transposing a directive; and (v) failure to implement, apply, and enforce regulations.[7] The Commission usually pursues specific cases of non-compliance. However, it may also pursue an administrative practice as such 'when it is, to some degree, of a consistent and general nature'.[8] In the 'Irish Waste' case, the Court of Justice looked to determine whether Ireland had taken all the measures necessary to ensure a whole range of directive provisions had been correctly implemented.[9]

2.1 *Pre-litigation procedure*

The procedure established under Article 258 TFEU consists of a pre-litigation phase and a litigation phase. The purpose of the pre-litigation phase 'is to enable the Member State to comply of its own accord with the requirements of the Treaty or, if appropriate, to justify its position'.[10] Thus, the Commission has at its disposal a tool to persuade the member state to comply voluntarily. However, if it is unsuccessful, the purpose of the pre-litigation phase becomes to define the subject-matter of the dispute.[11] It is settled case law that Article 258 TFEU does not empower the Commission

[7] While provisions of regulations generally have immediate effect in the national legal systems and do not require national authorities to adopt application measures, some provisions may nonetheless necessitate, for their implementation, the adoption of measures of application by the member states. See to this effect C-403/98 *Azienda Agricola Monte Arcosu* [2001] ECR I-103, para 26.

[8] C-494/01 *Commission v Ireland* [2005] ECR I-3331, para 27, with reference to, in particular, C-387/99 *Commission v Germany* [2004] ECR I-3751, para 42, and the case law cited.

[9] C-494/01 *Commission v Ireland* [2005] ECR I-3331. For analyses of the judgment, see P Wennerås, 'A New Dawn for Commission Enforcement under Articles 226 and 228 EC: General and Persistent (GAP) Infringements, Lump Sums and Penalty Payments' (2006) *Common Market Law Review* 43:1, 31–62; A Schrauwen, 'Fishery, Waste Management and Persistent and General Failure to Fulfil Control Obligations: The Role of Lump Sums and Penalty Payments in Enforcement Actions under Community Law' (2006) *Journal of Environmental Law* 18:2, 289–99; L Prete and B Smulders, 'The Coming of Age of Infringement Proceedings' (2010) *Common Market Law Review* 47:1, 9–61 (23–4); and R Macrory, *Regulation, Enforcement and Governance in Environmental Law* (Cameron May Ltd, 2008), 719–20.

[10] C-159/94 *Commission v France* [1997] ECR I-5815, para 103.

[11] Joined Cases 142/80 and 143/80 *Essevi and Salengo* [1981] ECR 1413, para 15.

to determine conclusively the rights and duties of a member state, or to give it guarantees concerning the compatibility of a given line of conduct with the EU Treaties. Only the Court of Justice is.[12] The implications of this division of power are discussed in more detail in chapter four.

Before analysing the stages of the pre-litigation phase, it should be mentioned that the Commission has initiated a so-called EU Pilot based on a 'partnership approach' between the Commission and the member states. It deals with questions concerning the correct application of EU law or the conformity of the law in a member state with EU law. Member states receive individual files, including a description and questions about a particular compliance issue. Within 10 weeks the national authorities shall reply to the questions raised and propose a solution to the identified infringement. Within a further 10 weeks, in principle, the Commission examines the answer and uploads an assessment in the confidential EU Pilot database.[13] The method has come about on the initiative of the Commission and it does not have a legal basis in the EU Treaties.[14] However, it has quickly turned into the Commission's main tool to communicate with the member states on infringements. Because EU Pilot, as a rule, applies before infringement proceedings are launched under Article 258 TFEU it constitutes a type of 'pre-infringement' phase. In cases that are not properly resolved and subsequently dealt with under the general EU infringement procedure, EU Pilot effectively constitutes a 'pre-pre-litigation' phase.

2.1.1 Letter of formal notice

If a case is not properly resolved through EU Pilot, the Commission may set the infringement procedure in motion by giving the member state the opportunity to submit observations. It does so by issuing a letter of formal notice.[15] This procedure provides the member state a right to submit its

[12] T-258/06 *Germany v Commission* [2010] ECR II-02027, para 153; Joined cases 142/80 and 143/80 *Essevi and Salengo* [1981] ECR 1413, para 16; C-393/98 *Gomes Valente* [2001] ECR I-1327, para 18.

[13] See Commission report *'Second Evaluation Report on EU Pilot'*, COM/2011/930 final with references.

[14] Commission Communication *'A Europe of Results—Applying Community Law'*, COM/2007/502 (section 2.2. 'Improving working methods').

[15] The term letter of formal notice is not used in Art 258 TFEU. Sometimes the Commission extends the legal assessment in the first letter of formal notice by issuing a supplementary letter of formal notice. See, eg, C-10/10 *Commission v Austria* [2011] not yet published in the ECR.

stand on the facts and legal assessment thereof to the Commission for further consideration. Hence, it constitutes an essential procedural guarantee in accordance with the doctrine of *audi alteram partem*.[16] The letter of formal notice is not subject to such strict requirements of precision though, since it cannot, of necessity, contain anything more than an initial brief summary of the complaints.[17]

2.1.2 Reasoned opinion

If the Commission considers the member state's response to the letter of formal notice to be inadequate and the member state has not altered its behaviour in a satisfactory manner, the Commission may follow up with a reasoned opinion. As mentioned, the Commission shall circumscribe the issue of its complaint in the letter of formal notice. The underlying purpose is to restrain the Commission so that it cannot alter, or extend, its complaints in a subsequent reasoned opinion. This, however, does not amount to a requirement of identical wording if the subject-matter has not been materially modified.[18] Thus, the Commission is free to set out in detail in the reasoned opinion the complaints which it has already made more generally in the letter of formal notice.[19] The issuing of a reasoned opinion does not have any binding legal effect for the addressee. It is merely a pre-litigation stage of a procedure which may lead to an action before the Court of Justice.[20]

In its reasoned opinion, the Commission requests the member state to take the measures necessary for it to comply. In doing so, it should observe a certain degree of specificity as to the subject-matter and make a 'coherent and detailed statement of the reasons which led the Commission to conclude that the State in question failed to fulfil one of its obligations under the Treaty'.[21] The requirement concerning coherence and detail

[16] Case 31/69 *Commission v Italy* [1970] ECR 25, para 13. K Lenaerts and D Arts, 'Action for Infringement of Community Law by a Member State' in K Lenaerts, D Arts, and R Bray (eds.), *Procedural Law of the European Union* (Sweet & Maxwell, 1999), 100–01. See also C-279/94 *Commission v Italy* ECR I-4743, para 15.

[17] C-20/09 *Commission v Portugal* [2011] not yet published in the ECR, para 20.

[18] C-280/02 *Commission v France* [2004] ECR I-8573, paras 29 and 30.

[19] See, eg, case 74/82 *Commission v Ireland* [1984] ECR 317, para 20; case 274/83 *Commission v Italy* [1985] ECR 1077, para 21; C-358/01 *Commission v Spain* [2003] ECR I-13145, para 29; and C-20/09 *Commission v Portugal* [2011] not yet published in the ECR, para 20.

[20] C-191/95 *Commission v Germany* [1998] ECR I-5449, para 44.

[21] C-289/94 *Commission v Italy* [1996] ECR I-4405, para 16.

does not, as some scholars have tentatively suggested,[22] amount to an obligation to specify what the Commission regards to be the measures and actions necessary to bring the concrete infringement to an end.[23] The Court of Justice would anyway not be able to rule on such specification. Notably, the Court of Justice is required to find only that a provision of EU law has been infringed.[24] If, however, the Commission would like to make failure to adopt measures to enable the infringement to be remedied the subject-matter of the infringement proceedings it has to specify those measures in the reasoned opinion.[25]

A literal interpretation of Article 258 TFEU suggests that the Commission is obliged to deliver a reasoned opinion if it considers a member state to be in default. Somewhat confusingly, this obligation is made dependent on the Commission's own view.[26] The Court of Justice has now clarified that the Commission's discretion to further a case at this point in time is unqualified.[27] Charges which have not been included in the reasoned opinion are inadmissible at the stage of proceedings before the Court of Justice.[28]

The Commission sets a deadline for the member state to reply in the reasoned opinion and the Court of Justice appraises member state conduct

[22] K Lenaerts and D Arts, 'Action for Infringement of Community Law by a Member State' in K Lenaerts, D Arts, and R Bray (eds.), *Procedural Law of the European Union* (Sweet & Maxwell, 1999), 102: 'The Commission also may—or possibly must—set forth the measures which need to be taken in order to bring the infringement to an end.' For a discussion whether the Commission and the Court respectively can state the specific measures that a member state must adopt, see also AJG Ibáñez, *The Administrative Supervision and Enforcement of EC Law* (Hart, 1999), 92–5.

[23] Cases C-458/08 *Commission v Portugal* [2010] not yet published in the ECR, para 51; C-559/07 *Commission v Greece* [2009] ECR I-47, para 23; C-328/96 *Commission v Austria* [1999] ECR I-7479, para 39; and C-247/89 *Commission v Portugal* [1991] ECR I-3659, para 22. See also AJG Ibáñez, 'A Deeper Insight into Article 169' *Harvard Jean Monnet Working Paper* 11/98.

[24] C-503/04 *Commission v Germany* [2007] ECR I-6153, para 15.

[25] C-394/02 *Commission v Greece* [2005] ECR I-4713, para 23.

[26] HAH Audretsch, *Supervision in European Community Law* (Elsevier Science Publishers BV, 1986), 35. See furthermore P Craig and G de Búrca, *EC Law: Text, Cases, and Materials* (3rd edn, Oxford University Press, 2003), 407.

[27] HAH Audretsch, *Supervision in European Community Law* (Elsevier Science Publishers BV, 1986), 35. Although the discretion is unqualified the Commission still has to observe the principle of sound administration. C-350/08, *Commission v Lithuania* [2010] ECR I-10525, para 38. An example could be that the Commission's decision to initiate a case is influenced by bribes. As will be discussed below, the Ombudsman argues that the Commission has a duty to state reasons vis-à-vis complainants when closing a case.

[28] C-305/03 *Commission v Luxembourg* [2006] ECR I-1213, para 22.

or omission prevailing in the member state at the end of that period.[29] Subsequent member state changes are immaterial.[30] Thus there is pressure on the member state to conform within this deadline.

The subject-matter of a dispute may however be extended to events which took place after the reasoned opinion was delivered if the events are of the same kind and constitute the same conduct as the events to which the opinion referred.[31] The situation may also arise that the member state significantly alters its behaviour after the time limit laid down by the Commission in its reasoned opinion expires, but before the Commission makes a referral to the Court of Justice and this may effectively render a judgment redundant. In such a situation, the Commission enjoys discretion as to whether it wishes to issue a revised reasoned opinion, taking the changed circumstances into considerations.[32]/Advocate General Colomer dubs the period following the issue of a reasoned opinion a 'period of grace' because the Commission undertakes not to start legal proceedings while the member state retains the option to alter its behaviour. After this period, he cautions, 'dialogue gives way to action'.[33] The Court of Justice however recognizes that bilateral compliance negotiations may continue during the court proceedings and up to the delivery of the judgment and that this is in accordance with the aim of the procedure, viz., to reach an amicable settlement.[34]

2.1.3 Time limits

Article 258 TFEU does not lay down time limits for a member state to respond to warning letters and reasoned opinions. As a general rule, the Commission operates with a 60-day deadline for member state response to a reasoned opinion. It is established case law that member states shall be

[29] Joined cases C-20/01 and C-28/01 *Commission v Germany* [2003] ECR I-3609, para 32. The question may however arise when an infringement ceases to subsist. See, eg, joined cases C-20/01 and C-28/01 *Commission* v *Germany* [2003] ECR I-3609.

[30] C-211/02 *Commission v Luxembourg* [2003] ECR I-2429, para 6.

[31] C-221/04 *Commission v Spain* [2006] ECR I-4515, para 28; with reference to Case 42/82 *Commission v France* [1983] ECR 1013, para 20; and 113/86 *Commission* v *Italy* [1988] ECR 607, para 11.

[32] C-177/03 *Commission v France* [2004] ECR I-11671, para 21; and C-266/94 *Commission v Spain* [1995] ECR I-1975, para 24.

[33] Opinion of Advocate General Colomer in C-362/01 *Commission v Ireland* [2002] ECR I-11433, point 21.

[34] T-36/04 *API v Commission* [2007] ECR II-3201, para 121; and T-191/99 *Petrie and Others v Commission* [2001] ECR II-3677, para 68.

given an opportunity to comply and that the member state's right of defence has to be respected.[35] All the particular circumstances of a case have to be considered when assessing whether the period granted of time is reasonable.[36] The relevant circumstances may relate to both the type of infringement and the member state's right of defence. The Court of Justice has, on occasion, taken into account whether the member state was already familiar with the Commission's viewpoints.[37] Likewise, short time limits of one month have been considered reasonable in situations where a member state has consistently objected to the Commission's allegations of a breach.[38]

Whereas the Court of Justice cannot prolong the time limit set by the Commission, the Commission itself may decide to make a suspension.[39] Member states sometimes request an extension of the period prescribed for its reply stating its intention to take the necessary action in response to the letter of formal notice, if need be by adapting the legislation, or citing internal problems; for instance of an institutional nature. Although the Commission is by no means bound by such a request, it may be persuaded by a sound action plan or by reasons it considers are politically or practically relevant as well as the member state's general repute in similar circumstances.

A member state cannot claim that the Commission excessively delayed initiation of the administrative proceedings provided for in Article 258 TFEU.[40] It may however succeed in arguing, in certain situations, that the excessive duration of the pre-litigation procedure has made it more difficult for it to refute the Commission's arguments and thus infringed the member state's rights of defence. The burden of proof in that regard rests on the member state.[41] This type of argument, if at some point successfully submitted, would only have procedural significance. That is to say, the member state's obligation to comply as directed by the EU Treaties will of course not be affected.

[35] C-473/93 *Commission v Luxembourg* [1996] ECR I-3207, para 19.

[36] C-328/96 *Commission v Austria* [1999] ECR I-7479, paras 34 and 51; and C-1/00 *Commission v France* [2001] ECR I-9989, paras 64 and 65.

[37] Case 85/85 *Commission v Belgium* [1986] ECR 1149, para 13; C-320/03 *Commission v Austria* [2005] ECR I-09871, para 33; and Case 293/85 *Commission v Belgium* [1988] ECR 305, para 14.

[38] C-247/89 *Commission v Portugal* [1991] ECR I-3659, para 25.

[39] Case 16/84 *Commission v Netherlands* [1985] ECR 2355, para 10.

[40] C-350/08, *Commission v Lithuania* [2010] ECR I-10525.

[41] C-96/89 *Commission v Netherlands* [1991] ECR I-2461, para 16; and C-546/07 *Commission v Germany* [2010] ECR I-439, para 22.

2.2 *The judicial phase*

2.2.1 *Procedural requirements: The Commission*

According to Article 258 TFEU the Commission has final recourse to the Court of Justice. The provision explicitly states that the Commission 'may' bring a matter before the Court of Justice. Thus, the Commission has the right, but not the obligation, to apply to the Court of Justice for a declaration establishing the member state's failure to comply.[42] In the words of Advocate General Alber, '[t]he structure of Treaty infringement proceedings, with their obligatory pre-litigation procedure, is designed to allow an amicable settlement at any stage of the proceedings'.[43] Notably, the vast majority of infringement cases are closed in the pre-judicial phase. 88 per cent of the 987 complaint-based and own initiative cases the Commission closed during 2010 did not reach the Court of Justice.[44] In 2010 the Court's average time to deal with a direct action was 16.7 months, down from 20 months in 2006.[45]

The Commission does not have to demonstrate a specific interest in bringing an action. This should not be conceived of as a Commission right, but rather a consequence of the Commission's particular function as guardian 'in the general interest of the Community'.[46] Moreover, the Court of Justice does not interfere with the Commission's decision on the appropriateness of launching a complaint and thus it cannot demand a withdrawal.[47] It may, however, examine the question as to whether the conditions laid down in Article 258 TFEU for the bringing of an action are satisfied and it can do so of its own motion.[48]

[42] See, eg, Case 247/87 *Star Fruit v Commission* [1989] ECR 291.

[43] Opinion of Advocate General Alber in C-185/96 *Commission v Greece* [1998] ECR I-6601, point 19.

[44] Commission '*28th annual report on monitoring the application of EU law*', COM/2011/588, 5.

[45] The Court of Justice of the European Union's 2010 Annual Report, 96. The report can be accessed at http://curia.europa.eu/jcms/jcms/Jo2_7000/. For a breakdown of cases according to subject-matter, see the report at 86.

[46] Joined cases C-20/01 and C-28/01 *Commission v Germany* [2003] ECR I-3609, para 29.

[47] C-236/99 *Commission v Belgium* [2000] ECR I-5657, para 28; and C-383/00 *Commission v Germany* [2002] ECR I-4219, para 19.

[48] C-362/90 *Commission v Italy* [1992] ECR I-2353, para 8; and C-417/02 *Commission v Greece* [2004] ECR I-7973, para 16.

The purpose of an application to the Court of Justice is to identify the complaints which the Court of Justice is requested to rule upon.[49] Thus, the Commission must indicate the specific complaints on which the Court of Justice is asked to rule and, at the very least in summary form, the legal and factual particulars on which those complaints are based.[50] The heads of claim must be set out unambiguously in order to warrant that the Court of Justice rule does not rule *ultra petita* or fail to rule on a complaint.[51] It is not permissible for a party to alter the very subject-matter of the case during the proceedings and the merits of the action must be examined solely in the light of the claims contained in the application initiating the proceedings.[52]

The reasoned opinion and the proceedings brought by the Commission must be based on the same complaints as those set out in the letter of formal notice initiating the pre-litigation procedure.[53] Any failure to do so cannot be remedied subsequently. It makes no difference in this regard if the defendant member state subsequently submits observations on the reasoned opinion. In such a case, the action will be deemed inadmissible altogether or in part.[54] At the same time, there is no requirement that the operative part of the reasoned opinion and the form of order sought in the application to the Court of Justice should be identical if the subject-matter of the proceedings as defined in the reasoned opinion has simply been limited.[55] The Commission is also free to clarify its initial grounds of complaint as long as it does not alter the subject-matter of the dispute.

[49] C-347/88 *Commission v Greece* [1990] ECR I-4747, para 28. See also C-160/08 *Commission v Germany* [2010] ECR I-3713, para 49.

[50] C-543/08 *Commission v Portugal* [2010] not yet published in the ECR, para 21, with reference to C-52/90 *Commission v Denmark* [1992] ECR I-2187, para 17; C-508/03 *Commission v United Kingdom* [2006] ECR I-3969, para 62; and C-487/08 *Commission v Spain* [2010] ECR I-04843, para 71.

[51] C-255/04 *Commission v France* [2006] ECR I-5251, para 24, with reference to joined cases 46/59 and 47/59 *Meroni v High Authority* [1962] ECR 411, 419, and C-296/01 *Commission v France* [2003] ECR I-13909, para 121.

[52] Article 42 of the Rules of Procedure of the Court of Justice; C-543/08 *Commission v Portugal* [2010] not yet published in the ECR, para 20; Case 232/78 *Commission v France* [1979] ECR 2729, para 3; C-256/98 *Commission v France* [2000] ECR I-2487, para 31; and C-508/03 *Commission v United Kingdom* [2006] ECR I-3969, para 61.

[53] C-191/95 *Commission v Germany* [1998] ECR I-5449, para 55; and C-422/05 *Commission v Belgium* [2007] ECR I-4749, para 25.

[54] Case 51/83 *Commission v Italy* [1984] ECR 2793, paras 6 and 7; and C-186/06 *Commission v Spain* [2007] ECR I-12093, para 15.

[55] C-441/02 *Commission v Germany* [2006] ECR I-3449, para 61.

This includes the possibility of producing fresh evidence to illustrate the grounds of complaint set out in its reasoned opinion.[56]

In some situations, the member state's behaviour may justify greater leeway to be given to the Commission. It could be that a member state alters its legislation during the pre-litigation period and also subsequent to the Commission bringing action. In that case, the Commission can choose to impute its complaints to the new circumstances during the course of the proceedings, as long as the subject-matter of the dispute remains the same.[57]

Claims are, however, rejected as inadmissible if they are put forward for the first time in the reply instead of in the application. The reason is that such claims modify the original subject-matter of the application and they are consequently regarded as new claims.[58] Another example of leeway given to the Commission is if the information provided by the member state is misleading or wrong. In this instance, the Commission may, under specific circumstances, make appropriate corrections. Sometimes member states wait to submit the correct adoption of a law transposing a directive until the Commission brings proceedings before the Court of Justice. Under such circumstances the Commission may, where relevant, specify in its reply that the implementation pleaded for the first time by the member state concerned in its defence is incorrect or incomplete so far as certain provisions of the directive are concerned.[59] As a general rule though, the objective of the pre-litigation procedure to protect the rights of the member state concerned must always be achieved.[60]

2.2.2 *The judgment*

There are no requirements that an infringement should be clear or manifest. The Court of Justice is not concerned with the nature or seriousness of an infringement.[61] Moreover, it does not consider whether a member state

[56] C-494/01 *Commission v Ireland* [2005] ECR I-3331, para 38, with reference to C-328/02 *Commission v Greece*, not published in the ECR, paras 32 and 36 (by analogy).

[57] C-177/04 *Commission v France* [2006] ECR I-2461, para 39, with analogy to C-42/89 *Commission v Belgium* [1990] ECR I-2821, para 11.

[58] C-160/08 *Commission v Germany* [2010] ECR I-03713, para 49.

[59] C-522/09 *Commission v Luxembourg* [2011] not yet published in the ECR.

[60] C-32/05 *Commission v Luxembourg* [2006] ECR I-11323, paras 54–6; and C-522/09 *Commission v Romania* [2011] not yet published in the ECR, para 19.

[61] C-359/93 *Commission v Netherlands* [1995] ECR I-157, para 14.

has been acting *in culpa*.[62] Judgments according to Article 258 TFEU are of a purely declaratory nature.[63] Thus, '[e]ither there is a failure to fulfil obligations and the Court can merely find accordingly, or there is none, and the action must be dismissed'.[64] Although the Court of Justice is only required to find that a provision of EU law has been infringed, judgments frequently suggest more or less implicitly what is required in order for the member state to comply.[65] Ibáñez considers it useful if the Commission and the Court of Justice indicate the measures that they expect a given member state to take. Because, he maintains, it 'would offer an opportunity to discuss the sustainability of these measures during the first judicial proceedings and not only the fact of lack of compliance'.[66] The extent to which the Court of Justice can provide such guidance and engage in a discussion of the sustainability of the proposed measures, though, is limited owing to the discretion enjoyed by the member states in transposing, implementing, and enforcing EU law. Even if a member state may be interested in rather concrete suggestions as to how to comply, such assistance by the judiciary is difficult to reconcile with division of powers between the Court of Justice and the member states. What is more, it may not be useful in general given the very different national contexts in which EU law needs to be effective. The roles played by the Court of Justice and the Commission in this respect are markedly different. As discussed in chapter one, the Commission engages in non-binding dialogue with the member states. Thus, there is ample room for the Commission to discuss with a member state

[62] This is not necessarily the case with implementation of structural funds where financial entitlement can be made conditional on compliance. See, eg, the culpability considerations in Regulation (EC) No 1655/1999 of the European Parliament and of the Council of 19 July 1999 amending Regulation (EC) No 2236/95 laying down general rules for the granting of Community financial aid in the field of trans-European networks [1999] OJ L197/1: 'Except where the Member States and/or the implementing authority provide proof that they were not responsible for the irregularity, the Member State shall be liable in the alternative for reimbursement of any sums unduly paid.'

[63] C-126/03 *Commission v Germany* [2004] ECR I-11197, para 26.

[64] Opinion of Advocate General Mischo in C-78/00 *Commission v Italy* [2001] ECR I-8195, point 65.

[65] AJG Ibáñez, *The Administrative Supervision and Enforcement of EC Law* (Hart, 1999), 94. In his opinion in case 124/81, Advocate General van Themaat proposed that the Court of Justice '. . . give the United Kingdom legislature guidance in its difficult task of complying with the judgment pursuant to Article 171 of the Treaty [Article 260 TFEU], and also in order to give the judgment the desirable effect of reducing existing trade restrictions'. See also HAH Audretsch *Supervision in European Community Law* (Elsevier Science Publishers BV, 1986), 130.

[66] AJG Ibáñez, *The Administrative Supervision and Enforcement of EC Law* (Hart, 1999), 95.

how it could comply during the pre-litigation phase and even during the court proceedings and up to the delivery of the judgment.

By clarifying the member states' obligations, a ruling under Article 258 TFEU may allow headway for citizens who wish to challenge a member state before national courts.[67] However, as Advocate General Stix-Hackl remarks, 'the rights accruing to individuals derive, not from that judgment, but from the actual provisions of Community [EU] law having direct effect in the internal legal order'.[68] Moreover, because the objectives and effects of the infringement procedure are different from proceedings before a national court, the 'existence of the remedies available through the national courts cannot prejudice the bringing of an action under Article 226 EC [Article 258 TFEU]'.[69]

Article 260 TFEU concerning repetitive non-compliance does not specify the period within which a judgment must be complied with. It is, however, settled case law that a member state shall take the necessary steps to give effect to a judgment immediately and the necessary action should be completed in the shortest possible period.[70] The remedies available to the Commission when a member state fails to take the necessary measures to comply with the judgment of the Court of Justice are discussed in chapter three.

The principle of *res judicata* applies to infringement proceedings under Article 258 TFEU. This works as a safeguard against judicial decisions being called into question. The principle, however, only extends to the matters of fact and law actually or necessarily settled by the judicial decision in question.[71]

[67] See P Craig and G de Búrca, *EU Law, Text, Cases and Materials* (2nd edn, Oxford University Press, 1998), 392. Individuals' remedies before national courts make up for the fact that the Commission is not obliged to monitor the member states' follow-up actions. It presupposes, of course, *locus standi* according to national law.

[68] Opinion of Advocate General Stix-Hackl in C-426/98 *Commission v Greece* [2001] ECR I-2793 with reference to joined cases 314/81, 315/81, 316/81, and 83/82 *Procureur de la République* [1982] ECR I-4337, point 15.

[69] C-508/03 *Commission v UK* [2006] ECR I-3969, para 71.On the relationship between the preliminary reference procedure and the general EU infringement procedure, see M Broberg and N Fenger, *Preliminary References to the Court of Justice* (Oxford University Press, 2010), 211–13.

[70] Case 69/86 *Commission v Italy* [1987] ECR 773, para 8; and C-568/07 *Commission v Greece* [2009] ECR I-4505, para 51.

[71] C-526/08 *Commission v Luxembourg* [2010] ECR I-6151, para 27; C-462/05 *Commission v Portugal* [2008] ECR I-4183, para 23, and the case law cited. For an analysis of the case and its implications for the relationship between Arts 258 and 260 TFEU, see see P Wennerås,

2.2.3 *Interim measures*

The Commission may seek interim measures according to Article 279 TFEU. An example of an interim measure could be an order that a member state should suspend operation of a traffic ban.[72] Two recent examples concern nature protection cases.[73] Ibáñez rightly points out that there is a contradiction between the Court of Justice's power to hand down declaratory judgments according to Article 258 TFEU and 'the power of the ECJ to impose concrete obligations on Member States when it adopts interim measures'.[74] The Commission seldom seeks interim measures. However when it does, an application for interim measures may in itself prompt a member state to change behaviour.[75]

2.2.4 *Member state defences*

The Court of Justice has accepted almost none of the defences submitted by member states over time.[76] First, a member state cannot plead that a directive or decision addressed to it is unlawful as a defence in an infringement case concerning its failure to implement that decision or comply with that directive.[77] Second, it is settled case law that a member state cannot plead failure to observe the principle of reciprocity or rely on a possible infringement of the Treaties by another member state to justify its

'Sanctions against Member States under Article 260 TFEU: Alive, but Not Kicking?' (2012) *Common Market Law Review* 49, 145–76

[72] C-320/03 R *Commission v Austria* [2003] ECR I-7929.

[73] C-76/08 R *Commission v Malta* [2008] ECR I-64; and C-503/06 R *Commission v Italy* [2007] ECR I-19.

[74] AJG Ibáñez, *The Administrative Supervision and Enforcement of EC Law* (Hart, 1999), 94.

[75] This was the case in C-193/07 *Commission v Poland* ([2007] OJ C 199, 14–16) where Poland agreed to halt a motorway project pending a judgment. See also Commission Staff Working Document *'Situation in Different Sectors'* accompanying document to the Report from the Commission 27th Annual Report on Monitoring the Application of EU Law (2009), SEC/2010/1143 final, 175.

[76] On member state defences, see, eg, L Borzsák, *The Impact of Environmental Concerns on the Public Enforcement Mechanism under EU* (Wolters Kluwer, 2011), 12–17, and L Prete and B Smulders, 'The Coming of Age of Infringement Proceedings' (2010) *Common Market Law Review* 47:1, 9–61 (41–3).

[77] See, eg, C-74/91 *Commission v Germany* [1992] ECR I-5437, para 10; and C-154/00 *Commission v Greece* [2002] ECR I-3879, para 28; and C-194/01 *Commission* v *Austria* [2004] ECR I-4579, para 41. The validity of directives and decisions can be disputed according to the procedure stipulated in Art 263 TFEU.

own infringement.[78] Third, given that a member state cannot rely on an infringement of EU law by another member state in order to justify its own default, it cannot under any circumstances unilaterally adopt, on its own authority, corrective or defensive measures.[79] Fourth, member states may not plead provisions, practices, or situations existing in its internal legal order to justify the failure to comply with obligations arising under EU law.[80] This includes those resulting from the member states' federal organization.[81] Fifth, arguments based on the direct effect of directives cannot be accepted either.[82] Sixth, a member state may not plead financial difficulties in order to justify non-compliance.[83] A member State may in principle rely on force majeure to justify non-compliance when it encounters temporarily insuperable difficulties preventing it from complying with its obligations under EU law. However, it may only do so for the period necessary in order to resolve those difficulties.[84]

2.2.5 *Burden of proof*

The burden of proof rests with the Commission.[85] It must provide the evidence necessary for the Court of Justice to establish that the obligation

[78] Case 232/78 *Commission v France* [1979] ECR 2729, para 9; Case 325/82 *Commission v Germany* [1984] ECR 777, para 11; C-101/94 *Commission v Italy* [1996] ECR I-2691, para 27.

[79] Case 232/78 *Commission v France* [1979] ECR 2729, para 9; Case 325/82 *Commission v Germany* [1984] ECR 777, para 11; C-146/89 *Commission v United Kingdom* [1991] ECR I-3533, para 47; C-5/94 *Hedley Lomas* [1996] ECR I-2553, para 20; and C-111/03 *Commission v Sweden* [2005] ECR I-8789, para 66.

[80] C-166/97 *Commission v France* [1999] ECR I-1719, para 13; C-212/99 *Commission v Italy* [2001] ECR I-4923, para 34; C-83/00 *Commission v Netherlands* [2001] ECR I-2351, para 10; C-195/02 *Commission v Spain* [2004] ECR I-7857, para 82.

[81] C-383/00 *Commission v Germany* [2002] ECR I-4219, para 18.

[82] Case 102/79 *Commission v Belgium* [1980] ECR 1473, para 12; C-433/93 *Commission v Germany* [1995] ECR I-2303, para 24; C-253/95 *Commission v Germany* [1996] ECR I-2423, para 13; and C-475/08 *Commission v Belgium* [2009] ECR I-11503, para 44.

[83] C-42/89 *Commission v Belgium* [1990] ECR I-2821, para 24.

[84] Case 101/84 *Commission v Italy* [1985] ECR 2629, para 16; and C-1/00 *Commission v France* [2001] ECR I-9989, para 131. According to settled case law, it is for the member states to show that the conditions permitting a derogation from Art 34 TFEU (free movement of goods) are satisfied. See, eg, C-165/08 *Commission v Poland* [2009] ECR I-6843, para 53. This however is not a member state defence concerning failure to comply. In cases like *Commission v Poland* the Court of Justice tries whether the material conditions stipulated in Art 36 TFEU are fulfilled. If so, the derogation is lawful.

[85] See generally K Lenaerts and D Arts, 'Action for Infringement of Community Law by a Member State' in K Lenaerts, D Arts, and R Bray (eds.), *Procedural Law of the European Union* (Sweet & Maxwell, 1999), 107; and AJG Ibáñez, *The Administrative Supervision and Enforcement of EC Law* (Hart, 1999), 99–101.

has not been fulfilled, and it may not rely on any presumption.[86] At the same time, the Court of Justice has emphasized that a member state cannot merely deny a failure to comply if the Commission produces 'sufficient' evidence. In that case the member state must 'contest substantively and in detail the information produced and the consequences thereof'.[87] Otherwise, the Court of Justice may consider that the charges indeed have been demonstrated. This implies that the member state must give details on how a particular law is applied.[88] This obligation was originally based on a reading of the fidelity clause in Article 10 of the EC Treaty (now repealed and replaced, in substance, by Article 4(3) TEU) in conjunction with Article 211 of the EC Treaty (replaced, in substance, by Article 17(1) TEU). In addition, if necessary, the national authorities may be obliged to conduct on-the-spot investigations.[89]

As mentioned above, the Commission may pursue failures in relation to an administrative practice as such 'when it is, to some degree, of a consistent and general nature'.[90] In cases concerning an administrative practice it is therefore the responsibility of the Commission to provide sufficient evidence that there is a repeated and persistent practice which is contrary to EU law.[91] This should contain sufficient documentation and detailed proof of the alleged practice. When the necessary evidence is provided the member state in turn has to challenge the information and that a repeated and persistent practice persists may be deduced from the information.[92] Again, the Commission may not rely on any presumption.[93]

2.3 *The principle of sincere cooperation*

The principle of sincere or loyal cooperation previously stipulated in Article 10 of the EC Treaty (now repealed and replaced, in substance, by

[86] See, eg, case 96/81 *Commission v Netherlands* [1982] ECR 1791, para 6; C-404/00 *Commission v Spain* [2003] ECR I-6695, para 26; and C-434/01 *Commission v United Kingdom* [2003] ECR I-13239, para 21; C-438/07 *Commission v Sweden* [2009] ECR I-09517.

[87] Case 272/86 *Commission v Greece* [1988] ECR 4875, summary and paras 30 and 31. See also C-297/08 *Commission v Italy* [2010] ECR I-01749, para 102.

[88] K Lenaerts, D Arts, and R Bray (eds.), *Procedural Law of the European Union* (Sweet & Maxwell, 1999), 108.

[89] C-494/01 *Commission v Ireland* [2005] ECR I-3331, para 45.

[90] C-494/01 *Commission v Ireland* [2005] ECR I-3331, para 27 with reference to, in particular, C-387/99 *Commission* v *Germany* [2004] ECR I-3751, para 42 and the case law cited.

[91] C-494/01 *Commission v Ireland* [2005] ECR I-3331, para 47.

[92] C-160/08 *Commission v Germany* [2010] ECR I-3713, para 108.

[93] C-489/06 *Commission v Greece* [2009] ECR I-1797, para 48.

Article 4(3) TEU) applies to the member states as well as to the Commission as an EU institution.[94] Although the principle is judiciable, the Court of Justice has held that it serves no purpose to rule upon this general obligation in addition to the question of non-compliance.[95] There may, however, be distinct occurrences of disloyalty in relation to infringement proceedings that can be pursued before the Court of Justice.

Loyal cooperation on the side of the member states is important, not least given that the Commission does not possess general powers to investigate infringements in the member states' territories. It is settled case law that member states shall cooperate in good faith with the Commission's enquiries and provide the Commission with all the information it requests.[96] Sometimes the Commission ends infringement proceedings because it considers an infringement to have been terminated or it has reached a satisfactory understanding on how the state shall fulfil its specific obligations. Such agreements shall take place in respect of the principle of loyal cooperation. A member state can therefore be held in breach of the principle of sincere cooperation in a separate case if it complies only initially when under the threat of judicial recourse without continuing to comply when the Commission has terminated proceedings.[97]

2.4 *The notion of member state*

2.4.1 *A broad notion*

The notion of member state according to Article 258 TFEU is interpreted broadly. The obligation to comply is not affected by any possible delegation of implementation power to, for instance, a federal or regional level of government.[98] In principle, a member state infringement may be established under Article 258 TFEU regardless of which agency of that state is the cause of the infringement. Also acts or omissions of *de jure* independent bodies such as private companies may, under certain conditions, be ascribed

[94] Joined cases C-63/90 and C-67/90 *Portugal and UK v Council* [2002] ECR I-5073, para 52.

[95] C-392/02 *Commission v Denmark* [2005] ECR I-9811, para 69.

[96] See, eg, C-490/09 *Commission v Luxembourg* [2011] not yet published in the ECR, para 59, case C-82/03 *Commission v Italy* [2004] ECR I-6635, paras 15–18.

[97] C-374/89 *Commission v Belgium* [1991] ECR I-367, paras 14–16.

[98] See case 96/81 *Commission v Netherlands* [1982] ECR 1791; case 97/81 *Commission v Netherlands* [1982] ECR 1819; joined cases 227/85, 228/85, 229/85, and 230/85 *Commission v Belgium* [1988] ECR 1, para 9; and case 131/88 *Commission v Germany* [1991] ECR I-825, para 71.

to a member state.[99] Moreover, a member state may be held responsible even in the case of a constitutionally independent institution.[100] In Case C-129/00 *Commission v Italy*, the Court of Justice established that a widely held judicial construction which had not been disowned by the Supreme Court, but rather confirmed by it, constituted a breach of EU law. Against this background, Italian legislation was not sufficiently clear to ensure its application in compliance with EU law.[101]

2.4.2 *Acts and omissions of national courts*

So far, the question as to whether a member state can be subject to infringement proceedings for acts or omissions of national courts has not been settled by the Court of Justice. Prete and Smulders maintain that: '... recent case-law appears to confirm clearly that infringement proceedings are, in principle, possible also against acts of the national judiciary'.[102] Ibáñez comments that infringement proceedings according to Article 258 TFEU would arguably '... not be the most appropriate way for the ECJ to change the decision of national court'.[103] As mentioned, judgments handed down according to Article 258 TFEU are of a declaratory nature and thus they would not, as such, change a decision of a national court. By contrast, according to settled case law it is important that judicial decisions which have become definitive after all rights of appeal have been exhausted or after expiry of the time limits provided to exercise those rights can no longer be called into question. The underlying purpose is to ensure stability of the law and legal relations, as well as the sound administration of justice.[104]

[99] See, eg, 249/81 *Commission v Ireland* [1982] ECR 4005 ('Buy Irish'); Case 222/82 *Apple and Pear Development Council* [1983] ECR 4083, para 17; C-325/00 *Commission v Germany* [2002] ECR I-9977, paras 17–20.

[100] Case 77/69 *Commission v Belgium* [1970] ECR 237, para 15.

[101] C-129/00 *Commission v Italy* [2003] ECR I-14637, paras 29–32. For a concise analysis of the case and the question whether acts or omissions by member state judiciaries can be addressed under the infringement procedure see Christian Timmermans, 'The Infringement Procedure and Judicial Errors' in JW de Zwaan et al (eds.), *The European Union: An Ongoing Process of Integration* (TMC Asser Press, 2004).

[102] L Prete and B Smulders, 'The Coming of Age of Infringement Proceedings' (2010) *Common Market Law Review* 47:1, 9–61 (25).

[103] AJG Ibáñez, *The Administrative Supervision and Enforcement of EC Law* (Hart, 1999), 141.

[104] C-507/08 *Commission v Slovakia* [2010] not yet published in the ECR, para 59; C-224/01 *Köbler* [2003] ECR I-10239, para 38; C-234/04 *Kapferer* [2006] ECR I-2585, para 20; and C-2/08 *Fallimento Olimpiclub* [2009] ECR I-7501, para 22. According to the judgment in C-40/08 *Asturcom Telecomunicaciones* [2009] ECR I-9579, para 37: EU law 'does not require a national court to disapply domestic rules of procedure conferring finality on a decision, even if to do so

Infringement proceedings targeting judicial practice would merely imply an objective review of legality in the general interest.[105]

Ruling on member state judiciaries' acts or omissions could arguably be a delicate matter for the Court of Justice given the heterarchical organization of national courts and the Court of Justice. Then again, the Court of Justice did not shy away from establishing that member states are obliged to make good any damage caused to individuals by infringements of EU law, including when the infringement stems from a decision of a member state court.[106] National courts undoubtedly play a pivotal role in ensuring the uniform interpretation and application of EU law. In view of case law explicitly emphasizing that the notion of member state according to Article 258 TFEU includes constitutionally independent institutions,[107] it seems to create a legal void if breaches of EU law in the form of judicial decisions should be exempted in this regard. Upholding that member states form a single entity which includes the judiciary would have at least two significant implications. Misapplication of EU law could be stopped prospectively and infringement cases could make headway for individuals in member state liability cases.[108] It is, however, useful to distinguish between two different types of breach by member state judiciaries, viz., (i) misapplication of EU law, and (ii) failure to make a preliminary reference according to Article 267 TFEU.

2.4.2.1 Misapplication of EU law It is settled case law that a national court which is called upon to apply provisions of EU law shall give full effect to those provisions. If necessary it shall furthermore refuse of

would enable it to remedy an infringement of [EU] law by the decision at issue'. Moreover, in the absence of EU legislation in this area, the rules implementing the principle of *res judicata* are a matter for the national legal order. This follows from the principle of the procedural autonomy of the member states (para 38). As M Broberg and N Fenger, *Preliminary References to the Court of Justice* (Oxford University Press, 2010), 266–7, point out, failure to make a preliminary reference may have consequences such as invalidity according to member state procedural law.

[105] C-445/06 *Danske Slagterier* [2009] ECR I-2119, para 67.

[106] C-224/01 *Köbler* [2003] ECR I-10239.

[107] Case 77/69 *Commission v Belgium* [1970] ECR 237, para 15.

[108] According to case law, harmed individuals have a right to reparation where the following conditions are met: (i) the rule of EU law infringed must be intended to confer rights on them; (ii) the breach of that rule must be sufficiently serious; and (iii) there must be a direct causal link between the breach and the loss or damage sustained by the individuals. See joined cases C-46/93 and C-48/93 *Brasserie du Pêcheur and Factortame* [1996] ECR I-1029, para 51; C-5/94 *Hedley Lomas* [1996] ECR I-2553, para 25; and joined cases C-178/94, C-179/94, and C-188/94 to C-190/94 *Dillenkofer and Others* [1996] ECR I-4845, para 21.

its own motion to apply any conflicting provision of national legislation. Significantly, it is not necessary for the court to request or to await the prior setting aside of that national provision by legislative or other constitutional means.[109] In principle, this obligation is unconditional. The question nevertheless remains whether any type of judicial infringement could be subject to infringement proceedings. Advocate General Warner maintains that:

> It is obvious... that a Member State cannot be held to have failed to fulfil an obligation under the Treaty simply because one of its Courts has reached a wrong decision. Judicial error, whether due to the misapprehension of facts or to misapprehension of the law, is not a breach of the Treaty. In the judicial sphere, Article 169 [Article 258 TFEU] could only come into play in the event of a court of a Member State deliberately ignoring or disregarding EU law.[110]

Advocate-General Warner's argument is sympathetic. However, it may not be sustainable in view of subsequent case law which establishes that judgments under Article 258 TFEU are declaratory. Thus, they are confined to the finding that a member state has not fulfilled an obligation under EU law.[111] Moreover, although not specifically in relation to national courts, there are infringement cases that address single instances of non-compliance. This could, for instance, be a public tender.[112] Advocate General Geelhoed, who makes a strong case why national case law can provide grounds for bringing infringement proceedings under Article 258 TFEU, argues: '... this finding does not mean to say that any judicial error is sufficient in this regard.'[113] He then discusses circumstances under which such action can and cannot be appropriate.[114] The Court of Justice did not address his propositions and it remains unsettled if any conditions can be

[109] Case 106/77 *Simmenthal* [1978] ECR 629, para 24; and C-314/08 *Filipiak* [2009] ECR I-11049, para 81; C-173/09 *Georgi Ivanov Elchinov* [2010] ECR I-08889, para 31.

[110] Opinion of Advocate General Warner in case 30/77 *Régina v Pierre Bouchereau* [1977] ECR 1999, at 2020.

[111] C-359/93 *Commission v Netherlands* [1995] ECR I-157, para 14.

[112] See, eg, C-243/89 *Commission v Denmark* [1993] ECR I-3353. See also and CWA Timmermans, 'Judicial Protection against Member States' in D Curtin and T Heukels (eds.), *Institutional Dynamics of European Integration. Essays in Honour of Henry G. Schermers. Volume II* (Martinus Nijhoff Publishers, 1994), 397, on individual cases of incorrect application of law.

[113] Opinion of Advocate General Geelhoed in C-129/00 *Commission v Italy* [2003] ECR I-14637, point 61.

[114] Opinion of Advocate General Geelhoed in case C-129/00 *Commission v Italy* [2003] ECR I-14637, points 62–5.

read into case law in this regard.[115] If so, it would appear to constitute a departure from the general jurisprudence on Article 258 TFEU.

The Commission does not consider acts of national courts to be outside the scope of Article 258 TFEU. Significantly, it has initiated infringement proceedings against the Netherlands concerning the reasoning of a concrete judgment delivered by *Hoge Raad der Nederlanden* (the Dutch Supreme Court) on freedom of movement for workers.[116] The case was discussed by the Association of the Councils of State and Supreme Administrative Jurisdictions of the European Union's 19th colloquium.[117] The majority of members giving their opinion on the case seem to be of the opinion that infringement proceedings are legally possible in the concrete case. However, they suggest that the Commission should exert self-restraint in this regard.[118] As will be discussed in more detail in this chapter (and more generally in chapter one), the Commission enjoys unfettered discretion under Article 258 TFEU. When it comes to enforcement against national courts it becomes particularly understandable why the Commission should enjoy political discretion and be able to choose not to initiate cases concerning, for instance, national courts' acts and omissions. At the least, the Commission should be empowered to reserve the possibility for situations where a court has deliberately or gravely ignored or disregarded EU law. A national court may always make a reference for a preliminary ruling to the Court of Justice according to Article 267 TFEU if it considers it desirable.[119] Against this background, infringement proceedings ought in principle to be a last option, if required at all.

2.4.2.2 Failure to make a preliminary reference according to Article 267 TFEU The preliminary ruling mechanism established under Article 267 TFEU obliges national courts, against whose decisions there is no judicial remedy under national law, to bring such matters before the Court of Justice. This general rule is moderated in a number of ways by

[115] C-129/00 *Commission v Italy* [2003] ECR I-14637, paras 29–32.

[116] Commission press release IP/04/178 issued on 9 February 2004. The infringement case (2003/2253) was closed by the Commission on 14/12/2004.

[117] The Hague, 14 and 15 June 2004.

[118] See General Report by Linda Senden entitled 'The Quality of European Legislation and its Implementation and Application in the National Legal Order', 86–8. The report can be accessed at http://www.juradmin.eu/colloquia/2004/gen_report_en.pdf.

[119] Joined cases 28/62 to 30/62 *Da Costa and Others* [1963] ECR 31, 38; 283/81 *Cilfit and Others* [1982] ECR 3415, para 15; and C-45/09 *Rosenbladt* [2010] ECR I-09391, para 31.

means of exemptions established in case law.[120] This includes situations where the answer to a question may be clearly deduced from existing case law and where it leaves no scope for any reasonable doubt.[121]

Given the division of functions between national courts and the Court of Justice, it is for the national courts to assess whether these criteria are met.[122] It arguably creates inroads into the national courts' competences established under Article 267 TFEU, if the procedure under Article 258 TFEU would apply to individual rulings by national courts not to make a preliminary reference to the Court of Justice of the European Union, when such decisions are based on the said criteria. It may at the same time be argued that the Court of Justice established the criteria in the first place and, consequently must be empowered to assess compliance with them.

A different situation occurs if a national court, against whose decisions there is no judicial remedy, refrains from submitting a reference for a preliminary ruling and fails to examine whether the strict conditions for not bringing the matters before the Court of Justice are indeed met. Likewise, there may be general practices or procedures that undermine the effectiveness of the procedure stipulated in Article 267 TFEU, ie, structural problems. Such situations do not raise similar questions concerning the division of power between national courts and the Court of Justice. Notably, the Commission has initiated proceedings against Sweden

[120] Joined cases 28/62 to 30/62 *Da Costa en Schaake and Others* [1963] ECR 31, at 38; case 283/81 *Cilfit and Others* [1982] ECR 3415, paras 14 and 16.

[121] Joined cases C-428/06 to C-434/06 *UGT-Rioja and Others* [2008] ECR I-6747, para 42.

[122] Case 283/81 *Cilfit and Others* [1982] ECR 3415. These situations should be distinguished from situations where either the Court of Justice or the referring court lack jurisdiction. Lack of jurisdiction occurs for instance, in situations where the interpretation of EU law that is sought bears no relation to the actual facts of the main action or its purpose or where the problem is hypothetical. See, eg, joined cases C-165/09 to C-167/09 *Stichting Natuur en Milieu and Others* [2011] ECR not yet published in the ECR, para 48 with reference to case C-379/98 *Preussen Elektra* [2001] ECR I-2099, para 39; and case C-169/07 *Hartlauer* [2009] ECR I-1721, para 25. Similarly, a national court is only empowered to bring a matter before the Court of Justice according to Art 267 TFEU if a case pending before the national court is capable of taking account of the preliminary ruling. Joined cases C-428/06 to C-434/06 *Unión General de Trabajadores de La Rioja (UGT-Rioja) and Others* [2008] ECR I-6747, paras 39–40. The *Cilfit*-exemptions do not deprive the Court of Justice of jurisdiction to rule on such a question. Joined cases C-428/06 to C-434/06 *Unión General de Trabajadores de La Rioja (UGT-Rioja) and Others* [2008] ECR I-6747, para 43.

concerning the Swedish Supreme Court's procedure as such concerning preliminary references.[123]

2.4.2.3 The Due Report The so-called Due Report on the Future of the European Communities' Court System from 2002 makes interesting reading in relation to acts and omissions of national courts. Among other things, the Working Party, composed primarily of former judges and Advocate Generals of the Court of Justice, proposed an amendment of Article 267(3) TFEU (then Article 234 EC) in order to make it more flexible. To anticipate claims that this would threaten the uniform application of EU law, the Working Party noted: 'There would still be two ways of remedying any breach by a court of final instance, *at least where such a breach resulted in a decision which conflicted with Community law*:... the second is for the Commission to bring an action for failure to fulfil its obligations against the Member State whose court has shown ignorance of Community law'.[124] (Emphasis added.) The remark suggests that the Working Party presupposes that at least situation (i) concerning misapplication of EU law, but not necessarily situation (ii) concerning failure to make a preliminary reference according to Article 267 TFEU could, in principle, be subject to infringement proceedings.

3. Confidentiality, Discretion, and the Position and Role of Individuals

3.1 *Vigilance of individuals*

Formally, individuals do not play a role under the general EU infringement procedure. However, they are important for enforcement of EU law. In its ruling *Francovich v Italy*, the Court of Justice ruled that member state

[123] Commission docket No 2003/2161, C(2004) 3899, dated 13 October 2004, summarized by Ulf Bernitz in 'Controlling Member State Courts under EU Law: The Duty to Refer Cases to the Court of Justice and the Köbler Doctrine on Member State Liability' (2005). The report can be accessed at www.law.harvard.edu. Bernitz' paper provides an interesting analysis and summary of the Commission's reasoned opinion, which was made public according to Swedish law on access to public documents.

[124] Report by the Working Party on the Future of the European Communities' Court System, 19 January 2000 (Due Report), 16. The report can be accessed at http://ec.europa.eu/dgs/legal_service/pdf/due_en.pdf.

liability is 'inherent in the system of the [EC] Treaty'.[125] The judgment strengthened what the Court of Justice first recognized in *van Gend & Loos*, when establishing the doctrine of direct effect, namely that '[v]igilance of individuals concerned to protect their rights amounts to an effective supervision in addition to the supervision entrusted by Articles 169 [now Article 258 TFEU] and 170 [now Article 259 TFEU] to the diligence of the Commission and of the Member States'.[126] Together the two judgments form part of case law that maximizes the effectiveness of supranational obligations through national procedures and helps to reduce the gap between national and EU law. The doctrine of liability is useful to keep in mind when discussing sanctions which are dealt with in more detail in chapter three. Although the principle of member state liability is essentially linked to reparation of loss and damage caused by the breach to nationals, ie protection of individuals,[127] it constitutes a pecuniary incentive to comply or, in other terms, a deterrent to infringements.

One of the conditions for member state liability is that the given breach of EU law is sufficiently serious. Significantly, the Court of Justice has established that a breach of EU law will clearly be sufficiently serious to cause member state liability if it has persisted despite a judgment finding the infringement in question to be established.[128] Thus, member state liability complements the Commission's action according to Article 260 TFEU.[129] Direct effect implies that actions before national courts, to some extent, can complement the Commission's task under Article 258 TFEU.[130] Empirically, the doctrine of direct effect and the principle of member state liability corroborate Fisher's proposition that internalization of international law through national courts fosters compliance.[131] The range of conditions for

[125] Joined cases C-6/90 and C-9/90 *Francovich v Italy* [1991] ECR I-5357 para 35.

[126] Case 26/62 *van Gend & Loos* [1963] ECR 1, 13.

[127] C-224/01 *Köbler* [2003] ECR I-0, para 45.

[128] Joined cases C-46/93 and C-48/93 *Brasserie du Pêcheur and Factortame* [1996] ECR I-1029, para 57.

[129] K Lenaerts, 'The Rule of Law and the Coherence of the Judicial System of the European Union' (2007) *Common Market Law Review* 44, 1636–59, 1641.

[130] In relation to EU environmental law see P Wennerås, *The Enforcement of EC Environmental Law* (Oxford University Press, 2007), 304.

[131] R Fisher, *Improving Compliance with International Law* (University Press of Virginia, 1981). See also A Burley and W Mattli, 'Europe before the Court: A Political theory of Legal Integration' (1993) *International Organization* 47:1: '[T]he Court created a pro-Community constituency of private individuals by giving them a direct stake in promulgation and implementation of Community Law.'

establishing direct effect and member state liability does, however, limit the dissuasive effect in certain policy areas, thereby minimizing the mechanism's general capacity to induce member state compliance.[132] In addition, some argue that actors in the private sector may hesitate to challenge a member state anxious that it could have negative ramifications on, for example, their market prospects.[133] In such situations there is the option for the private actor to contact the Commission directly. This is however not a guarantee that the Commission will initiate proceedings.[134]

3.2 *Mounting pressure on the Commission's discretion*

The Court of Justice has consistently confirmed the Commission's exclusive competence to decide on the initiation of infringement proceedings.[135] The Commission's discretionary decision-making power precludes the right of individuals to require the Commission to take a particular position.[136] It may nevertheless be considered whether case law on non-contractual liability on the part of the EU could bring about such rights through the backdoor. The answer differs between situations where the Commission has not initiated infringement proceedings and where it has.

Since the Commission is not bound to commence infringement proceedings under Article 258 TFEU 'its decision not to institute such proceedings is not in any event unlawful'. Consequently it cannot give rise to non-contractual liability on the part of the EU.[137] The only conduct which might possibly be adduced as a source of damage in this situation is the

[132] P Wennerås downplays this problem in relation to direct effect of environmental law. P Wennerås, *The Enforcement of EC Environmental Law* (Oxford University Press, 2007).

[133] Final Report of the Committee of Wise Men on the Regulation of the European Securities Markets, 15 February 2001 (the Lamfalussy Committee), 40.

[134] R Macrory, *Regulation, Enforcement and Governance in Environmental Law* (Cameron May Ltd, 2008), 720, suggests that the Commission could improve the current system by only responding to responding to complainants that have exhausted the national remedies available to them and more generally that it should divert its resources to areas of EU law characterized by weak decentralized enforcement.

[135] Joined cases T-479/93 and T-559/93 *Commission v Giorgio Bernardi* [1994] ECR II-01115.

[136] Joined cases C-205/10 P, C-217/10 P, and C-222/10 P *Heinz Helmuth Eriksen, Bent Hansen and Brigit Lind v Commission*, [2011] not yet published in the ECR, para 42; Order of 6 April 2006 in C-408/05 P *GISTI v Commission*, para 14 and case law cited.

[137] T-202/02 *Makedoniko Metro and Michaniki v Commission* [2004] ECR II-181, para 43 and case law cited.

conduct of the member state concerned.[138] In the case of *Asia Motor France*, the Court of Justice ruled that an application for damages is 'patently inadmissible' insofar as it concerns liability arising from the Commission's inaction in relation to the alleged infringement.[139]

It cannot, however, be entirely overlooked that, when the Commission has initiated infringements it can give rise to non-contractual liability.[140] In the judgment *Arizmendi and Others* the General Court noted that in principle, a reasoned opinion can adversely affect an individual due to its content. This may, for instance, be the case if the Commission divulges confidential information obtained from complainants or if a reasoned opinion contains inaccurate information about certain persons.[141] These examples, however, do not appear to extend to decisions to terminate infringement cases as such. Thus, the Commission's crucial discretion in this regard remains unfettered.

The preliminary investigations and the consecutive conciliatory phase of the administrative stage of Articles 258 TFEU allow infringements to be dealt with bilaterally and somewhat discretely between the Commission and the member states. Likewise, complainants do not have general procedural rights enabling them to require the Commission to inform them and to grant them a hearing.[142] Confidentiality and diplomacy thus enable the Commission to seek amicable solutions with member states and, if necessary, to exert pressure on a member state. As discussed in chapter one, this discretion reflects that the Commission acts as a semi-political institution. Notably, the College of Commissioners bears collective responsibility at a political level for central decisions related to the

[138] T-202/02 *Makedoniko Metro and Michaniki v Commission* [2004] ECR II-181, para 43 and case law cited.

[139] C-72/90 *Asia Motor France v Commission* [1990] ECR I-2181, paras 13 and 15. See also T-201/96 *Smanor and Others v Commission* [1997] ECR II-1081, para 31; and case T-202/02 *Makedoniko Metro and Michaniki v Commission* [2004] ECR II-181, para 44. Wennerås argues that there might nevertheless be circumstances under which liability could potentially occur. P Wennerås, *The Enforcement of EC Environmental Law* (Oxford University Press, 2007), 300.

[140] Joined cases T-440/03, T-121/04, T-171/04, T-208/04, T-365/04, and T-484/04 *Jean Arizmendi and Others v Council and Commission* [2009] ECR II-04883, para 68. See also K Gutman, 'The Evolution of the Action for Damages against the European Union and Its Place in the System of Judicial Protection' (2011) *Common Market Law Review*, 48:3, 695–750 (707–8).

[141] Joined cases T-440/03, T-121/04, T-171/04, T-208/04, T-365/04, and T-484/04 *Jean Arizmendi and Others v Council and Commission* [2009] ECR II-04883, para 69.

[142] T-202/02 *Makedoniko Metro and Michaniki v Commission* [2004] ECR II-181, para 46.

management of infringement cases. This includes political responsibility for the majority of cases that are settled in an amicable manner.

The Commission can choose to exert political pressure on the member state, for instance, by informing the broader public about pending cases.[143] This serves instrumental objectives of exposure and shaming and, in addition, it informs citizens of potential rights and liability claims enforceable before national courts.[144] Despite these practices, the Commission has an interest in maintaining the general EU infringement procedure as one of confidentiality, especially because Article 258 TFEU merely provides the Commission with a 'warning procedure'.[145]

3.3 *The Commission's handling of complaints*

The Commission's discretion and also the secrecy surrounding the pre-litigation phase have come under some pressure. This is, in part, due to the general and incremental focus on greater transparency within the EU. It also reflects that the Commission to a high degree relies on complaints from citizens as a means to detect possible compliance problems. Complainants and private bodies (as well as the press) constitute important sources of information in addition to the information submitted by the member states.[146] Ultimo 2009, the Commission was handling circa 2900 complaints and infringement files; complaints accounting for not less than 54 per cent of the total.[147]

[143] The information from the letter of formal notice stage onwards is available on the Commission's web-page at http://ec.europa.eu/eu_law/infringements/infringements_decisions_en.htm.

[144] According to the Commission, raising citizens' awareness regarding their rights obviously prevented the opening of infringement proceedings and the Commission has put considerable effort into improving communication tools to inform the citizens about their EU rights. Commission Staff Working Document '*Situation in Different Sectors*' accompanying document to the Report from the Commission 27th Annual Report on Monitoring the Application of EU Law (2009), SEC/2010/1143 final. See also J Tallberg, *European Governance and Supranational Institutions—Making States Comply* (Routledge, 2003).

[145] Joined cases 2/62 and 3/62 *Commission v Luxembourg and Belgium* [1962] ECR 793, 430.

[146] C-494/01 *Commission v Ireland* [2005] ECR I-3331, para 43; C-135/05 *Commission v Italy*, para 28; C-297/08 *Commission v Italy* [2010] I-01749, para 101.

[147] Commission '*27th Annual Report on Monitoring the Application of EU Law*', COM/2010/538, section 2.2. At the same time, the number of cases initiated on the Commission's own initiative decreased by 11 per cent compared to 2008.

The Commission has published a set of rules on its handling of complaints,[148] and in 2009 it introduced a complaints and enquiries registration system (CHAP).[149] According to these, complaints which the Commission considers incompatible with EU law must be examined within a month to decide if it should be classified as a complaint. In addition, the Commission endeavours to take a decision on the substance of a complaint within 12 months of its registration with the Secretariat-General. Thus, in principle, the complainant is told within a year whether the Commission will open infringement proceedings or close the case.[150] These measures, and specifically the publication of the Commission's internal procedural rules, have led Advocate General Mengozzi to comment that '[t]here is . . . a tendency towards progressive depoliticisation of the infringement procedure and towards proceduralisation of it, at least in cases where a complaint by an individual is at the origin of the Commission's action'.[151] Along the same lines, Prete and Smulders, both Commission officials, argue that '. . . from a rarely used, opaque and policy-driven procedure, it [the infringement proceedings] has now become a common, fairly transparent and highly technical procedure'.[152]

Whether the general EU infringement procedure is sufficiently transparent is contested. Rawlings and Smith, among others, moreover problematize the Commission's lack of procedural recognition of private complainants and the absence of a clearly defined policy for its use of

[148] See the Commission's web-page at http://ec.europa.eu/eu_law/your_rights/your_rights_en.htm. In 1999 the Commission published a notice containing a standard form for complaints to be submitted to it where a member state fails to comply with EU (then, Community law) in the context of the infringement procedure laid down by Art 258 TFEU, [1999] OJ C 119/5. See also Commission Communication to the European Parliament and the European Ombudsman on relations with the complainant in respect of infringements of Community law, COM/2002/141; and Commission '*27th Annual Report on Monitoring the Application of EU Law*', COM/2010/538 (Introduction).

[149] The Commission terms CHAP and EU Pilot 'management (pre-infringement) tools'. See Commission '*28th Annual Report on Monitoring the Application of EU Law*', COM/2011/588, 3.

[150] See the Commission's web-page at http://ec.europa.eu/eu_law/your_rights/your_rights_en.htm. Wennerås points out the risk that this internal rule is used as a 'formalistic justification for closing cases'. P Wennerås, *The Enforcement of EC Environmental Law* (Oxford University Press, 2007), 294.

[151] Opinion of Advocate General Mengozzi in C-523/04 *Commission v The Netherlands* [2007] ECR I-3267, fn 49.

[152] L Prete and B Smulders, 'The Coming of Age of Infringement Proceedings' (2010) *Common Market Law Review* 47:1, 9–61 (13).

discretion.[153] Both the European Ombudsman[154] and the European Parliament[155] have criticized the Commission's complaint handling and advocated citizen rights in the administrative phase of Article 258 TFEU. This would include access to documents where a complainant is affected, right to be heard, and a compulsory explanation as to why a case has been terminated.[156] In her analysis of Article 258 TFEU from the perspective of good governance, Smith argues that '[t]he key tension in the current operation of Article 226 [Article 258 TFEU] is that it is split between being a legal and political mechanism of enforcement, but does not possess the requisite controls demanded by either a political or legal mechanism in order to be compatible with good governance and legitimacy'.[157]

3.3.1 The emergence of supplementary, practical problem-solving programmes

Regardless of the Commission's in-house rules for dealing with complaints, the general EU infringement procedure is not a remedy for citizens and enterprises against member state infringements. Consequently, the Commission can reserve the procedure for priority cases and structural issues.[158] At the same time, the Commission attempts to assist citizens and enterprises to tackle compliance obstacles through other channels. These include practical, problem-solving programmes such as SOLVIT, created in 2002 (concerning internal market law) and EU Pilot. SOLVIT centres established in the member states cooperate directly via an on-line database to

[153] See R Rawlings, 'Engaged Elites: Citizen Action and Institutional Attitudes' in C Kilpatrick, T Novitz, P Skidmore (eds.), *The Future of Remedies in Europe* (Hart Publishing, 2000), 268; and M Smith, *Centralised Enforcement, Legitimacy and Good Governance in the EU* (Routledge, 2009).

[154] Decision of the European Ombudsman in the own initiative inquiry 303/97/PD into the Commission's administrative procedures in relation to citizens' complaints about national authorities—Commission reference: Letter of 11 August 1997 PhG/es SG/D(97) 35503; and R Rawlings and C Harlow, 'Accountability and Law Enforcement: the Centralised EU Infringement Procedure' (2006) *European Law Review* 31, 447–75, 466.

[155] See also European Parliament Report on the Commission's 21st and 22nd Annual reports on monitoring the application of Community law (2003 and 2004) (2005/2150(INI)).

[156] For an analysis of the European Ombudsman's impact on the Commission's interaction with complainants, see M Smith, *Centralised Enforcement, Legitimacy and Good Governance in the EU* (Routledge, 2009), 161–202.

[157] M Smith, *Centralised Enforcement, Legitimacy and Good Governance in the EU* (Routledge, 2009), 211.

[158] Commission Staff Working Document *'Situation in Different Sectors'* accompanying document to the Report from the Commission 27th Annual Report on Monitoring the Application of EU Law, SEC/2010/1143 final.

solve problems submitted by citizens and businesses.[159] EU Pilot is a confidential on-line database for communication between Commission services and member state authorities. The system is operated through a network of contacts that oversee practical solutions of complaints as well as Commission own-initiative cases, and cases raised by the European Parliament Petitions' Committee or individual members of the European Parliament. EU Pilot is not used to manage issues that are subject to infringement proceedings. However, cases not properly resolved may afterwards be pursued according to the general EU infringement procedure.[160] This comprehensive system of heterarchical cooperation between the Commission and national authorities as a means of ensuring member state compliance (sometimes referred to as 'partenariat') is only institutionalized now; however, the idea was tabled two decades ago in the 'Sutherland Report'.[161]

Clearly, supplementary methods such as the CHAP and EU Pilot programmes can bring to light structural non-compliance and thus provide some degree of synergy between them and the general EU infringement procedure.[162] In addition, complaints also constitute a policy tool that connects the Commission with citizens and business.[163] Furthermore,

[159] See generally Commission staff working document *'SOLVIT 2006 Report—Development and Performance of the SOLVIT network in 2006'*, SEC(2007)585. According to the Commission's report *'Development and performance of the SOLVIT network in 2008'*, the average case handling time for SOLVIT in 2008 was just under two months. The report (at 6) also compares the number of complaints resolved through infringement proceedings and through SOLVIT. In 2007 and 2008 the majority of cases were solved through SOLVIT. The report can be accessed at http://ec.europa.eu/solvit/site/docs/solvit2008_report_en.pdf. The Commission's annual SOLVIT reports and background information can be found at http://ec.europa.eu/solvit/site/background/index_en.htm.

[160] Commission *'28th Annual Report on Monitoring the Application of EU Law'*, COM/2011/588, 8–9; Commission *'EU Pilot Evaluation Report'*, COM/2010/70 final; and Commission Staff Working Document *'Facts on the functioning of the system up to beginning of February 2010'* accompanying document to the Commission's EU pilot evaluation report, SEC(2010) 182. See also the Commission's web-page at http://ec.europa.eu/eu_law/infringements/application_monitoring_en.htm. For a critical appraisal of the scheme and the implications of the new process, see M Smith, *Centralised Enforcement, Legitimacy and Good Governance in the EU* (Routledge, 2009), 152–60.

[161] P Sutherland, *The Internal Market after 1992: Meeting the Challenge*. Report presented to the Commission by the High Level Group on the functioning of the Internal Market (1992).

[162] Commission *'27th Annual Report on Monitoring the Application of EU Law'* (2009), COM/2010/538 (Introduction).

[163] R Macrory, *Regulation, Enforcement and Governance in Environmental Law* (Cameron May Ltd, 2008), 731.

they have potential to remedy concrete instances of non-compliance in a swift manner. According to the Commission 4035 cases were created in CHAP in 2010. Of those cases, 83 per cent were complaints and 17 per cent were enquiries. 52.5 per cent of complaints were closed directly in CHAP 'on the basis of a comprehensive response by the Commission' and a further 14 per cent were closed on the grounds of a lack of EU competence. For 17 per cent of the cases the examination continued via EU Pilot and only 9 per cent were transferred into infringement proceedings.[164] At the same time, the Commission notes that EU Pilot might explain the decrease of ongoing infringement cases in 2010 compared to previous years and it intends to broaden the scope to include all member states.[165]

According to Smith, the Commission may however also seek to employ these alternative methods as a means to separate complainants from the general EU infringement procedure. This could be one way to sidestep some of the criticism pertaining to transparency and good governance in relation to Article 258 TFEU.[166] Smith points out a number of what she considers to be 'worrying implications' of the EU Pilot. These include prolonging the procedure under Article 258 TFEU and eventually 'complaint fatigue'. Moreover, Smith argues, it is problematic that the Commission essentially outsources 'its responsibility to deal with complainants *to the very entity committing the alleged infraction*'.[167]

At the same time, the EU Pilot method of dealing with non-compliance issues is very much aligned with the purpose of Article 258 TFEU, namely to ensure effective application of EU law through amicable settlement. Like the administrative phase of Article 258 TFEU, it relies on dialogue and technical and legal exposition. In addition, the mere initiation of an EU Pilot procedure implies a degree of pressure through exposure to the Commission. Thus, EU Pilot is consonant with the flexible and deliberative

[164] Commission '*28th Annual Report on Monitoring the Application of EU Law*', COM/2011/588.

[165] Commission '*28th Annual Report on Monitoring the Application of EU Law*', COM/2011/588, 6 and 15.

[166] M Smith, *Centralised Enforcement, Legitimacy and Good Governance in the EU* (Routledge, 2009). The European Parliament Committee on Legal Affairs has voiced a similar concern in Report on the 26th Annual Report on Monitoring the Application of European Union Law (2008) (2010/2076(INI)).

[167] M Smith undertakes a critical appraisal of EU Pilot and its implications in 'Enforcement, monitoring, verification, outsourcing: the decline and decline of the infringement process' (2008) *European Law Review* 33:6, 777–802, 798.

tradition of enforcement in the EU and the central role attributed to the member states in this connection. In particular regarding the latter point, the perhaps most important invention of EU Pilot is that it requires the member states to play a decidedly proactive role in solving potential infringements. According to Article 258 TFEU the burden of proof rests with the Commission. It must provide the evidence necessary for the Court of Justice to establish that the obligation has not been fulfilled, and it may not rely on any presumption. EU Pilot is less about proving an infringement. Therefore, it does not activate the procedural steps and requirements established under Article 258 TFEU with a view to guaranteeing the member state's interest in submitting its observations and preparing a defence. It more simply asks the member state to address and tackle a concrete, practical problem. This resonates well with the member states' primary responsibility for ensuring implementation, application, and enforcement of EU law.

3.4 *Access to documents*

3.4.1 A balancing act

The Amsterdam IGC made citizen right of access to the central EU institutions' documents a general rule.[168] Prior to that, the Maastricht IGC stressed the importance of transparency in the decision-making process as a means to strengthen the democratic nature of the institutions and the public's confidence in the administration.[169] According to the Commission Decision on public access to Commission documents, no longer in force, the Commission would however refuse access to any document where disclosure could undermine the protection of the 'public interest' including inspections and investigations.[170] The case of T-309/97 *The Bavarian Lager Company* shed light on this notion.[171] Notably, it holds, the general rule of citizen access to documents is to some extent countervailed by member state expectations of 'confidentiality from the Commission during investigations which may lead to an infringe-

[168] Article 255 of the EC Treaty.

[169] Declaration (No 17) attached to Final Act of the Treaty on European Union signed in Maastricht on 7 February 1992.

[170] Decision 94/90/ECSC, EC, Euratom on public access to Commission documents ([1994] OJ L 46/58).

[171] T-309/97 *The Bavarian Lager Company Ltd v Commission* [1999] ECR II-3217.

ment procedure'.[172] The disclosure of documents relating to the investigation stage, during the negotiations between the Commission and the member state concerned, could undermine the proper conduct of the infringement procedure and its purpose. That is to say, to enable the member state to comply of its own accord with the requirements of the Treaty or, if appropriate, to justify its position.[173] According to the Court of Justice, the safeguarding of that objective warrants the refusal of access to a preparatory document relating to the investigation stage of the procedure. It did so under the heading of protection of the public interest.[174]

According to the second indent of Article 4(2) of Regulation No 1049/2001, the Commission shall refuse access to a document where disclosure would undermine the protection of court proceedings and legal advice. Furthermore, the third indent of Article 4(2) of Regulation No 1049/2001 now stipulates that the institutions shall refuse access to a document, where disclosure would undermine the protection of the purpose of inspections, investigations, and audits.[175] According to the last sentence of the second subparagraph of Regulation No 1049/2001 this applies, unless there is an overriding 'public interest' in disclosure.[176] There are two notable differences between the Commission's Decision on public access to Commission documents from 1994 and Regulation No 1049/2001. Whereas the Commission's Decision provided for the possibility of excluding from public access any document whose disclosure 'could undermine'

[172] Cases T-309/97 *The Bavarian Lager Company Ltd v Commission* [1999] ECR II-3217, para 46 with reference to case T-105/95 *WWF UK v Commission* [1997] ECR II-313, para 63. See also case T-191/99 *Petrie and Others v Commission* [2001] ECR II-3677, para 68.

[173] Cases T-309/97 *The Bavarian Lager Company Ltd v Commission* [1999] ECR II-3217, para 46 with reference to C-191/95 *Commission v Germany* [1998] ECR I-5449, para 44.

[174] Cases T-309/97 *The Bavarian Lager Company Ltd v Commission* [1999] ECR II-3217, para 46.

[175] The Commission submitted a proposal for recasting Regulation (EC) No 1049/2001 on 30 April 2008 (COM(2008) 229). Subsequently, when realizing that there was no short-term possibility that a new regulation would be adopted, it tabled a proposal amending Regulation (EC) No 1049/2001 (COM(2011) 137 final). The Commission's annual reports on the application of the Regulation are published on the Commission's web-page on openness and access to documents. The web-page can be accessed at http://ec.europa.eu/transparency/access_documents/index_en.htm#. See also Commission Green Paper '*Public access to documents held by institutions of the European Community—A review*', COM/2007/185.

[176] The previous Commission Decision on public access to Commission documents did not provide that an overriding public interest could override the interest in the protection of the purpose of the investigations. Commission Decision of 8 February 1994 on public access to Commission documents [1994] OJ L 46/58.

the activities of the investigation, the Regulation refers to the case where disclosure 'would undermine' those activities. Moreover, the Commission's Decision does not provide that an overriding public interest could override the interest in the protection of the purpose of the investigations.[177]

Case law has consistently upheld the objective of reaching an amicable settlement in infringement cases. Notably, the requirement of confidentiality remains even after the matter has been brought before the Court of Justice, on the grounds that bilateral compliance negotiations may continue during the court proceedings and up to the delivery of the judgment.[178] Thus, the purpose of obtaining an amicable settlement remains at the very heart of the infringement procedure and it serves as the justification for confidentiality. The aim of the exception is not to protect the investigations as such.[179] By the time a case is ruled upon by the Court of Justice, the member state can no longer resort to voluntary compliance. Hence, the proper conduct of the pre-litigation procedure no longer warrants confidentiality.

It cannot be presumed though that disclosure of documents lodged in a procedure which ultimately led to the delivery of a judgment undermines investigations leading to proceedings being brought under Article 260 TFEU (concerning failure to comply with a judgment establishing a breach of obligations). At this point in time, the continuation of negotiations between that member state and the Commission is no longer designed to establish the existence of the infringement, but to determine whether the necessary conditions for the bringing of an action under Article 260 TFEU are met. Hence, an amicable settlement is no longer possible.[180] Once the Court of Justice hands down a judgment, the case is, as a general rule, no longer within the semi-political sphere of bilateral negotiation that justifies confidentiality.[181] According to Article 4(5) of Regulation No 1049/2001,

[177] T-36/04 *API* v *Commission* [2007] ECR II-3201, para 119.

[178] T-36/04 *API v Commission* [2007] ECR II-3201, para 121; and T-191/99 *Petrie and Others v Commission* [2001] ECR II-3677, para 68.

[179] T-36/04 *API v Commission* [2007] ECR II-3201, para 133.

[180] T-36/04 *API v Commission* [2007] ECR II-3201, paras 135 to 140; and joined cases C-514/07 P, C-528/07 P, and C-532/07 P *Sweden v API and Commission* [2010] ECR I-08533, paras 118–23.

[181] In joined cases C-514/07 P, C-528/07 P, and C-532/07 P *Sweden v API and Commission* [2010] ECR I-08533, the Commission put forward an additional argument as to why the exemption should apply even after the Court had ruled on the infringement. It maintained that disclosure of the documents relating to the 'Open Skies' cases (discussed in chapter one) would have endangered the negotiations for a new international agreement on air transport which, at the

a member state may request the institution not to disclose a document originating from that member state without its prior agreement.[182]

3.4.2 The importance of sincere dialogue

In the case T-309/97 *The Bavarian Lager Company*, the Commission pleaded that the objective of the procedure under Article 258 TFEU (then Article 169 EC) is to ensure that member states comply with EU law:

> by means, initially, of a process of negotiation centred around sincere dialogue with the State concerned. The interest of the member states and that of the investigation itself require that dialogue to take place without any publicity at all and those States to be assured that compromises may be reached in confidence.[183]

The Commission's line of reasoning is buttressed by case law that confirms that confidentiality is inextricably linked to the very purpose of the pre-litigation phase; that is to say, the search for an amicable settlement whereby the member state can conform to its Treaty obligations.

The merits of transparency, in terms of bringing greater openness to the work of the institutions and strengthening the principle of democracy and respect for fundamental rights, are specifically acknowledged in Regulation No 1049/2001.[184] What is more, the Court of Justice holds, in relation to the legislative procedure, that openness is critical for citizens' confidence in the institutions.[185] At the same time, it should be kept in mind that only the Court of Justice is empowered to interpret EU law and assess member

time when the contested decision was adopted, the Commission was conducting in the name of the EU with the member states and with non-member States. The Court held this part of the Commission's plea inadmissible for procedural reasons. Thus, it remains unclear whether such consideration could indeed be invoked in favour of confidentiality. The argument appears to require a very broad interpretation of the purpose of Art 258 TFEU, viz., to ensure the effective application of EU law. In view of pertinent case law, it is doubtful whether this purpose should be understood as a reference to the effective application of EU law more generally and not just in relation to the concrete case.

[182] The European Ombudsman has urged the Commission to inform citizens that they can also apply for access to documents in infringement procedures by applying directly to the authorities of the member state concerned, in addition to the Commission. In that case it is national law which applies. See Decision of the European Ombudsman closing his own-initiative inquiry OI/2/2009/MHZ concerning the European Commission.

[183] T-309/97 *The Bavarian Lager Company Ltd v Commission* [1999] ECR II-3217, para 32.

[184] Points 3 and 10 in the preamble.

[185] Joined cases C-39/05 P and C-52/05 P *Sweden and Maurizio Turco v Council* [2008] ECR I-4723, para 59.

state behaviour according to Article 258 TFEU.[186] Consequently, there are factors that militate in favour of confidentiality. Notably, there is a risk of prematurely politicizing cases at EU and domestic levels. That is to say, member states frequently enjoy a margin of discretion concerning *how* to comply. At the same time, infringement cases are often about contested norms and the Commission does not possess prescriptive powers under Article 258 TFEU and it cannot establish infringements. These procedural features require the Commission to engage in a responsive dialogue with member states. This dialogue essentially presupposes some degree of secrecy.

On a related and more practical note, there are frequently parallel domestic cases involving several stakeholders, which hold conflicting viewpoints on the correct interpretation and application of EU law.[187] The risk of creating legal uncertainty and the potential political and economic cost for member states by engaging in an open and frank dialogue may therefore outweigh the benefits. The alternative (ie, more openness and individual access to case-files) could well be that more non-compliance cases are dealt with informally, which would make the processes even less transparent, or that cases are dealt with more formally and thus at the expense of the practice of amicable settlements. This would in turn jeopardize the effectiveness of the infringement procedure as a means to remedy non-compliance informally.

3.5 *The European Parliament*

The European Parliament increasingly attempts to hold the Commission in its role as guardian accountable. The Commission's annual reports on the monitoring of the application of EU law, for instance, are made in response

[186] Article 17(1) TEU. It is established case law that the Commission is not empowered to determine conclusively, by reasoned opinions formulated pursuant to Art 258 TFEU, the rights and duties of a member state or to afford that member state guarantees concerning the compatibility of a given line of conduct with the Treaty. According to the system embodied in Arts 258 to 260 TFEU, the rights and duties of member states may be determined and their conduct appraised only by a judgment of the Court. C-191/95 *Commission v Germany* [1998] ECR I-5449, para 45 and the case law cited.

[187] According to the Report from the Commission on the application in 2010 of Regulation (EC) No 1049/2001 regarding public access to European Parliament, Council and Commission documents, COM/2011/492 final, most applications for access are made by the academic sector, by NGOs, interest groups, and law firms. The report provides statistics relating to the application of Regulation (EC) No 1049/2001.

to requests made by the European Parliament.[188] There are several ways in which the Commission can be held accountable, including when the members of the Commission are subject, as a body, to a vote of consent by the European Parliament in connection with the confirmation hearings according to Article 17(7) TEU.[189] Moreover, according to Article 230 TFEU the Commission shall reply orally or in writing to questions put to it by the European Parliament or by its members. These questions frequently pertain to alleged infringements. According to Article 227 TFEU, EU citizens and organizations have the right to address a petition to the European Parliament on a matter which comes within the Union's fields of activity and which affects him, her, or it directly. This may also prompt the European Parliament's Petition Committee to ask the Commission to conduct a preliminary investigation or to contact SOLVIT.[190] Furthermore, the European Parliament can issue non-legislative resolutions and urge the Commission to pursue specific cases of alleged infringements. Finally, the European Parliament has obtained certain rights of information in the Framework Agreement on relations between the European Parliament and the European Commission. Specifically, the Commission shall provide information concerning infringement procedures from the letter of formal notice and, by request of the European Parliament, on the issues to which the infringement procedure relates. The wording makes sure though that the general rules, in particular as established in case law, concerning access to documents apply.[191]

The European Parliament furthermore puts pressure on the Commission to take action to ensure procedural rights of complainants and to enter a dialogue with the Parliament about the Commission's enforcement

[188] Resolution of 9 February 1983. See also point 2 of Declaration No 19 annexed to the Treaty signed at Maastricht on 7 February 1992. The reports can be accessed at http://ec.europa.eu/eu_law/infringements/infringements_annual_report_en.htm.

[189] On the basis of this consent the European Council appoints the Commission, acting by a qualified majority. Craig calls the confirmation hearings 'senate-like'. For an analysis see P Craig, 'The Role of the European Parliament under the Lisbon Treaty' in S Griller and J Ziller (eds.), *The Lisbon Treaty: EU Constitutionalism without a Constitutional Treaty?* (Springer, 2008). See also Framework Agreement on relations between the European Parliament and the European Commission, [2010] OJ L 304/47, Section 44.

[190] On petitions, see the European Parliament's web-page, which can be accessed at www.europarl.europa.eu. The Commission accounts for petitions in its annual report on monitoring the application of EU law.

[191] Framework Agreement on relations between the European Parliament and the European Commission (2010) OJ L 304/47–62, Section 44. See also '*28th Annual Report on Monitoring the Application of EU Law*' (2010), COM 2011/588.

priorities. It advocates both general political commitments, but also legal rights. Thus, the European Parliament maintains, the Commission's discretionary powers entail a duty of transparency and accountability. In addition, it argues, the Commission should use its right of initiative to propose that genuine legal rights to complainants are established.[192] Generally, the European Parliament stresses that there should be ways to find a 'more transparent approach and a more structured access for the European Parliament to the Commission's decisions, without interfering into the discretionary power the Commission has in deciding how to deal with specific infringement cases'.[193] This includes access to information about why decisions are taken, including not least decisions not to pursue complaints.[194]

The European Parliament has also argued that it should gain access to individual infringement files, including details of the correspondence exchanged with the member states.[195] The distinction between general rights and rights of access to documents in individual cases merits critical appraisal. It raises a number of questions pertaining to the role and responsibility of the European Parliament if it were to be granted access to individual case details. Clearly, the European Parliament could not reserve such type of powers to individual cases of interest to their constituents. Moreover, whereas the Commission makes decisions as a college and, significantly, under its political remit the European Parliament does not have, at the moment at least, mechanisms whereby it can act as a unitary institution in relation to individual infringement cases. This is significant

[192] The question whether the 'EU legislators' can establish such rules in secondary legislation is beyond the scope of this chapter. The European Parliament at least argues that it is a possibility. Thus, it: 'Calls on the Commission to propose a "procedural code" in the form of a regulation under the new legal basis of Article 298 TFEU, setting out the various aspects of the infringement procedure, including notifications, time-limits, the right to be heard, the obligation to state reasons, etc., in order to enforce citizens' rights and transparency.' The European Parliament Committee on Legal Affairs' Report on the 26th Annual Report on Monitoring the Application of European Union Law (2008) (2010/2076(INI)), point 11.

[193] European Parliament Report on the Commission's 21st and 22nd Annual reports on monitoring the application of Community law (2003 and 2004) (A6–0089/2006 Final), explanatory statement at p 16.

[194] European Parliament Report on the Commission's 21st and 22nd Annual reports on monitoring the application of Community law (2003 and 2004) (A6–0089/2006 Final), point 25.

[195] European Parliament Report on the Commission's 21st and 22nd Annual reports on monitoring the application of Community law (2003 and 2004) (A6–0089/2006 Final) generally and point 30 specifically.

because infringement cases often concern contested norms rather than manifest non-compliance.

3.6 *Preliminary conclusions*

Despite the criticism articulated, among others, by the Ombudsman and the European Parliament, case law is unequivocal; in the context of proceedings under Article 258 TFEU, the Commission exercises the powers conferred on it by Article 17 TEU in the general EU interest, in order to ensure the application of EU law. It does so as an autonomous institution. It is not the handmaiden of individual complainants, member states, or institutions. Moreover, the Commission does not have to commit itself to pursue certain infringements or to justify its methods. Individuals do not have legal rights of access to the Commission's internal documents in specific cases or to the Commission's more general internal procedures on complaints handling and investigation principles.

At the same time, the Commission's reform of its enforcement working methods of 1998 implies a policy objective of 'greater transparency'. Above all, the Commission now notifies citizens before closing a file and provides the complainant an opportunity to submit comments concerning the grounds on which the case is being closed.[196] Moreover, the Commission publishes on its website summary information on all infringement proceedings from the stage of letter of formal notice.[197] According to the European Ombudsman the Commission 'has come a long way since those early days [where it would merely react to inquiries by insisting on its discretion and by pointing out that complainants do not possess any specific procedural rights]'.[198] The introduction of EU Pilot does not bring greater transparency to the general EU infringement procedure. However, from the Commission's information at least, it appears to be a very effective means to resolve non-compliance. This is in line with the purpose of the general

[196] Commission Communication to the European Parliament and the European Ombudsman on relations with the complainant in respect of infringements of Community law, COM/2002/141, [2002] OJ C 244. See also the Commission's web-page at http://ec.europa.eu/eu_law/your_rights/your_rights_en.htm for an overview of administrative guarantees established by the Commission.

[197] Can be accessed at http://ec.europa.eu/eu_law/infringements/infringements_decisions_en.htm.

[198] Speech by the European Ombudsman, Mr Diamandouros, at the event organized by Institute of International and European Affairs (Dublin, Ireland, 24 February 2011). The speech can be accessed at www.ombudsman.europa.eu.

EU infringement procedure, viz., to solve alleged infringements in an amicable manner.

By request, the Commission has also undertaken to provide the European Parliament with information on the issues the infringement procedure relates to. This will take place 'on a case-by-case basis and respecting the confidentiality rules, in particular those acknowledged by the Court of Justice of the European Union'.[199] More generally, the Commission nevertheless insists on maintaining 'confidentiality on the content and timing of contacts with Member States while the relevant issues are under investigation'.[200]

4. Article 258 TFEU in Perspective

4.1 *Managing non-compliance*

The remainder of this chapter analyses the general EU infringement procedure in view of managerial compliance theory and the number of defined successive stages it prescribes. The methodologically distinct questions of enforcement and effectiveness deserve a preliminary remark. The focus here is solely on the manner in which the law structures the interaction between the investigated member states and the Commission acting as a semi-diplomatic, semi-legal institutional actor. No attempts are made to assess the extent to which the process has brought about compliance in the concrete cases or generally.

Whereas enforcement theorists adhere to sanctions as part of a coercive enforcement strategy which is ultimately assumed to compel observance, management theorists in turn advocate capacity-building, formal and informal dispute settlement, and continuous adaptation of treaty norms.[201] In short, the managerial approach aims at consensual observance of treaty norms through discourse. The penultimate stage of the process comprises threats to invoke the regime's dispute settlement mechanisms or actual

[199] Framework Agreement on relations between the European Parliament and the European Commission, [2010] OJ L 304/47–62, Section 44.

[200] Commission Communication '*A Europe of Results—Applying Community Law*', COM/2007/502, 10.

[201] A Chayes and AH Chayes, *The New Sovereignty: Compliance with International Regulatory Agreements* (Harvard University Press, 1995), ch 2.

recourse whilst the final stage consists of mere considerations as to the legitimacy of the treaty provision itself.[202] The processes up to and including the penultimate stage and their logic of succession resemble the general EU infringement procedure as stipulated in Article 258 TFEU. Chayes and Chayes build their managerial approach on a variation of state-interdependency theory. With the explanatory notion of the 'New Sovereignty', they seek to distance themselves from the traditional meta-language of sovereignty and the centrality of nation-states as ultimate authorities.[203] This is, at least theoretically speaking, a mode whereby states act to realize national objectives unhindered by the influence of other states and without external interference. It is exactly the inadequacy of autonomous action to achieve, for example, economic and security ends that provokes Chayes and Chayes' claim that 'sovereignty no longer consists in the freedom of States to act independently, in their perceived self-interest, but in membership of and reasonably good standing with the regimes that make up the substance of international life'.[204] From the starting point that dependency on other states has increased and that transnational interaction has become crucial for the realization of domestic policy objections, Chayes and Chayes maintain that membership and good standing with other participants of transnational treaty regimes constitutes a fundamental gauge of contemporary statehood. Therefore, they hold, states are in principle willing to comply. The authors' contrasting of sovereignty and interdependency is germane to the history of the EU.

Chayes and Chayes suggest a number of main causes why non-compliance nevertheless occurs, namely, ambiguous treaty language, capacity problems (including lack of knowledge) and comprehension of treaty obligations and excessively short transposition periods.[205] These factors, all present in the EU compliance picture, will be briefly commented on. Against this backdrop, Article 258 TFEU is contrasted with the main

[202] A Chayes and AH Chayes, *The New Sovereignty: Compliance with International Regulatory Agreements* (Harvard University Press, 1995), 7.

[203] A Chayes and AH Chayes, *The New Sovereignty: Compliance with International Regulatory Agreements* (Harvard University Press, 1995), 26: 'Traditionally, sovereignty has signified the complete autonomy of the state to act as it chooses, without legal limitation by any superior entity.'

[204] A Chayes and AH Chayes, *The New Sovereignty: Compliance with International Regulatory Agreements* (Harvard University Press, 1995), 27.

[205] A Chayes and AH Chayes, *The New Sovereignty: Compliance with International Regulatory Agreements* (Harvard University Press, 1995), 15.

components of managerialism. Significantly, the Commission considers lack of knowledge and substantive comprehension of EU provisions to be a considerable source of non-compliance.[206] The EU Council has also, on several occasions, raised the issue that implementation suffers from overly complicated or unclear legal drafting.[207] In 2002, the Commission launched an action plan on 'a strategy for further coordinated action to simplify the regulatory environment' with a view to making EU law more readily understandable.[208] The Commission has continued these efforts to ensure 'clarity, simplicity, operability and enforceability of legislation'.[209]

Excessively short transposition deadlines, the 'time factor', explain some EU law infringements. The Commission however also cautions that overly long transition periods 'can deprive directives of their effect'.[210]

Finally, there does seem to be a link between lack of capacity and compliance in the EU. Ibáñez, for instance, notes: '... the different quality and quantity of administrative and financial resources available in the individual Member States directly influences the application of Community law.'[211] Börzel et al find empirical evidence that variations in longitudinal non-compliance patterns can be ascribed to differences in capacity and power. Consequently, they argue, capacity-building in terms of financial resources and managerial know-how 'might actually be a feasible way to substantially reduce the persistence of non-compliance the stages of the

[206] See, eg, answer given by Bolkestein on behalf of the Commission to Written Question P-2950 in the area of public procurement: '[T]he Commission also believes that non-compliance is to a large extent caused by a lack of knowledge and understanding of the rules.'

[207] Conclusions of the European Council summits at Lisbon (23–24 March 2000), Stockholm (23–24 March 2001), Laeken (8–9 December 2001) and Barcelona (5–16 March 2002).

[208] Communication from the Commission, Action plan '*Simplifying and Improving the Regulatory Environment*', COM/2002/278 final.

[209] Commission Communication '*A Europe of Results—Applying Community Law*', COM/2007/502, point 1.1. See also Commission Communication on '*Better Monitoring of the Application of Community Law*', COM/2006/689 final; Commission Communication '*Second strategic review of Better Regulation in the European Union*', COM/2008/32 final; Commission Communication '*Third strategic review of Better Regulation in the European Union*', COM/2009/15 final; and Commission Communication '*Smart Regulation in the European Union*', COM/2010/543 final.

[210] White Paper on Governance, Preparatory work, '*Recommendations for the Improvement of the Application of Community Law by the Member States and its Enforcement by the Commission*', September 2001, 5. In the Inter-Institutional Agreement on Better Law-making of December 2003 (2003/C 321/01), point 33, the European Parliament, the Council, and the Commission vow to insert as short as possible transposition deadlines that, generally, do not exceed two years.

[211] AJG Ibáñez, *The Administrative Supervision and Enforcement of EC Law* (Hart, 1999), 152–4.

infringement proceedings'.[212] Jensen demonstrates that failure to comply with EU labour policy comes down to the member state governments' ability rather than willingness.[213]

4.2 *Cooperation*

Literature on market governance, in particular theories of self-regulation, suggests that regulatees faced with only one deterrence option are more likely to be in opposition and that enforcement approaches founded on punishment bear the risk of undermining a cooperative position where it is motivated by a sense of responsibility.[214] This line of thought is also present in the managerial approach according to which prohibitory rules enforced in a speedy and pre-emptory manner are likely to be counterproductive. Instead the authors perceive treaties and regimes as 'institutions for the management of an issue area over time'[215] and this framework also includes a strategy to manage failures to comply. The dual role of the Commission as both policy initiator and guardian of the EU Treaties supports a reading of the general EU infringement procedure as a subset of a coherent policy cycle to manage certain policy areas over time.

Infringement proceedings frequently concern politically sensitive matters and the type of interaction that takes place between the Commission and a given member state may harden during the negotiations. At the same time, a ruling by the Court of Justice is of a purely declaratory nature; the principle of loyal cooperation applies to the Commission as an EU institution and not merely to the supervisees;[216] the judicial phase of Article 258 TFEU does not imply a culpability test and, significantly, the burden of proof in infringement procedures lies with the Commission alone.[217] Significantly, there is no presumption of non-compliance in the procedural

[212] T Börzel, T Hofmann, and D Panke, 'Caving in or Sitting it Out? Longitudinal Patterns of Non-compliance in the European Union' (2011) *Journal of European Public Policy*, 1–18, 14.

[213] CB Jensen, 'Implementing Europe. A Question of Oversight' (2007) *European Union Politics* 8:4, 451–77.

[214] I Ayres and J Braithwaite, *Responsive Regulation: Transcending the Deregulation Debate* (Oxford University Press, 1992), 19.

[215] A Chayes and AH Chayes, *The New Sovereignty: Compliance with International Regulatory Agreements* (Harvard University Press, 1995), 227–8.

[216] Case 2/88 *Zwartveld* [1990] ECR I-489, para 18.

[217] Cases C-96/81 *Commission v Netherlands* [1982] ECR 1791. See, however, C-272/86 *Commission v Greece* [1988] ECR I-4875, para 21, clarifying that where the 'Commission has produced sufficient evidence ... [it is] incumbent on ... [the Member State] to contest substantively and in detail the information produced and the consequences thereof'.

design of Article 258 TFEU.[218] Given the somewhat soft powers of the Commission, a contextual understanding of the enforcement mechanism and the implied function of the Commission suggests a role as a loyal cooperator endorsing and assisting national compliance. Overt violations of Treaty obligations aside, the pre-litigation and also the judicial phases are more usefully thought of as forums for clarification. This is both in relation to substantive questions and to member state behaviour. Where it becomes apparent that a member state has misread its Treaty obligations or failed to conform to them, it shall loyally arrange itself in accordance with the obligations.[219] The Commission likewise underscores that the overall purpose of the general infringement procedure and the specific purpose of the pre-litigation phase, is to encourage voluntary compliance. Thus, as a complement to its treaty-based enforcement measures, the Commission has encouraged member state cooperation through non-binding arrangements and thereby expanded the scope for cooperative interaction.[220] The CHAP and EU Pilot 'management (pre-infringement) tools' are examples thereof.[221] Moreover, by focusing on its capacity to accommodate and assist member states' compliance, the Commission defines the infringement procedure as one of cooperativeness and portrays its own role as that of a managerial supervisor.

The distinction between compliance and effectiveness set out in chapter one is useful to have in mind when comparing the managerial approach *towards* compliance and the general EU infringement procedure. Central to the approach is a range of activities that take treaty norms as a point of reference rather than perceiving them as pre-fixed obligations to be imposed in a rigid manner. That the Court of Justice issues declaratory judgments, suggests a need for interpretive clarification and an assumption that states will meet the terms voluntarily. The Commission does presume, implicitly[222] and explicitly,[223] that member states are generally willing to

[218] C-287/03 *Commission v Belgium* [2005] ECR I-3761, para 27.

[219] This general obligation is codified in the fidelity clause (Art 4, para 3, TEU).

[220] Commission '*22nd Annual Report from the Commission on Monitoring the Application of Community Law*' (2004), COM/2005/570, 3.

[221] The term is borrowed from Commission '*28th Annual Report on Monitoring the Application of EU Law*', COM/2011/588.

[222] Eg, by setting up 'package meetings' where member states are provided an opportunity to comply voluntarily.

[223] The Commission's understanding of most non-compliance as being benign appears from interviews conducted by Börzel in 2001 with Commission officials from a range of DGs. T Börzel, 'Guarding the Treaty. The Compliance Strategies of the Commission' in T Börzel

comply[224] and it asserts that judicial recourse is 'not the only nor necessarily the most efficient way to ensure compliance'.[225]

In practice, the Commission's endeavours to ensure compliance primarily rest on informal and formal approaches to obtain an amicable agreement, in accordance with the purpose of the pre-litigation phase. The range of complementary compliance measures institutionalized unilaterally by the Commission[226] includes, among others, 'benchmarking, peer pressure, annual reporting on implementation of Community law',[227] naming and shaming, SOLVIT-programmes, IMPEL (the EU Network for the implementation and enforcement of environmental law), EU Pilot, as well as preventive measures such as implementation plans.[228] These instruments and practices are continuously evaluated and adapted.[229] Other soft-law tools have become available thanks to secondary legislation.[230] Together, these formal and informal procedures resemble core elements of the managerial model. Judicial recourse is, however, a significant part of the overall monitoring regime,[231] and the Commission recognizes it as a vital feature of the procedure.[232]

and R Cichowski (eds.), *State of the European Union Volume 6: Law Politics and Society* (Oxford University Press, 2003), 207.

[224] The managerial model presumes that states are in principle prone to comply. See A Chayes and AH Chayes, *The New Sovereignty: Compliance with International Regulatory Agreements* (Harvard University Press, 1995); and H Koh, 'Why Do Nations Obey International Law? (1997) *Yale Law Journal* 106, 2599–659.

[225] 'Implementation of EU Environmental Law: Survey Highlights Serious Shortcomings', IP/04/1038, Brussels, 19 August 2004.

[226] See, eg, Commission scoreboards.

[227] Commission paper, '*Towards the Enlarged Union—Strategy Paper and Report of the European Commission on the Progress towards Accession by each of the Candidate Countries*', COM/2002/700 final, 25.

[228] See, eg, Commission '*28th Annual Report on Monitoring the Application of EU Law*', COM/2011/588.

[229] See, eg, Commission Communication '*A Europe of Results—Applying Community Law*', COM/2007/502, point 2.2.

[230] See, eg, Decision No 3052/95/EC of the European Parliament and of the Council of 13 December 1995 establishing a procedure for the exchange of information on national measures derogating from the principle of the free movement of goods within the Community, [1995] OJ L 321/1, Art 9.

[231] See, eg, Second Forum on Implementation and Enforcement of Community Environmental Law, *Intensifying our Efforts to Clean Urban Waste Water*, closing remarks of Commissioner Wallström, 2. More generally, see Commission Communication '*Better Monitoring of the Application of Community Law*', COM/2002/725, 10–12.

[232] See, eg, Answer given by Mr Prodi on behalf of the Commission to Written Question P-3784/2002.

4.3 *Identification and justification*

Active management starts with identifying infringements[233] and the Commission has classified behaviour it considers to be particularly grave. The three main categories of infringements are prioritized in the following order: (i) infringements that undermine the foundations of the rule of law; (ii) infringements that undermine the smooth functioning of the EU legal system; and (iii) infringements consisting in the failure to transpose or the incorrect transposal of directives.[234] Rapid changes in situations may render obligations inapt and become a cause of non-compliance. The Commission maintains that *ex post* evaluation is a useful tool to identify shortcomings and argues that, where appropriate, review clauses should be included in legislative acts.[235] This enables the Commission to table legislative proposals when a provision is non-operational or needs amendment.

The procedural structure starting with a 'warning letter', guarantees member state interest in submitting its observations. It also allows for an exchange of interpretations of particular provisions, jurisprudence, etc, and, significantly, it prevents the Commission from acting as a vindicative prosecutor by automatically initiating infringement proceedings. It thus compels the parties to seek out pre-judicial conflict solution during the preliminary as well as the consecutive phase.

4.4 *Technical assistance*

At EU level technical assistance is provided, for instance, through so-called package meetings involving also national expert civil servants. Moreover, the reciprocal nature of the principle of sincere cooperation arguably entails that member states can request assistance from the Commission.[236]

[233] A Chayes and AH Chayes, *The New Sovereignty: Compliance with International Regulatory Agreements* (Harvard University Press, 1995), 110.

[234] Commission Communication *'Better Monitoring of the Application of Community Law'*, COM/2002/725, 11–12. Concerning the Commission's priority criteria, see also Commission Communication *'A Europe of Results—Applying Community Law'*, COM/2007/502 final, mentioned in chapter one. The criteria are, in principle, continuously reviewed and adapted.

[235] Communication from the Commission, *'Action plan "Simplifying and Improving the Regulatory Environment"'*, COM/2002/278 final, 8 and Part IV.

[236] Case 94/87 *Commission v Germany* [1989] ECR 175, para 9. Note that the case concerns state aid. See furthermore Case 2/88, *Zwartveld* [1990] ECR I-489, para 18.

4.5 *Discourse and persuasion—elitist settlements*

The general EU infringement procedure, as well as the managerial approach, attributes a central role to structured discourse.[237] When infringement cases concern conflicting interpretations by the Commission and the member state, the administrative phases consist of exchanges of arguments and expositions[238] rather than technical advice. Often, the Commission manages to generate behavioural changes on the side of the member states. Elitist settlements can differ considerably from a hypothetic potential ruling, had the Commission referred the case to the Court of Justice. Significantly, the Commission has no authority to interpret EU law in a binding manner and friendly settlements do not influence the member states' material obligations.[239] However, the possibility for a member state to negotiate a favourable understanding with the Commission constitutes an incentive to engage in bilateral dialogue. The method of recurring exchanges based on facts and law resembles the 'iterative process of discourse' central to managerialism.[240] Moreover, the aim of the problem-solving exercise is to obtain a practical elimination of defections and their consequences.[241] 'Member States' responses, arguments and, where appropriate, intentions of rectifying the situation' are decisive to the Commission's follow-up action.[242] It is, of course, significant that this negotiation takes place in the shadow of formal adjudication. The Commission, thus, has a significant advantage throughout the process given that it decides on the advancement of the case.

[237] A Chayes and AH Chayes, *The New Sovereignty: Compliance with International Regulatory Agreements* (Harvard University Press, 1995), 229.

[238] At least from Commission side given its obligation to set out in the reasoned opinion 'a coherent and detailed statement of the reasons which persuaded the Commission that the state concerned had failed to fulfil one of its obligations under the Treaty'. See C-247/89 *Commission v Portugal* [1991] ECR I-3659, para 22.

[239] C-393/98 *Ministério Público and António Gomes Valente v Fazenda Pública* [2001]ECR I-1327, C-142 and C-143/80 *Amministrazione delle Finanze dello Stato v Essevi SpA and Carlo Salengo* [1980] ECR 1413.

[240] A Chayes and AH Chayes, *The New Sovereignty: Compliance with International Regulatory Agreements* (Harvard University Press, 1995), 25.

[241] See Case 70/72 *Commission v Germany* [1973] ECR 813.

[242] Answer given by Mr Flynn on behalf of the Commission to Written Question E-3681/97.

4.6 *Dispute settlement*

Although only a relatively small number of infringement proceedings initiated result in referral to the Court of Justice, formal dispute settlement constitutes a central element of Article 258 TFEU.[243] Awareness that there is a final, impartial body to undertake normative interpretation and to appraise member state conduct restricts the scope for idiosyncratic and non-cooperative conduct by the parties. This is negotiation in the shadow of law. As seen from case law on, for instance, economic freedoms, there are a significant number of provisions that leave ample room for genuine interpretational doubt.[244] This matter of legal indeterminacy, discussed in more detail in chapter one, is not unique to EU law. In a regime based on the rule of law, some disputes will inevitably call for final clarification.

4.7 *Transparency (between the member states)*

Whereas the member states have engaged in a legal system on the 'basis of reciprocity',[245] compliance with EU law does not rest on reciprocity.[246] The immediate purpose of ensuring compliance is two-fold; first, to obtain the collective benefits that sparked off the institution of the Treaty. The other, interrelated, purpose is to prevent free-riding. Member states are clearly concerned about the costs of complying in a defective enforcement milieu. This can be seen from the proceedings before the Court of Justice where member states invoke other treaty parties' failure to comply, even though such arguments have no legal bearings on their own obligation to comply. It is also reflected in the piecemeal strengthening of the general EU infringement procedure. Weatherill points out that the possible implications of such member state apprehension may be serious, in addition to

[243] The Commission's annual reports with statistical annexes can be accessed at http://ec.europa.eu/eu_law/infringements/infringements_annual_report_en.htm. According to Commission Communication *'A Europe of Results—Applying Community Law'*, COM/2007/502, 4, the Commission closes around 93 per cent of all infringement cases before a ruling from the Court of Justice.

[244] See, eg, K Lenaerts, D Arts, and R Bray (eds.), *Procedural Law of the European Union* (Sweet & Maxwell, 1999), 84: 'The "finding" serves principally to enforce the actual application of Community law . . . The action may also be used as a means of determining the exact nature of the obligations of a Member State in the event of differences of interpretation of Community law.'

[245] Case 6/64 *Costa v ENEL* [1964] ECR I-585, para 3.

[246] Cases C-142/01 *Commission v Italy* [2002] ECR I-4541, para 7; and C-163/99 *Portugal v Commission* [2001] ECR I-2613, para 22.

being very hard to detect. Thus, he notes, there is an inherent risk of directives, and framework directives in particular, giving incentives to 'a more subtle form of retaliation based on reduction in domestic costs of compliance'.[247] Weatherill's point transcends isolated instances of non-compliance. Rather, he is concerned with the intrinsic risk of competitive under-implementation. This practice is furthered by the perceived risk that other member states benefit from opportunistic behaviour to the detriment of compliant member states.[248] 'Gold-plating' by adding 'layers of complexity and red-tape' when transposing directives, is one way the member states can under-implement.[249]

Transparency in this regard could deter states from considering non-compliant behaviour in the first place. Similarly, the obligation for member states to make transposition notifications has preventive effects. These methods bring about transparency and serve as means to reassure compliance. They may thereby persuade other states to undertake genuine implementation. However, although the Commission's statistical breakdowns may constitute a source of information, which enables the member states to monitor one another, the practice of publicity may also have negative repercussions for overall compliance. This is also true for the Commission's shaming strategies and the public pressure on defaulting member states. Börzel has suggested that the serious compliance deficit identified by the Commission is mainly a statistical artefact.[250] Insofar as her assessment is correct, the Commission's complaints that member states do not comply satisfactorily may indeed cause the same member states to perceive some of their peers as free-riders. If the reaction to the Commission's public shaming and negative compliance assessments is non-compliance as a means of tacit retaliation or self-protection, the Commission's shaming strategy risks becoming a self-perpetuating cause of non-compliance. Whereas, this chapter has argued, the secrecy characterizing the

[247] S Weatherill, 'Addressing Problems of International Implementation in EC Law' in C Kilpatrick, T Novitz, and P Skidmore (eds.), *The Future of Remedies in Europe* (Hart Publishing, 2000), 113.

[248] S Weatherill, 'Addressing Problems of International Implementation in EC Law' in C Kilpatrick, T Novitz, and P Skidmore (eds.), *The Future of Remedies in Europe* (Hart Publishing, 2000).

[249] Handling the Process of Producing and Implementing Community Rules: Report of the Working Group 'Better Regulation' (Group 2c) May 2001 (White Paper on European Governance, Work Area no 2).

[250] T Börzel, 'Non-compliance in the European Union: Pathology or Statistical Artefact?' (2001) *Journal of European Public Policy* 8:5, 803–24.

infringement procedure has advantages in terms of effectiveness in individual cases, secrecy generally does little to assure member states that other member states *do* comply. As will be discussed in more detail in chapter six, the Commission increasingly supplements action according to the general infringement procedure with non-binding measures such as peer-review and expert groups on compliance. These forums can function, among other things, as a means for member states to verify compliance. The shift towards more transparency among the member states seems laudable in this regard.

5. Conclusion

This chapter described and analysed the general EU infringement procedure stipulated in Article 258 TFEU, including case law concerning the Commission's powers and obligations towards member states during the pre-litigation and judicial stages. It then discussed the pressure on the Commission to make the general EU infringement procedure more transparent and accessible to individuals. In addition, it looked at a range of non-binding, practical, problem-solving tools established by the Commission. Their purpose is to deal with complainants and alleged member state infringements outside the scope of Article 258 TFEU. Finally, it analysed the general EU infringement procedure in view of managerial compliance theory.

A central trait of the general EU infringement procedure is that it leaves room for amicable settlements between the Commission and a given member state. This type of dialogue is not explicitly mentioned in Article 258 TFEU. However, it is viable owing to a number of characteristics of the procedural framework. Notably, the Commission enjoys unfettered discretion whether to pursue alleged infringements and it may terminate proceedings at any point in time.

The Commission's heavy reliance of individual complaints as a tool to detect member state infringements has generated demands for greater recognition of complainants and transparency. In response to this criticism, the Commission has taken a range of steps over the last decades to formalize relations with complainants and to promote transparency. However, it stresses that this will happen within the legal and judicial limits described in this chapter. More recently the Commission has begun to filter complaints through EU Pilot. It remains to be seen whether this will enable the Commission to disengage complainants from the general infringement procedure. If so, the Commission can continue to employ complaints as a means to detect infringements. Moreover, it can address the underlying compliance problems proactively, while reserving the general EU infringement procedure for priority cases.

The procedural review in this chapter demonstrated that Article 258 TFEU does not contain any citizen rights. Besides, the relevant provisions pertaining to access to documents protect confidentiality to the extent necessary for the Commission to reach an amicable settlement with a given member state. At this point in time, the Commission can thus opt to conduct the administrative phase in confidentiality. Not surprisingly, it has consistently defended its right to secrecy stating that there is a broader public interest in keeping negotiations at this stage undisclosed. The vast majority of infringement cases are terminated via the practice of reaching a friendly settlement and thus before they reach the Court of Justice. Hence, diplomatic, bilateral settlements continue to constitute a primary and proportionate, initial means of enforcement. Final recourse to the Court of Justice is however significant, both for the initial search for friendly settlement and per se.

A number of features of Article 258 TFEU suggest an assumption of voluntary compliance and that defection should be managed rather than sanctioned. These include the general EU infringement procedure's non-coercive nature, the significance attached to discourse and to technical assistance, the lack of transparency during the administrative stage, and the declaratory nature of rulings from the Court of Justice. Moreover, it was argued, the general EU infringement procedure relies on an instrumental logic similar to that of the managerial theory of enforcement. It foresees the range of prescribed measures and activities to 'separately and in intricate combination press toward compliance'.[251] Similarly, the various *de facto* and *de jure* phases of the EU infringement procedure have isolated functions. Yet, they form part of a comprehensive enforcement strategy intended to anticipate compliance. As Snyder also points out, the pre-judicial compliance negotiation and adjudication should be considered as complementary

[251] A Chayes and AH Chayes, *The New Sovereignty: Compliance with International Regulatory Agreements* (Harvard University Press, 1995), 110.

forms of dispute settlement.[252] Significantly, the administrative and judicial phases provide forums for discursive interaction where treaty norms are interpreted and member states induced to make the necessary behavioural changes in order to conform to their obligations. Aiming at non-punitive friendly settlements, voluntary member state compliance may take place at any point of the process. Key words in this respect are argumentation, technical and legal exposition, persuasion, pressure through exposure, and juridical recourse.

[252] F Snyder, 'The Effectiveness of European Community Law. Institutions, Processes, Tools and Techniques' (1993) *Modern Law Review* 56, 30.

3

Failure to Comply with a Judgment of the Court: Article 260 TFEU[1]

1. Introduction

Chapter two discussed Article 258 TFEU concerning member state failure to comply with EU law. This chapter examines Article 260 TFEU concerning failure to comply with judgments of the Court of Justice according to Article 258 TFEU. This type of infringement is among one of the Commission's enforcement priorities.[2] Because Article 260 TFEU is designed only to induce the member state to comply with the judgment, it has a much narrower ambit than Article 258 TFEU.[3] Originally the procedures stipulated in Articles 258 and 260 TFEU were largely similar although tackling different types of non-compliance. However, the Maastricht Treaty and the Lisbon Treaty amend Article 260 TFEU in a number of important ways, introducing pecuniary sanctions and omitting the Commission's obligation to issue a reasoned opinion. Thus, the Commission is granted a more potent and easily employable tool against repetitive infringements. In addition, the Lisbon Treaty empowers the Commission to request that the Court of Justice award sanctions against member states that fail to notify measures transposing a directive. Notably,

[1] This chapter is based on my article entitled 'Procedural Overview and Substantive Comments on Articles 226 and 228 EC' published in 2009 in (2008) *Yearbook of European Law* 27, 121–66.

[2] Commission Communication '*A Europe of Results—Applying Community Law*', COM/2007/502.

[3] T-36/04 *API* v *Commission* [2007] ECR II-3201, para 137. On the material aspect and the relationship to Art 258 TFEU, see P Wennerås, 'Sanctions against Member States under Article 260 TFEU: Alive, but Not Kicking?' (2012) *Common Market Law Review* 49, 145–76.

it can do so already when initiating proceedings according to Article 258 TFEU.[4]

This chapter analyses Article 260 TFEU. The aim is two-fold. First, it accounts for the procedural steps involved in the light of pertinent case law. Secondly, it appraises the procedure against contemporary international law and international relations compliance theory. It argues that Article 260(2) TFEU proposes a durable procedural framework for awarding pecuniary sanctions. Thus, the Commission has been granted a tool to put sustained pressure on defaulting member/states while maintaining them in a process towards compliance. Critically, the procedure accomplishes to do so without undermining the treaty regime's legitimacy.

This chapter is structured as follows: it discusses briefly some of the early Community deliberations on sanctions and the eventual introduction of sanctions. Then it examines Article 260(2) TFEU, including the amendments introduced by the Maastricht Treaty and the Lisbon Treaty. In doing so, it explains central procedural clarifications provided in case law. The penultimate section appraises the *lex specialis* provision stipulated in Article 260(3) TFEU concerning failure to notify measures transposing a directive. Drawing from international law literature, the final section discusses the characteristics that make EU sanctions relatively mobile, legitimate, and functional in comparison to sanctions in many international treaty regimes.

2. Pecuniary Sanctions—the Maastricht and Lisbon Treaty Amendments

The idea of member state sanctions was contemplated at a relatively early point in the European Economic Community's history.[5] For instance, the Court of Justice proposed that sanctions should be introduced already in the 1970s.[6] On later occasions Spinelli and the European Parliament too

[4] Article 260(3) TFEU.

[5] G Tesauro, 'Remedies for Infringement of Community Law by Member States' in W van Gerwen and M Zuleeg (eds.), *Sanktionen als Mittel zur Durchsetzung des Gemeinschaftsrechts* (Bundesanzeiger, 1996), 19–20.

[6] L Borzsák, *The Impact of Environmental Concerns on the Public Enforcement Mechanism under EU* (Wolters Kluwer, 2011) provides an excellent analysis of Art 260 TFEU. Among other things, the author sets out in detail the historical attempts by different actors (including the Court of

envisaged that the Court of Justice should be conferred powers to suspend member state Community rights; and in the case of persistent and particularly grave infringements, to suspend Council voting rights.[7] The first proposal was in stark contrast to the procedure in place under Article 171 of the EEC Treaty as it was then (now Article 260 TFEU). Significantly, it provided no other remedy than obtaining a declaratory judgment that a member state had failed to comply with a judgment of the Court of Justice.

Article 258 TFEU, it was argued in chapter two, can usefully be explained through the lenses of managerialism. However, more generally, Downs et al argue that managerialism critically fails to appreciate the link between enforcement and compliance when there is a considerable incentive to defect.[8] Moreover, there is a real risk that non-compliance and weak enforcement mechanisms will deter the Council and also the member state governments from taking on new and deep commitments.[9] Given the depth and breadth of legal integration in the EU it was perhaps to be expected that the member state governments eventually introduced pecuniary sanctions. The Maastricht Treaty which entered into force in 1993 empowered the Commission to request the Court of Justice to impose a lump sum or penalty payment on a member state, in addition to a declaration that it has failed to comply with a ruling under Article 258 TFEU. A lump sum is a 'single sum of money that serves as complete payment'.[10] Penalty payments are sums of money to be paid periodically from the date the Court of Justice awards them until the member state breach has been brought to an end. The Lisbon Treaty further amended Article 260 TFEU in two respects. It omitted the reasoned opinion in the administrative phase (Article 260(2) TFEU) and introduced a new provision concerning failure to notify measures transposing a directive (Article 260(3) TFEU). The Commission may now request that the Court of Justice awards a pecuniary penalty already during the Article 258 TFEU procedure for failure to notify measures

Justice and the European Parliament) to have sanctions introduced as well as some of the early academic thoughts on this matter.

[7] Draft Treaty Establishing the European Union [1984] OJ C77/33, Art 44.

[8] GW Downs, D Rocke, and PN Barsoom, 'Is the Good News about Compliance Good News for Cooperation?' (1996) *International Organization* 50:3, 379–406.

[9] Compare GW Downs, D Rocke, and PN Barsoom 'Is the Good News about Compliance Good News for Cooperation?' (1996) *International Organization* 50:3, 379–406. The authors address the theory in general and not in relation to the EU specifically.

[10] *The American Heritage Dictionary of the English Language* (4th edn, Houghton Mifflin Company, 2004).

transposing a directive. In doing so the Court of Justice's discretion in deciding on the amount of pecuniary penalties has been restricted.

Article 260 TFEU reads:

1. If the Court of Justice of the European Union finds that a Member State has failed to fulfil an obligation under the Treaties, the State shall be required to take the necessary measures to comply with the judgment of the Court.
2. If the Commission considers that the Member State concerned has not taken the necessary measures to comply with the judgment of the Court, it may bring the case before the Court after giving that State the opportunity to submit its observations. It shall specify the amount of the lump sum or penalty payment to be paid by the Member State concerned which it considers appropriate in the circumstances.

   If the Court finds that the Member State concerned has not complied with its judgment it may impose a lump sum or penalty payment on it.

   This procedure shall be without prejudice to Article 259.
3. When the Commission brings a case before the Court pursuant to Article 258 on the grounds that the Member State concerned has failed to fulfil its obligation to notify measures transposing a directive adopted under a legislative procedure, it may, when it deems appropriate, specify the amount of the lump sum or penalty payment to be paid by the Member State concerned which it considers appropriate in the circumstances.

   If the Court finds that there is an infringement it may impose a lump sum or penalty payment on the Member State concerned not exceeding the amount specified by the Commission. The payment obligation shall take effect on the date set by the Court in its judgment.

The reluctance to introduce sanctions prior to the Maastricht Treaty has by and large been explained with reasons pertaining national sovereignty.[11] Audretsch, for instance, notes that sanctions would amount to more than 'certain sacrifices of sovereignty'. It would signify creation of 'a real federal power'.[12] Commentators were also puzzled to learn that it was the traditionally anti-federalist UK which ultimately proposed the insertion of a

[11] K Alter, 'Who are the "Masters of the Treaty"?: European Governments and the European Court of Justice' (1998) *International Organization* 52:1, 121–47, 127; and J Tallberg, 'Supranational Influence in EU Enforcement: the ECJ and the Principle of State Liability [2000] *Journal of European Public Policy* 7:1, 104–21, 108–9.

[12] HAH Audretsch, *Supervision in European Community Law* (Elsevier Science Publishers BV, 1986), 140.

pecuniary penalty provision in the EC Treaty.[13] One possible explanation is that the UK feared that non-compliance would undermine the internal market and in addition, that its own record of compliance was relatively good.[14] Moreover, there had been an increase in the number of repetitive infringements in a five-year period leading up to the Maastricht IGC. A more general explanation might be found in the perception of EU law—or Community law as it was then. When the House of Lords in 1983 reflected on the status of Community law vis-à-vis national law, Community law was addressed as a 'subject matter of an international obligation'.[15] However, a comparative study on implementation of Community law based on interviews with national civil servants, first published in 1988, suggests that national administrations 'do not consider the Community law implementation of the Community substance of directives as the application of foreign imposed law'.[16] To the extent EU norms are perceived as part of national law per se at the implementation stage, the demands articulated by the Commission under Articles 258 and 260 TFEU are less intrusive. Finally, given the span of EU law, the cost of defection to the internal market and the EU generally may also outweigh concerns that sanctions have a federal appearance.

Whereas the Court of Justice endorsed the UK proposal, somewhat surprisingly the Commission was sceptical. The Commission proposed that the principle of member state liability should be strengthened and codified in the Treaty thus invigorating decentralized enforcement.[17]

[13] J Tallberg, *European Governance and Supranational Institutions—Making States Comply* (Routledge, 2003), 77. For a discussion of the various proposals that surfaced during the IGC, see I Kilbey, 'Financial Penalties under Article 228(2) EC: Excessive Complexity?' (2007) *Common Market Law Review* 44:3, 743–59. The author notes that the UK's submission was a slightly revised version of a suggestion tabled by the Court of Justice.

[14] J Tallberg, *European Governance and Supranational Institutions—Making States Comply* (Routledge, 2003); and Maria Mendrinou, 'Non-Compliance and the European Commission's Role in Integration' (1996) *Journal of European Public Policy* 3:1, 14.

[15] P Mead, 'The Obligation to Apply European Law: Is Duke Dead?' (1991) *European Law Review* 16, 490–501, 491.

[16] H Siedentopf, 'The Implementation of Directives in the Member States' in H Siedentopf and J Ziller (eds.), *Making European Policies Work* (SAGE, 1988), 178.

[17] Member State liability does constitute a deterrent to infringements and is by some considered a type of sanction. It is, strictly speaking, linked to the protection of individuals and reparation of loss and damage caused by a Member State breach rather than to enforcement. See, eg, W van Gerven and M Zuleeg, 'Einführung in die Problemstellung' in Walter van Gerven (ed.), *Remedies and Sanctions for the Enforcement of European Community Law* (Bundesanzeiger Verlag, 1996), 12. See also C-224/01 *Gerhard Köbler v Österreich* [2003] ECR I-10239, para 45.

It also voiced concern over the fact that repetitive infringements often express a lack of resources and that imposing pecuniary sanctions would merely aggravate the cause of non-compliance.[18] Additional and more concrete problems in terms of making sanctions effective were brought up. Timmermans notes that in 'reading the Commission's contribution to the Conference in this respect one gets the impression that the Commission did not consider the introduction of a sanction mechanism a priority'.[19]

3. Article 260(1) TFEU

According to Article 260(1) TFEU the member state shall be required to take the necessary measures to comply with the judgment of the Court of Justice. The importance of immediate and uniform application of EU law means according to settled case law, that the process of compliance must be initiated at once and completed as soon as possible.[20]

4. Article 260(2) TFEU

Jurisprudence from the Court of Justice provides important points of procedural clarification on Article 260(2) TFEU. It explains the powers of the Court of Justice and the Commission respectively and the possibility of imposing periodic and lump sum penalties cumulatively. After more than a decade of case law the contours of a mature procedural framework begin

As discussed in chapter two, supremacy and particularly the doctrine of direct effect contribute to blurring the interface between domestic law and EU law and they constitute part of a sophisticated set of compliance pressures on Member States.

[18] There actually was a correlation between wealth and patterns of non-compliance with EU law. L Borzsák, *The Impact of Environmental Concerns on the Public Enforcement Mechanism under EU* (Wolters Kluwer, 2011), 81. See also T Börzel, T Hofmann, and D Panke, 'Caving in or Sitting it Out? Longitudinal Patterns of Non-compliance in the European Union' (2011) *Journal of European Public Policy*, 1–18.

[19] CWA Timmermans, 'Commentary' in MK Bulterman and M Kuijer (eds.), *Compliance with Judgments of International Courts* (Martinus Nijhoff Publishers, 1996), 115.

[20] See, eg, C-387/97 *Commission* v *Greece* [2000] ECR I-5047, paras 81 and 82; and C-278/01 *Commission v Spain* [2003] ECR I-14141, paras 26 and 27; C-568/07 *Commission v Greece* [2009] ECR I-4505, para 51.

to materialize.[21] However, there are also unresolved issues, including how to establish and confirm that a member state has taken adequate action to comply with rulings under Article 260(2) TFEU.[22] This section discusses the implications of the most recent treaty amendment, ie, omitting the reasoned opinion from the pre-litigation phase. It then provides a procedural overview of Article 260(2) TFEU with reference to relevant jurisprudence and to the Commission's communications on the provision.

4.1 *Omitting the reasoned opinion and the search for amicable settlement*

Similar to Article 258 TFEU the procedure established under Article 260 TFEU consists of a pre-litigation and a litigation phase. The purpose of the pre-litigation phase according to Article 258 TFEU was explained in detail in chapter two. The purpose of the pre-litigation phase according to Article 260(2) TFEU is similar. That is to say, it gives the member state the opportunity to fulfil its obligations under EU law, or to put its case properly against the complaints set out by the Commission as regards its continued failure to fulfil its obligations.[23] Prior to the Lisbon Treaty, the pre-litigation phase under Article 260 TFEU required the Commission to issue a letter of formal notice and subsequently a reasoned opinion. Both the letter of formal notice and the reasoned opinion delimit the subject-matter of the dispute, so that it cannot be extended afterwards. The Convention Discussion Circle on the Court of Justice proposed omitting the reasoned opinion from Article 260(2) TFEU 'to bring about greater effectiveness and simplicity in the machinery for sanctions for failure to comply with a judgment of the Court'.[24] This amendment was eventually introduced by the Lisbon Treaty. It raises a number of questions concerning the

[21] This is reflected in the fact that the chambers rather than the Grand Chamber sometimes rule in cases involving pecuniary sanctions. See, eg, C-109/08 *Commission v Greece* [2009] ECR I-4657. L Borzsák, *The Impact of Environmental Concerns on the Public Enforcement Mechanism under EU* (Wolters Kluwer, 2011), 198 and chapter seven, discusses some unresolved issues and proposes solutions to them.

[22] C-292/11 P: Appeal brought on 9 June 2011 by the European Commission against the judgment delivered on 29 March 2011 by the General Court in T-33/09 *Portugal v Commission* [2011] OJ C 252/19.

[23] C-457/07 *Commission v Portugal* [2010] ECR I-08091, para 55.

[24] Praesidium '*Articles on the Court of Justice and the High Court*', CONV 734/03, 12 May 2003, 16.

procedural guarantees of member states and the scope for finding friendly settlement.

The first question is whether the amended procedure establishes adequate member state guarantees. Although the reasoned opinion has now been omitted under Article 260(2) TFEU, the subject-matter of proceeding shall still be delimited by the pre-litigation procedure.[25] By analogy to case law concerning the reasoned opinion, the warning letter and the action provided for in Article 260(2) TFEU must 'set out the Commission's complaints coherently and precisely in order that the member state and the Court may appreciate exactly the extent to which the judgment finding a failure to fulfil obligations has been complied with'.[26] As mentioned in chapter two, the letter of formal notice according to Article 258 TFEU is not subject to strict requirements of precision, since it cannot, of necessity, contain anything more than an initial brief summary of the complaints.[27] The Commission may lack initial knowledge about the relevant factual and legal circumstances under Article 258 TFEU proceedings. By contrast, cases against repetitive infringements are necessarily more concrete. Notably, the Commission need only specify the points on which the member state has failed to comply with the Court of Justice's judgment. Thus, the amended pre-litigation procedure provides the member states with robust procedural guarantees, as long as the Commission executes its powers in accordance with the objectives of the procedure.

The second question concerns the scope for finding friendly settlement. As discussed in chapter two, this is a central element of Article 258 TFEU. The General Court has even called 'the objective of reaching an amicable settlement... the *raison d'être* for the pre-litigation stage'.[28] Although Article 260 TFEU has a much narrower ambit than Article 258 TFEU, there may still be need for some interpretation and thus dialogue between the Commission and a member state. This is particularly so owing to the fact that judgments are of a declaratory nature. Negotiations at this point concern whether the necessary conditions for the bringing of an action under Article 260 TFEU are met.[29]

[25] Compare, eg, C-457/07 *Commission v Portugal* [2010] ECR I-08091, para 57.

[26] Compare, eg, C-457/07 *Commission v Portugal* [2010] ECR I-08091, para 68.

[27] C-20/09 *Commission v Portugal* [2011] not yet published in the ECR, para 20.

[28] T-36/04 *API* v *Commission* [2007] ECR II-3201, para 132.

[29] Joined cases C-514/07 P, C-528/07 P, and C-532/07 P *Sweden* v *API and Commission*, not published in the ECR, paras 118–20. According to the judgment, negotiations between that

With the amendment of Article 260(2) TFEU the member state governments have attempted to strike a balance between the member states' right to prepare an adequate defence, on the one hand, and timely enforcement, on the other. However, the scope for finding an amicable settlement is not narrowed down by the Lisbon Treaty amendments. Only the process is. Significantly, the Commission can still act responsively towards member states it deems to be cooperative. According to the Commission the amendment will automatically reduce the average duration of the procedure to between eight and 18 months.[30]

4.2 *Procedural clarifications*

4.2.1 *Dates of relevance*

When examining whether a member state has taken the necessary measures to comply with a judgment under Article 258 TFEU, the Court of Justice considers the situation on expiry of the date prescribed by the Commission in its formal notice under Article 260 TFEU.[31] Thus, the Court of Justice cannot take account of any subsequent changes even if they bring the member state into compliance.[32] In relation to the possible imposition of a penalty payment, it is the date on which the Court examines the facts that is relevant.[33] If the state has brought itself into compliance before Court proceedings are initiated and the facts have been verified, the member state, as a rule, no longer risks this type of sanction.[34] The Court of Justice may however still impose the payment of a lump sum.[35]

member state and the Commission under Art 258 TFEU are, by contrast, designed to establish the existence of the infringement.

[30] Commission Communication '*Implementation of Article 260(3) of the Treaty*' [2011] OJ C12/1.

[31] Prior to the Lisbon Treaty amendment, the reference date was established in the reasoned opinion. C-304/02 *Commission v France* [2005] ECR I-6263, para 30; C-119/04 *Commission v Italy* [2006] ECR I-6885, para 27; and C-503/04 *Commission v Germany* [2007] ECR I-6153, para 19.

[32] C-475/08 *Commission v Belgium* [2009] ECR I-11503, para 30; and C-340/09 *Commission* v *Spain* [2010] not yet published in the ECR, para 39.

[33] C-119/04 *Commission v Italy* [2006] ECR I-6885, paras 33, 45, and 46; C-503/04 *Commission v Germany* [2007] ECR I-6153, para 40; C-177/04 *Commission v France* [2006] ECR I-2461, para 21, and C-304/02 *Commission v France* [2005] ECR I-06263, para 31.

[34] See, to that effect, C-369/07 *Commission v Greece* [2009] ECR I-5703, para 59; C-121/07 *Commission v France* [2008] ECR I-9159, para 27; and C-119/04 *Commission v Italy* [2006] ECR I-6885.

[35] C-121/07 *Commission v France* [2008] ECR I-9159, para 60.

4.2.2 Member state defences

The strict case law on member state defences was discussed in chapter two. Notably, a member state cannot plead provisions, practices, or situations prevailing in its domestic legal order to justify the failure to observe obligations arising under Community law.[36]

4.2.3 Lump sum and penalty payments—exclusive or complementary

Article 260(2) TFEU reads that the Commission shall 'specify the amount of the lump sum *or* penalty payment to be paid by the Member State concerned which . . . [it] considers appropriate in the circumstances' (emphasis added). The Commission initially took the standpoint that periodic penalty payments were 'more appropriate than lump sum payments as a means of achieving the essential objective of infringement proceedings, namely . . . compliance at the earliest possible opportunity'.[37] The underlying rationale was that penalty payments are forward-looking. This position should be seen against the background that the Commission seemingly understood the two types of sanction to be mutually exclusive, as a strict literal interpretation of Article 260 TFEU would arguably suggest.[38]

Applying a broad and teleological interpretation Advocate General Geelhoed first recommended that a member state should be ordered to pay both a lump sum and a penalty payment.[39] The case was against France and concerned controls measures for the conservation of fishery resources.[40] The opinion prompted the Court of Justice to re-open the oral procedure. This allowed the parties and other member states to express their views and

[36] C-121/07 *Commission v France* [2008] ECR I-9159, para 72; C-369/07 *Commission v Greece* [2009] ECR I-5703, para 45; C-503/04 *Commission v Germany* [*2007*] ECR I-6153, para 38; C-70/06 *Commission v Portugal* [2008] ECR I-1, para 22.

[37] Commission '*13th Annual Report on Monitoring the Application of Community Law*', COM/96/600, 1. See also Information from the Commission '*Memorandum on Applying Article 171 of the EC Treaty*', [1996] OJ C242/6. The illegal French ban on British beef made the Commission consider the option of a lump sum fine. See Commission '*20th Annual Report on Monitoring the Application of Community Law*', COM 2003/669, 9.

[38] The Court of Justice (supported by the Commission and the Danish, Netherlands, Finnish, and UK Governments) maintains that 'or' may, linguistically, have an alternative or a cumulative sense.

[39] Opinion of Advocate General Geelhoed [2004] in C-304/02 *Commission v France* [2005] ECR I-6263, point 38.

[40] C-304/02 *Commission v France* [2005] ECR I-6263.

France to prepare a new defence.[41] The Commission had initially requested the Court to order France to pay a pecuniary penalty. The question now arose whether the Court could deviate from the penalty type considered most appropriate by the Commission. Several governments argued that such an interpretation would be incompatible with the principles of legal certainty, predictability, transparency, and equal treatment.[42] Germany moreover argued that the Court of Justice (as opposed to the Commission) lacked the 'political legitimacy necessary to exercise such a power in a field where assessments of political expediency play a considerable role'. In addition, given the extensive nature of the power it would be against the 'general principle of civil procedure common to all the Member States that courts cannot go beyond the parties' claims'.[43] The Court of Justice however maintained that the judicial procedure under Article 260(2) TFEU is *sui generis* and cannot be compared to civil procedure principles.[44] In addition, it made a definite distinction between the administrative and judicial phases of Article 260 TFEU. The Commission operates in a political realm in which it benefits from unfettered discretion. The Court of Justice however enjoys absolute jurisdiction under Article 260(2) TFEU. Therefore, questions concerning fines and their appropriateness and suitability are entirely within the Court of Justice's judicial function once a case has been referred to it.[45]

The two types of penalty have distinct functions yet serve the identical objective of inducing compliance with a judgment.[46] The purpose of penalty payments is to induce 'a Member State to put an end as soon as possible to a breach which, in the absence of such measure, would tend to persist'.[47] Penalty payments should thus be purposively justified. Lump sums are 'based more on assessment of the effects on public and private interests of

[41] In the second round of submissions, the Commission and the Danish, Netherlands, Finnish, and UK Governments answered in the affirmative to the question of the possibility of imposing both a penalty payment and a lump sum. The French, Belgian, Czech, German, Greek, Spanish, Irish, Italian, Cypriot, Hungarian, Austrian, Polish, and Portuguese Governments argued against such an interpretation.

[42] France, Belgium, Denmark, Germany, Greece, Spain, Ireland, Italy, the Netherlands, Austria, Poland, and Portugal. The Commission and the Czech, Hungarian, and Finnish Governments answered in the affirmative.

[43] C-304/02 *Commission v France* [2005] ECR I-6263, para 88.

[44] C-304/02 *Commission v France* [2005] ECR I-6263, para 91.

[45] C-304/02 *Commission v France* [2005] ECR I-6263, para 103.

[46] C-304/02 *Commission v France* [2005] ECR I-6263, para 80 in conjunction with para 84.

[47] C-304/02 *Commission v France* [2005] ECR I-6263, para 81.

the failure... to comply'.[48] When assessing such effect the Court of Justice takes into account, in particular, the duration of the breach after the judgment initially establishing it was delivered.[49] It may also warrant a lump sum payment if a member state repeatedly infringes sector-specific EU law.[50] Penalty payments and lump sum payments constitute means of coercion and deterrence respectively.[51] Consequently, they should be employed according to their particular capacity to meet those purposes and consistent with the circumstances of a given case.[52]

When penalty payments are applied in isolation the member state in question may altogether avoid sanctions. The reason is that member states are liable from the date of delivery of the second judgment. The time passing from initiation of the infringement procedure for failure to comply with a judgment of the Court of Justice to the consecutive judgment is thus cost-free, so to speak. This is also the case when a member state complies after the Commission refers a case to the Court of Justice, but before judgment is handed down. In making the lump sum fine operational the Court of Justice has remedied this systemic deficiency.[53] Consequently, the Commission has changed its practice and no longer withdraws its action automatically when member states comply before the judgment.[54]

4.2.4 Method of calculation

As discussed in chapter two, the Commission is subject to claims that its actions according to Article 258 TFEU are non-transparent. The

[48] C-304/02 *Commission v France* [2005] ECR I-6263, para 81; and C-121/07 *Commission v France* [2008] ECR I-9159.

[49] C-121/07 *Commission* v *France* [2008] ECR I-9159, para 58.

[50] C-121/07 *Commission* v *France* [2008] ECR I-9159, para 69. See also C-496/09 *Commission v Italy* [2011] not yet published in the ECR, paras 89–91.

[51] For a different analysis and conclusion, see L Borzsák, *The Impact of Environmental Concerns on the Public Enforcement Mechanism under EU* (Wolters Kluwer, 2011), 182–7. In Communication from the Commission '*Application of Article 228 of the EC Treaty*', SEC/2005/1658, the Commission talks about lump sums 'penalising the continuation of the infringement between the first judgment on non-compliance and the judgment delivered under Article 228'.

[52] C-121/07 *Commission v France* [2008] ECR I-9159, para 81.

[53] In Communication from the Commission '*Application of Article 228 of the EC Treaty*', SEC/2005/1658, the Commission explains that it will 'from now include' both types of sanctions in its applications to the ECJ. See point 10.3. There may be situations where the Commission will exclusively ask for a lump sum to be imposed. See point 10.5.

[54] Commission MEMO/05/482, 'Financial Penalties for Member States who fail to comply with judgments of the European Court of Justice: European Commission Clarifies rules', Brussels, 14 December 2005, p 5.

Commission enjoys wide discretion under Article 260 TFEU generally and in relation to sanctions specifically.[55] However, it has issued two communications, in 1996 and 1997, concerning its approach to calculating fines. Thus, the Commission's actions according to the third subparagraph of Article 260(2) TFEU are by contrast relatively transparent, foreseeable, and consistent with legal certainty.[56] The communications are recast and amended in view of subsequent jurisprudence and in order to update the data used in the calculations.[57]

The method of calculating penalty payments proposed by the Commission allows for variation consistent with the seriousness of the infringement, the duration of the infringement, and the need to ensure that the penalty functions as a deterrent to further infringements. A flat-rate amount of 630 euros[58] per day is index-linked to a GDP deflator, rounded off, and multiplied by a coefficient scaling from 1 to 20 reflecting the seriousness of the breach and with a coefficient between 1 and 3, depending on the duration of the infringement.[59] Where appropriate, the Court of Justice acknowledges that immediate member state compliance may be difficult to achieve. This is accommodated for in the coefficient that reflects the duration.[60] To ensure the effectiveness of the penalty, the final amount is multiplied by a coefficient supposed to match the member state's ability

[55] C-121/07 *Commission v France* [2008] ECR I-9159, para 63.

[56] C-369/07 *Commission v Greece* [2009] I-05703, para 112. See also M Smith, 'Inter-institutional Dialogue and the Establishment of Enforcement Norms: A Decade of Financial Penalties under Article 228 EC (now Article 260 TFEU)' (2010) *European Public Law* 16:4, 547–70.

[57] Information from the Commission 'Memorandum on Applying Article 171 of the EC Treaty' [1996] OJ C242/6; and Information from the Commission 'Method of Calculating the Penalty Payments Provided for Pursuant to Article 171 of the EC Treaty' [1997] OJ C63 were replaced by Communication from the Commission '*Application of Article 228 of the EC Treaty*', SEC/2005/1658. The latter communication was amended by European Commission Communication SEC/2010/923. Commission Communication SEC/2011/1024 updates the data used to calculate lump sum and penalty payments in infringement proceedings.

[58] Commission Communication SEC/2011/1024 '*Updating of data used to calculate lump sum and penalty payments to be proposed by the Commission to the Court of Justice in infringement proceedings*'.

[59] The date of reference is the time the Court of Justice assesses the facts. See, eg, C-496/09 *Commission v Italy* [2011] not yet published in the ECR, para 58.

[60] The Commission has likewise acknowledged that it takes more time and energy to bring some infringements to an end than others. According to case law the duration is assessed by reference to the time when the Court of Justice assesses the facts. C-304/02 *Commission v France* ECR I-6263, para 71; and C-70/06 *Commission v Portugal* [2008] ECR I-1, para 45.

to pay. It is based on the member states' GDP and votes in the Council.[61] This geometric mean, the 'n' factor, is, for instance, 0.60 for Estonia and 21.37 for Germany.[62] The Court has taken the Commission's basic measures on board.[63] However, the Commission's propositions are merely considered to be 'useful point[s] of reference'.[64] Thus, the Court of Justice is by no means bound by them.[65] Finally, the Court of Justice ensures that the penalty payment is appropriate to the circumstances and proportionate to the infringement and the member state's ability to pay.[66]

When the Commission proposes a lump sum fine, it proposes a minimum fixed lump sum payment established on the basis of the same 'n' factor. For Estonia this basic amount is 314,000 euros and for Germany, for instance, it is 11,120,000 euros.[67] In addition, the Commission operates with a method of calculation that resembles the approach it takes to penalty payments. The Commission only applies this method if it exceeds the established minimum lump sum. The Commission multiplies a flat-rate amount[68] by a coefficient reflecting the seriousness of the infringement on a scale of 1 to 20, and by factor 'n', which reflects the capacity of each member state to pay. It then proposes a lump sum by 'multiplying a daily amount by the number of days the infringement persists between the date of delivery of the judgment under Article 226 [Article 258 TFEU] and the date the infringement comes to an end, or, failing compliance, the date of delivery of the judgment

[61] The Council votes are politically determined and hence do not necessarily reflect genuine ability to pay. The 'n' factor was revised in Commission Communication SEC/2011/1024.

[62] Communication from the Commission *'Application of Article 228 of the EC Treaty'*, SEC/2005/1658, point 18.1; and Commission Communication *'Updating of data used to calculate lump sum and penalty payments to be proposed by the Commission to the Court of Justice in infringement proceedings'*, SEC/2011/1024.

[63] C-369/07 *Commission v Greece* [2009] ECR I-5703, para 115.

[64] C-387/97 *Commission v Greece* [2000] ECR I-5047, para 92; and C-278/01 *Commission v Spain* [2003] ECR 2003 I-14141, para 52.

[65] C-387/97 *Commission v Greece* [2000] EC 2000 I-5047, para 89; and C-278/01 *Commission v Spain* [2003] ECR I-14141, para 41.

[66] C-369/07 *Commission v Greece* [2009] ECR I-5703, para 114.

[67] Communication from the Commission *'Application of Article 228 of the EC Treaty'*, SEC/2005/1658; and Commission Communication *'Updating of data used to calculate lump sum and penalty payments to be proposed by the Commission to the Court of Justice in infringement proceedings'*, SEC/2011/1024.

[68] The standard flat rate for the lump sum payment is currently fixed at 208 euros per day. Communication from the Commission *'Application of Article 228 of the EC Treaty'*, SEC/2005/1658, 9; and Commission Communication *'Updating of data used to calculate lump sum and penalty payments to be proposed by the Commission to the Court of Justice in infringement proceedings'*, SEC/2011/1024, 3.

under Article 228 [Article 260 TFEU]'.[69] In the first case where the Court of Justice awarded a lump sum fine the amount came to 20 million euros. The Commission, supported by Advocate General Geelhoed, had proposed a significantly larger lump sum of more than 115 million euros.[70] In C-121/07 *Commission v France*, France was ordered to pay a lump sum of 10 million euros, and in C-407/09 *Commission v Greece* the Court of Justice imposed a lump sum of 3 million euros.[71]

4.2.5 Frequency

Initially the Commission maintained that periodic payments should be imposed on a daily basis.[72] This was also the case in the first judgment case C-387/98 *Commission v Greece*. The Court of Justice however rejects the assumption that periodic payments should necessarily be imposed with respect to each day's delay. In view of the particular circumstances in the case *Commission v Spain*, the Court of Justice imposed pecuniary penalties on an annual basis.[73] Penalty payments can also, for instance, be imposed every six months of delay in complying with a judgment.[74] Finally, the Court of Justice may decide to defer the point at which the penalty payment takes effect. The member state thus gains time to demonstrate that it has brought the infringement to an end. In C-369/07 *Commission v Greece* for instance, the penalty payment was deferred until one month after delivery of the judgment.[75]

4.2.6 When the infringement comes closer to an end—adjustability

The importance of immediate and uniform application of EU law means that the process of compliance with the Court of Justice's judgment under Article 258 TFEU must be initiated at once and completed as soon as possible.[76] Sometimes though, infringements are only gradually remedied. Advocate General Colomer first raised the question how to deal with these

[69] Communication from the Commission '*Application of Article 228 of the EC Treaty*', SEC/2005/1658, 21.

[70] C-304/02 *Commission v France* [2005] ECR I-6263, para 116.

[71] C-407/09 *Commission v Greece* [2011] not yet published in the ECR.

[72] Information from the Commission—Method of Calculating the Penalty Payments Provided for Pursuant to Article 171 of the EC Treaty, OJ C63, 28.02.1997, para 1.

[73] C-278/01 *Commission v Spain* [2003] ECR I-14141, para 46.

[74] C-496/09 *Commission v Italy* [2011] not yet published in the ECR, para 68.

[75] C-369/07 *Commission v Greece* [2009] ECR I-5703, para 125.

[76] C-387/97 *Commission v Greece* [2000] ECR I-5047, para 82.

situations.[77] This is an issue of importance in view of the general EU principle of proportionality, which requires that fines should be proportional to a given breach and appropriate in view of a case's circumstances.[78] The question was addressed in C-278/01 *Commission v Spain*, where the Court of Justice acknowledged that awarding a static fine would potentially be inappropriate to the circumstances and non-proportionate to the breach. It has now been clarified that the amount can decrease and thus, take account of gradual progress.[79] The Court of Justice thus established a more nuanced conception of compliance in relation to the penalty payment instead of the absolute distinction between compliance and non-compliance advocated by the Commission.[80] In the concrete case, which concerned an obligation to ensure the quality of inshore bathing water,[81] the gradation was made contingent on the percentage of bathing areas in compliance with a directive.[82] By analogy, in C-496/09 *Commission v Italy* Italy was ordered to pay a periodic payment calculated by multiplying a basic amount by a percentage of unlawful aid that had not yet been recovered compared to the total amount not yet recovered on the date of delivery of the judgment.[83] The particular types of obligation and also the access to control the relevant measures were fairly plain in both these cases. Compliance with other types of obligations may turn out to be more problematical to monitor fully and in particular to graduate.

4.2.7 The measures to be taken

The member states generally enjoy a broad margin of discretion concerning how to comply. This is in accordance with the doctrine of proportionality. It also reflects that EU law sometimes is the result of diplomatic craftsmanship. The Court of Justice's judgments are of a declaratory nature and thus restricted to affirming whether or not a member state is complying.[84] It is

[77] Opinion of Advocate General Colomer in C-387/97 *Commission v Greece* [2000] ECR I-05047.

[78] C-278/01 *Commission v Spain* [2003] ECR I-14141, para 52.

[79] C-278/01 *Commission v Spain* [2003] ECR I-14141, para 49.

[80] On this distinction, see furthermore opinion of Advocate General Mischo in C-278/01 *Commission v Spain* [2003] ECR I-14141, point 77.

[81] Council Directive 76/160/EEC of 8 December 1975 concerning the quality of bathing water [1976] OJ L31/1–7.

[82] C-278/01 *Commission v Spain* [2003] ECR I-14141, para 50.

[83] C-496/09 *Commission v Italy* [2011] ECR not yet published in the ECR, para 52.

[84] Albeit unsuccessfully, the Court of Justice, supported by the Commission, has itself proposed that it should gain powers to clarify exactly what measures a member state should take in

nevertheless assumed that the Court of Justice may suggest how a member state can comply. In cases where penalty payments are awarded, the question of when the member state is complying becomes of paramount significance.

The Commission has no general powers to interpret EU law or to appraise member state conduct[85] and consequently no authority to reach a binding decision that an infringement has been brought to an end.[86] However, the Commission Legal Service has issued an in-house note clarifying that it shall notify member states about exactly what they are expected to do in order to be considered compliant. Given that the Commission's indications do not amount to acts of authoritative interpretation, they have no bearing on private individuals' ability to challenge member states before national courts. In some cases though, the Court of Justice carefully indicates what is required from the member states in terms of evidence.[87]

4.2.8 Burden of proof

The burden of proof rests with the Commission and continues to do so after the amendment of Article 260 TFEU. Thus, the Commission shall provide the Court of Justice with the information necessary to determine whether a member state has complied with a judgment.[88] However, if the Commission provides sufficient evidence to suggest that the alleged breach persists,

order to comply. CWA Timmermans, 'Commentary' in MK Bulterman and M Kuijer (eds.), *Compliance with Judgments of International Courts* (Martinus Nijhoff Publishers, 1996), 116. See also I Kilbey, 'Financial Penalties under Article 228(2) EC: Excessive Complexity?' (2007) *Common Market Law Review* 44:3, 743–59.

85 C-393/98 *Ministério Público and António Gomes Valente v Fazenda Pública* [2001] ECR I-1327; joined cases 142 and 143/80 *Amministrazione delle Finanze dello Stato v Essevi SpA and Carlo Salengo* [1980] ECR, 1413.

86 See T-33/09 *Portugal v Commission* [2011] not yet published in the ECR; and C-292/11 P: Appeal brought on 9 June 2011 by the European Commission against the judgment delivered on 29 March 2011 by the General Court in T-33/09 *Portugal v Commission* [2011] OJ C 252/19, concerning, inter alia, the powers of the Commission with regard to compliance with judgments of the Court of Justice made pursuant to Art 260(2) TFEU. See also T-139/06 *France v Commission* [2011] not yet published in the ECR; and P Wennerås, 'Sanctions against Member States under Article 260 TFEU: Alive, but Not Kicking?' (2012) *Common Market Law Review* 49, 145–76, 170.

87 See, eg, C-496/09 *Commission v Italy* [2011] not yet published in the ECR, paras 69–78.

88 C-387/97 *Commission v Greece* [2000] ECR I-5047, para 73.

the member state shall challenge, in a detailed manner, the substantive content of that evidence and prove that the breach has ceased.[89]

5. Article 260(3) TFEU: a *Lex Specialis* Fast-Track Enforcement Procedure

The Commission had reservations about the effectiveness of sanctions prior to the Maastricht Treaty, however eventually proclaimed it a useful enforcement tool. Later the Commission submitted a proposal to the Convention Discussion Circle on the Court of Justice concerning enforcement of transposition of directives. It suggested a mechanism whereby the Commission could initiate before the Court—both in the same procedure —proceedings for failure to fulfil an obligation and an application to impose a sanction in cases of failure to communicate a national transposition measure.[90] The Lisbon Treaty introduced such special, fast-track enforcement procedure aimed at failure to notify measures transposing a directive adopted under a legislative procedure. According to Article 260(3) TFEU the Commission may request that the Court of Justice impose a lump sum or penalty payment already when bringing a case before the Court pursuant to Article 258 TFEU. The adopted procedure thus breaks with the traditional method of enforcement whereby pecuniary sanctions were reserved for repetitive infringements.

The amended system distinguishes between types of infringements that concern interpretation of EU law and failure to notify the Commission of measures transposing a directive. The two situations raise questions of substantive compliance and procedural compliance, respectively. Article 260(3) TFEU concerns the latter situation only. In this way, the Commission still pursues wrongful implementation according to the procedure established in Article 260(2) TFEU.[91] Timely transposition does not necessarily bode substantive compliance. However delayed transposition is per se

[89] C-304/02 *Commission v France* [2005] ECR I-6263, para 56; and C-365/97 *Commission v Italy* [1999] ECR I-7773, paras 84–7.

[90] European Convention, Final Report of the discussion circle on the Court of Justice, CONV 636/03, 25 March 2003; and Praesidium 'Articles on the Court of Justice and the High Court', CONV 734/03, 12 May 2003, 16.

[91] P Wennerås, 'Sanctions against Member States under Article 260 TFEU: Alive, but Not Kicking?' (2012) *Common Market Law Review* 49, 145–76, 166–7, points out that the scope of the

disruptive for the EU legal order. It creates uncertainty for citizens and legal individuals alike and it prevents the Commission from monitoring correct application.[92] Moreover, transposition is an indispensable condition for compliance with exception of those situations where there is a perfect fit between EU law and already existing domestic legislation.[93]

As discussed in chapter two, the member states enjoy various degrees of autonomy in implementing and enforcing EU law. Interpretation of EU law and appraisal of member state behaviour can be a complex exercise. The duty to fulfil an obligation to notify measures transposing a directive adopted under a domestic legislative procedure is more straight-forward. Consequently, there is good reason to single out non-transposition and maintain the normal framework for other infringements generally.

As mentioned in chapter one, non-communication of national measures transposing directives is one of the Commission's enforcement priorities. This is in line with the Maastricht IGC's political call for vigorous enforcement of transposition of directives.[94] The Commission publishes information on the measures taken by the national authorities in each member state to incorporate EU directives into their national law on a monthly basis as well as timetable for implementing EU law nationally.[95]

According to Article 260(3) TFEU the Commission 'may, when it deems appropriate' request pecuniary sanctions. Thus, the wording sustains the wide discretion enjoyed by the Commission according to Article 260 TFEU. The Commission has issued a communication explaining how it intends to make use of the procedure.[96] After asserting its wide discretion according to the procedure, the Commission notes that the 'instrument should be used as a matter of principle in all cases of failure to fulfil an obligation covered by this provision . . . The importance of ensuring

obligation to notify 'measures transposing a directive' and the scope of the notion 'notify' can be ambiguous.

[92] The general practice of correlation tables constitutes an important means for individuals to obtain information on the national implementation of directives. See Commission Communication *'A Europe of Results—Applying Community Law'*, COM/2007/502.

[93] The obligation to implement directives persists irrespective whether provisions of a directive have direct effect. See, eg, C-197/96 *Commission v France* [1997] ECR I-1489, paras 14 and 15.

[94] 'Treaty on European Union—Declaration on the implementation of community law' [1992] OJ C 191/102.

[95] See the Commission's web-page at http://ec.europa.eu/eu_law/directives/directives_communication_en.htm and http://ec.europa.eu/eu_law/directives/directives_echeancier_en.htm.

[96] Commission Communication *'Implementation of Article 260(3) of the Treaty'* [2011] OJ C12/1.

transposition by Member States within the deadlines laid down applies equally to all legislative directives, there being in principle no reason to distinguish between them'.[97] Whether this is motivated by a wish to ensure some degree of equality or for enforcement reasons is unclear.[98] In any case, as Timmermans points out, there are no objective grounds to treat differently when it comes to failures to notify.[99]

Article 260(3) TFEU undoubtedly implies a strengthening of the Commission's enforcement powers. The same applies to the Court of Justice, although its powers are curtailed in comparison with the powers it enjoys according to Article 260(2) TFEU. Thus, Article 260(3) TFEU specifically stipulates that the Court of Justice may impose a lump sum or penalty payment 'not exceeding the amount specified by the Commission'.[100]

The question remains whether the special procedure will bring about timely transposition. Peers has endorsed the amendment of Article 260(2) TFEU. However, he argues, the fast-track sanction-mechanism stipulated in Article 260(3) TFEU is

> unnecessary in light of the speedier application of Article 228 [Article 260 TFEU]; if the Commission frequently applies for fines within the context of Article 226 [Article 258 TFEU] it will take more time for the Court to adjudicate these frequent cases as Member States will contest them more, and the Commission will have to spend much time arguing about the collection of the fines.[101]

[97] Commission Communication '*Implementation of Article 260(3) of the Treaty*' [2011] OJ C12/1.

[98] Since the late 1970s the Commission has attempted to ensure some degree of equality of treatment of member states. CWA Timmermans, 'Judicial Protection against Member States' in D Curtin and T Heukels (eds.), *Institutional Dynamics of European Integration. Essays in Honour of Henry G. Schermers. Volume II* (Martinus Nijhoff Publishers, 1994), 396.

[99] CWA Timmermans, 'Judicial Protection against Member States' in D Curtin and T Heukels (eds.), *Institutional Dynamics of European Integration. Essays in Honour of Henry G. Schermers. Volume II* (Martinus Nijhoff Publishers, 1994).

[100] Moreover, it follows from Art 260(3) TFEU that the payment obligation shall take effect on the date set by the Court of Justice in its judgment. According to the Praesidium's explanatory notes this allows for a period of grace where the member state can comply without being sanctioned. Praesidium 'Articles on the Court of Justice and the High Court', CONV 734/03, 12 May 2003. However, the Commission considers that the obligation to pay, as a rule, should be the day on which the judgment is handed down. Commission Communication '*Implementation of Article 260(3) of the Treaty*' [2011] OJ C12/1, para 30.

[101] House of Lords Select Committee, Session 2007–08, Tenth Report, printed 26 February 2008, para 4.161.

These are insightful points. At the same time there are factors that militate in favour of the special procedure stipulated in Article 260(3) TFEU. In cases concerning failure to notify measures transposing a directive, the Court of Justice establishes a manifest infringement. Significantly, the vast majority of cases, if not all, involve no substantive interpretation. Moreover, it involves no appraisal of the particular member state's behaviour beyond the mere assertion of the failure to notify. Thus, the purpose of the procedure is of a purely coercive nature. Late transposition is already one of the Commission's enforcement priorities. Significantly, it pursues all failures in this regard and, when necessary, refers them to the Court of Justice. Thus, whereas the Court of Justice is in any case required to pass judgments the element of coercion and deterrence has been accelerated. Assessing compliance and thus collecting the fine should be relatively easy in comparison with cases dealt with according to Article 260(2).[102] Member states will presumably seldom, of necessity, deny their failure to transpose a directive. In this respect, the preparation of cases according to Article 260(3) TFEU should be undemanding for the Judge-Rapporteur and, if one is appointed, the Advocate General. Then again, Lenaerts cautions, these types of cases probably 'warrant a full hearing on the matter and a detailed assessment as regards the amount' and it would normally require Chambers of five judges.[103]

The perhaps biggest merit of the fast-track procedure may not be a large scale imposition of fines, but better compliance rates prior to sanctions being actually imposed. In relation to Article 260(2) TFEU, the Commission has argued that sanctions have a more general dissuasive effect and thus ability to increase the general efficacy of the infringement procedure.[104] Thus, the Commission argues, member states comply rapidly before the Court of Justice has delivered a second judgment when there is the pressure of a fine payment.[105]

[102] Compare, eg, C-292/11 P: Appeal brought on 9 June 2011 by the European Commission against the judgment delivered on 29 March 2011 by the General Court in T-33/09 *Portugal v Commission*, OJ C 252, 27 August 2011, p 19.

[103] K Lenaerts, 'The Rule of Law and the Coherence of the Judicial System of the European Union' (2007) *Common Market Law Review* 44:6, 1636–59, 1639.

[104] See, eg, Commission '*14th Annual Report on Monitoring the Application of Community Law*', COM 97/299.

[105] Answer given by Wallstrom on behalf of the Commission to Written Question E-2776/01. See also S Weatherill, 'Addressing Problems of International Implementation in EC Law' in C Kilpatrick, T Novitz, and P Skidmore, *The Future of Remedies in Europe* (Hart Publishing, 2000), 93, on adding teeth to the procedure.

6. Sanctions in Perspective

The two dominant strands within contemporary compliance theory, namely the enforcement and managerial approaches, rely on rational choice theory[106] and on 'constructivist logic of appropriateness'[107] respectively. More recently, both political scientists and international lawyers have questioned whether the managerial and enforcement models (both discussed in chapter one) are necessarily mutually exclusive. Thus, Koh finds support in domestic enforcement practices that discourse leading to compliance can take place in the shadow of sanctions—and often succeed exactly because the two strategies complement each other.[108] Tallberg sees the EU as an example of how the two approaches successfully function *in concerto.*[109] Albeit to a lesser extent than originally, the procedure established under Article 260 TFEU resembles Article 258 TFEU. As discussed in chapter two, the managerial model of enforcement provides a useful framework for analysing Article 258 TFEU. It builds on the legal process tradition and thus emphasizes capacity building, etc, rather than sanctions. At the same time, the Commission maintains that the shadow of sanctions has a dissuasive effect more generally. Thus, it increases the general effectiveness of the infringement procedure.[110] Specifically, the Commission argues, the threat of fines make member states comply faster than they would otherwise do.[111]

[106] Compare, eg, GW Downs, D Rocke, and PN Barsoom, 'Is the Good News about Compliance Good News for Cooperation?' (1996) *International Organization* 50:3, 379–406.

[107] K Raustiale and A Slaughter, 'International Law, International Relations and Compliance' in W Carlsnaes, T Risse, and BA Simmons (eds.), *Handbook of International Relations* (SAGE, 2002), 548.

[108] H Koh, 'Why Do Nations Obey International Law?' (1997) *Yale Law Journal* 106, 2599–659. See R Fisher, *Improving Compliance with International Law* (University Press of Virginia, 1981), 7, for a critical comment on the appropriateness of applying domestic compliance theories to compliance with international obligations and in particular analogues to domestic criminal law.

[109] J Tallberg, *European Governance and Supranational Institutions—Making States Comply* (Routledge, 2003), 14 and 143 ff. See also T Börzel, T Hofmann, D Panke, and C Sprungk, 'Obstinate and Inefficient: Why Member States Do Not Comply with European Law' (2010) *Comparative Political Studies* 43:11, 1363–90.

[110] See, eg, '*14th Annual Report on Monitoring the Application of Community Law*' COM/97/299.

[111] Answer given by Wallstrom on behalf of the Commission to Written Question E-2776/01. See also S Weatherill, 'Addressing Problems of International Implementation in EC Law' in

In this section, the system of pecuniary sanctions under Article 260 TFEU will be set out and discussed in the light of managerialism. Many international lawyers argue that sanctions often fail.[112] Chayes and Chayes, the originators of managerialism, likewise point out a number of problems with treaty-based sanctions. This section argues that the sanctioning mechanism established in Article 260(2) TFEU to some extent remedies those problems. More specifically, the procedural structure of Article 260 TFEU proposes a way of incorporating sanctions into a managerial process that leads towards compliance. Moreover, it accomplishes this without undermining the treaty regime's legitimacy.

6.1 *Mobilization*

One of the main obstacles to effective sanctions concerns the mobilization of the sanctioning treaty parties, ie, problems of collective action. Each national decision is likely to be taken in view of a broad range of dispersed interests and pressures, be that of an economic or political nature. Ensuring compliance will not necessarily prevail among those considerations.[113] The members of the Commission College, ie, the EU commissioners, may not pursue partisan interests. Thus, the College as a unit does not suffer comparable constrictions. To the extent that there are competing interests the Commission makes decisions in the general interest of the EU.

6.2 *Legitimacy*

A second problem is that of assembling and maintaining the consensus 'necessary for the legitimacy of sanctions'.[114] In the context of centralized EU enforcement, the decision to initiate proceedings (the question of assembling), lies with the Commission as an institution set up to protect

C Kilpatrick, T Novitz, and P Skidmore, *The Future of Remedies in Europe* (Hart Publishing, 2000), 93, on adding teeth to the procedure.

[112] S Weintraub (ed.), *Economic Coercion and US Foreign Policy: Implications of Case Studies from the Johnson Administration* (Westview Press, 1982), 23; G Clyde Hufbauer and JJ Schott, *Economic Sanctions Reconsidered: History and Current Policy* (Institute for International Economics, 1990), 2; and Jean Amphoux, 'Recours en constatation des manquements des États, les traités CEE et Euratom' (1969) *Droit des Communautés Européennes*, 1042–88.

[113] A Chayes and AH Chayes, *The New Sovereignty: Compliance with International Regulatory Agreements* (Harvard University Press, 1995), 64.

[114] A Chayes and AH Chayes, *The New Sovereignty: Compliance with International Regulatory Agreements* (Harvard University Press, 1995), 64.

and promote EU interests as a whole.[115] The Commission acts in the interest of the EU[116] and it draws on general political support by the regime parties.[117] Legitimacy considerations might arise in relation to the way the Commission exercises its discretion. This applies both to the decision to make a second referral to the Court of Justice and to the amount of the fines it proposes. The former, ie, the matter of intermittent sanctioning practice is, however, a consequence of the anti-legalistic nature of Article 260 TFEU. Rather than meticulously prescribing how the Commission shall exercise its enforcement powers, the procedure leaves room for the Commission to pursue ends by other means than a rigid, rule-centred approach.[118] The latter matter concerning the amount of fines is countered by the considerable procedural guarantees on the side of the member states, including the principle of proportionality.

6.3 *Maintaining the sanction*

For sanctions to work there needs to be not just initial, but continual consensus for maintaining them up until the point of compliance. Under many multilateral sanctioning schemes this comes down to the sum of political willingness of the sanctioning states. EU sanctions do not depend upon any such consensus. Where a sanction takes the form of a periodic penalty payment it will be imposed until the infringement has been terminated. Significantly, this is a legal rather than political assessment.

6.4 *Boycotts versus fines*

Chayes and Chayes' objections against economic sanctions primarily relate to sanctions in the form of boycotts, which are likely to place the heaviest burdens on parties least able to meet them. This latent dysfunction together with the general risk of evasion, they argue, will often feed 'pressure for

[115] A Dashwood and R White, 'Enforcement Actions under Articles 169 and 170 EEC' (1989) *European Law Review* 14, 288–412, 389.

[116] CWA Timmermans, 'Judicial Protection against Member States' in D Curtin and T Heukels (eds.), *Institutional Dynamics of European Integration. Essays in Honour of Henry G. Schermers. Volume II* (Martinus Nijhoff Publishers, 1994), 397.

[117] Article 17(7) TEU.

[118] F Snyder, 'The Effectiveness of European Community Law. Institutions, Processes, Tools and Techniques' (1993) *Modern Law Review* 56:1, 19–54, 30.

relaxation of the sanctions'.[119] This in turn undermines the sanctions' effectiveness. There are significant differences between boycotts and EU sanctions. Article 260(2) TFEU prescribes a positive amount to be paid without any further implications for the defaulting state. In addition, the member state's ability to pay measured in GDP[120] constitutes a core variable of the fine amount.[121] Finally, the principle of legality stipulated in Article 13(2) TEU and Court of Justice precedents suggests that a non-compliant member state cannot negotiate a friendly settlement with the Commission after a judgment has been delivered in accordance with Article 260 TFEU.[122] The compliance process, therefore, enters a more technical phase without distracting interventions by the Commission or the other treaty parties.

The equilibrium between actual non-compliance and the amount to be paid established by the Court of Justice allows for appreciation not only of full compliance, but also gradual progress.[123] This supports the interpretation put forward by Advocate General Michos that the objective of the penalty provision is to constitute 'a positive incentive, in accordance with the logical basis underlying the penalty payment, to encourage the Member State to remedy the situation in the shortest possible timescale'.[124] Thus the penalty provision, rather than creating deadlock situations, also rewards smaller behavioural changes.

6.5 *Preliminary conclusions on EU sanctions*

The managerialist critique of treaty-based sanctions, in particular of their effectiveness and legitimacy, should be read in their proper context.

[119] A Chayes and AH Chayes, *The New Sovereignty: Compliance with International Regulatory Agreements* (Harvard University Press, 1995), 66.

[120] For a critical account of the method of calculation, see MA Theodossiou, 'An Analysis of the Recent Response of the Community to Non-compliance with Court of Justice Judgments: Article 228(2) E.C.' (2002) *European Law Review* 27, 25–46.

[121] C-278/01 *Commission v Spain* [2003] ECR I-14141, para 52.

[122] Joined cases 142 and 143/80 *Amministrazione delle Finanze dello Stato v Essevi SpA and Carlo Salengo* [1980] ECR 1413, para 18; and C-278/01, *Commission v Spain* [2003] ECR I-14141. See also joined cases C-514/07 P, C-528/07 P, and C-532/07 P *Sweden* v *API and Commission* [2010] ECR I-8533, paras 119–21.

[123] C-496/09 *Commission v Italy* [2011] not yet published in the ECR, para 52; and C-278/01 *Commission v Spain* [2003] ECR I-14141, para 49.

[124] Opinion of Mr Advocate General Mischo in C-278/01 *Commission v Spain* [2003] ECR I-14141, para 98.

It concerns general 'characteristics of the international system'[125] and not necessarily those of the EU, which is often characterized as a *tertium quid*. Thus, to question Chayes and Chayes' conclusions with reference to the general EU infringement procedure does not seriously address the core premises of their critique. Nevertheless, there are good reasons for examining the merits of the general EU infringement procedure by comparing it to international law compliance theory. Significantly, the Treaty on the Functioning of the European Union proposes a procedural architecture where sanctions are not an arbitrary consequence of the relative strength of the regime participants. It is a mechanism whereby proportional fines put sustained pressure on the defaulting state. The member states' rights of participation remain intact as do all their general obligations Thus, the sanctioning mechanism does not stymie the normal relations between the member states and the Treaty-regime. Consequently, the EU avoids some of the negative economic and political implications often connected with sanctions against states.

7. Conclusion

This chapter discussed the Commission's general enforcement powers against repetitive infringements, including the introduction of pecuniary sanctions, and the special fast-track enforcement procedure concerning non-transposition of directives. It outlined case law pertaining to the operability of Article 260(2) TFEU and argued that the scope for friendly settlements persists even though the reasoned opinion has been omitted in the Lisbon Treaty. With the amendments the Commission's powers have become easier to employ and speedier. This is laudable, in particular owing to the relatively narrow scope of Article 260 TFEU. This closing section provides more policy-oriented conclusions and comment on the viability of the EU infringement procedure and in particular on Article 260(2) TFEU and member state sanctions.

The examined case law sets out the boundaries of the member states' procedural guarantees. For the Commission, the case law is decisive to the procedure's capability as a remedy against repetitive non-compliance.

[125] A Chayes and AH Chayes, *The New Sovereignty: Compliance with International Regulatory Agreements* (Harvard University Press, 1995), 67.

The Court of Justice has established a strict separation between the administrative and judicial phases of Article 260 TFEU. Whereas the Commission enjoys broad and semi-political discretion throughout the administrative phase, the Court of Justice has wide discretion after a case has been referred to it for a judgment. This is both with regards to the initial awarding of sanctions, the sanctioning type, the amount and the frequency with which, periodic penalties are imposed. Moreover, the Court of Justice has taken a noticeably strict stance on failure to comply under Article 260 TFEU. This includes imposing both lump sum and penalty payments on its own motion and also awarding sanctions in situations, where the Commission no longer requested so.

As discussed in chapter one, the EU polity cannot satisfactorily be conceptualized in terms of international law. Yet, the infringement procedure in isolation can usefully be analysed drawing on international law compliance theory. Specifically, it concerns a matter between an international (or rather, supranational) organization and a state and it relies primarily on confidential, bilateral, diplomacy. In chapter two it was argued that a comparison with managerialism helps unpack why the procedure in Article 258 TFEU is a particularly robust enforcement mechanism. The argument extends to Article 260 TFEU. At the same time, member state governments and the Commission acclaim pecuniary sanctions against repetitive infringements.

At first sight, successful enforcement through coercion and deterrence seems at odds with managerialism. However, this chapter argued that sanctions complement managerial types of enforcement of EU law for a number of reasons. The principal starting point of the procedures established in Articles 258 and 260 TFEU presumes that member states are in principle willing to comply. Infringements are primarily to be overcome through discursive, problem-solving processes in which the Commission assists the member state. The Commission is only empowered to employ a coercive approach against repetitive infringements. That is to say, against infringements already established by the Court of Justice in the judicial phase of Article 258 TFEU. At this point, the general compliance expectation has been gravely upset. Thus, sanctions are not foreseen as an immediate response to infringements. They constitute a last resort where the various stages of Article 258 TFEU have been used. In addition, Article 260(2) TFEU remedies some of the drawbacks often attributed to sanctions against states. They concern matters pertaining to (i) mobilization, (ii) legitimacy, (iii) maintenance of sanctions, and (iv) boycotts versus fines.

Against this backdrop, the real significance of Article 260(2) TFEU is its capacity to bolster the interactive process of discourse and problem-solving between the Commission and a given member state in the period prior to actual judgment. However, when such an approach fails, the supervisor can fall back on sanctions without compromising basic considerations of legitimacy and effectiveness. Moreover, it can do so while retaining the state in a constructive process of engagement leading to compliance.

4

The Commission's Quest for Stronger Powers of Enforcement

1. Introduction

The Commission has on different occasions proposed that stronger enforcement powers should be conferred on it to establish member state infringements and to take punitive and reparative action against member states.[1] In 2002, the Commission issued a communication preceding the proposal for a Constitutional Treaty. One of several proposals concerning the future institutional architecture concerned an amendment of the general EU infringement procedure. According to the proposal the Commission should be empowered to establish infringements. The procedure would thus come to resemble Article 88 of the Treaty establishing the

[1] Commission *'For the European Union: peace, freedom, solidarity—Communication of the Commission on the institutional architecture'*, COM/2002/728 final; Proposal for a Council Regulation (EC) creating a mechanism whereby the Commission can intervene in order to remove certain obstacles to trade, COM/97/619, [1998] OJ C 10/14; and Commission Communication of 4 June 1997 to the European Council: *'Action plan for the single market'* [Commission Communication to the European Council CSE (97)1 final—Not published in the Official Journal]. See also Art 45 in the Penelope Feasibility Study, a Working Document produced at the request of former Commissioner Prodi on the Constitution of the European Union, dated 4 December 2002. The study can be accessed at http://ec.europa.eu/economy_finance/emu_history/documents/treaties/Penelope%20pdf_en.pdf. The provision suggests that the Commission shall ensure the application of EU law and determine infringements of it, subject to review by the Court of Justice. In 1990 and 1996 the Commission proposed amendments of Art 258 TFEU and Art 260 TFEU, respectively. None of the proposals that both aimed at strengthening the Commission's direct powers of enforcement were successful. For a description and analysis of the proposals, see M Smith, *Centralised Enforcement, Legitimacy and Good Governance in the EU* (Routledge, 2009); and J Tallberg, *European Governance and Supranational Institutions—Making States Comply* (Routledge, 2003).

European Coal and Steel Community (ECSC).[2] In the proposal there was no question, though, that the general power to impose sanctions should continue to rest with the Court of Justice.[3] The principal reasons invoked by the Commission for a general reinforcement of the treaty procedure concerned the recent EU enlargement and considerations pertaining to the efficient operation of the internal market.[4] In addition to the proposal for a comprehensive amendment, the Commission has suggested to the Council that ad hoc enforcement procedures should be established in secondary legislation. The rationale underpinning these proposals—redolent of the more vigorous enforcement powers granted to the Commission in the Accession Treaty[5]—is one of effectiveness. Such ad hoc enforcement procedures give rise to both legal and extra-legal questions. Thus, the regime implications that would follow from institutionalizing Commission powers to establish member state failures to comply, to specify how the states should live up to their obligations, or to impose sanctions on the states merit further consideration. Clearly, the real significance would reach beyond the immediate effect on the vertical and horizontal division of power in the EU. This chapter focuses more closely on the legality dimension. Specifically, it investigates whether the Treaty on the Functioning of the European Union (and prior to that, the EC Treaty) in fact provide adequate legal basis for the 'EU legislator' to establish binding enforcement mechanisms in secondary legislation.[6]

[2] The procedure is discussed in chapter one. The Treaty expired on 23 July 2002. See further Council Decision 2002/596/EC of 19 July 2002. The 2002 Working Party on the Future of the European Communities' Court System has likewise suggested that a procedure similar to the former ECSC infringement procedure should be introduced. However, the Working Party notes, 'it is clear that the Court of justice would retain its powers under Article 228(2) [Article 260(2) TFEU]...to impose a penalty payment on any Member State which has not complied with a decision recording its failure to fulfil its obligations which had become final'. *'Report by the Working Party on the Future of the European Communities' Court System'* (2000), 26. The report can be accessed at http://ec.europa.eu/dgs/legal_service/pdf/due_en.pdf.

[3] Commission *'For the European Union: peace, freedom, solidarity—Communication of the Commission on the institutional architecture'*, COM/2002/728 final.

[4] Commission *'For the European Union: peace, freedom, solidarity—Communication of the Commission on the institutional architecture'*, COM/2002/728 final, 14.

[5] Treaty of Accession of the Czech Republic, Estonia, Cyprus, Latvia, Lithuania, Hungary, Malta, Poland, Slovenia and Slovakia [2003] OJ L 236. Act concerning the conditions of accession and the adjustments to the Treaties on which the European Union is founded, Arts 37, 38, 39.

[6] The notion of 'EU legislator' refers to the Council or the Council and the European Parliament, depending on the decision-making rules that apply in the concrete case.

2. The Context

As discussed in chapter one, the Commission's general enforcement powers according to the Treaty establishing the European Economic Community (EEC) are comparably more flexible, but also weaker than the High Authority's powers according to the Treaty establishing the European Coal and Steel Community (ECSC). Whereas the High Authority made binding compliance decisions (subject to judicial review), the Commission is merely empowered to initiate and advance infringement proceedings. Clearly, striving for absolute supervision would be excessive from a cost/benefit perspective, given the scope of the Treaty establishing the EEC and now the EU Treaties. Moreover, and perhaps more importantly, considerable sovereignty considerations came into play with the establishment of the EEC treaty system. Significantly, it had law-making capacity and introduced to some degree majority voting. The implications of the latter element are exacerbated by the fact that law-making in the EU traditionally has been characterized by compromises. The result is legislation which deals with matters with various degrees of comprehensiveness and which either sidesteps taxing questions or leaves them for interpretive resolution by the member states, the Commission, and ultimately the Court of Justice of the European Union. This practice, discussed in chapter one, is symptomatic of much international law negotiation. However, it has a constitutional dimension in the EU context. Notably, according to the doctrine of proportionality, action by the EU shall not go beyond what is necessary to achieve the objectives of the Treaties.[7] In areas where the EU does not have exclusive competence, the legislator must also balance the principle of proportionality with the principle of subsidiarity and comply with the requirement that 'measures should leave as much scope for national decision as possible, consistent with securing the aim of the measure and observing the requirements of the Treaty'.[8]

[7] Protocol on the Application of the Principles of Subsidiarity and Proportionality annexed to the Treaty of Amsterdam establishing the European Community, para 7. See also Protocol (no 2) on the Application of the Principles of Subsidiarity and Proportionality annexed to the Treaty on European Union and to the Treaty on the Functioning of the European Union.

[8] Protocol (no 2) on the Application of the Principles of Subsidiarity and Proportionality annexed to the Treaty of Amsterdam establishing the European Community, para 6. See also Art 5(3) TEU.

These principles are distinct from the above-mentioned circumstance that international, diplomatic compromises can lead to imprecise, or even conflicting, legal drafting. Significantly, the constitutionally secured scope for the member states to leave an imprint on the law in the implementation and enforcement phase is an additional and *sui generis* legal feature of EU law. This dimension in turn means that enforcement of EU law for the most part is more complex than simply a matter of increasing pressure on a member state. By contrast, enforcement of EU law often necessitates interpretation and careful analytical appraisal of the concrete member state's behaviour. As discussed in chapters one, two, and three, the Commission's unfettered discretion in this regard implies significant room for manoeuvre and reflects the Commission's role as a semi-administrative, but also a politically responsible and responsive organ.

In chapter one it was argued that many of the procedural characteristics of Articles 258 and 260 TFEU reflect the EU polity's *de facto* dependency on a dual source of authority (the member states' and the EU's, respectively) and its lack of genuine, self-sufficient steering capacity.[9] Consequently, it is both particularly suitable and to a high degree necessary that the general EU infringement procedure is process-oriented and relies on reiterated discourse of an interpretative and political/pragmatic nature. The procedural framework requires the Commission to display legal and political responsiveness towards the member states. The final objective, it was argued in chapter one, is to reach a normative consensus on how to give effect to EU objectives. This element of enforcement of EU law and the role of the Commission is further explored in chapter six.

Against the backdrop of these more general comments on enforcement of EU law, this chapter examines the legal basis for establishing enforcement measures in secondary law. The argument proceeds in three parts. First, it considers the principle of attribution of power and its implications for the Council, the Commission, and the Court of Justice with regard to the establishment of ad hoc infringement procedures in secondary legislation. Subsequently, it examines concrete cases where the Commission proposed that this type of provision should be established. The Commission's and the

[9] The Court of Justice too acknowledges that formal law depends on actual recognition. '*Report of the Court of Justice on Certain Aspects of the Application of the Treaty on European Union*', Luxembourg, May 1995 (published in the Court's 1995 Annual Report) thus states: 'The Union, like the European Communities on which it is founded, is governed by the rule of law. Its very existence is conditional on recognition by the Member States, by the Institutions and by individuals of the binding nature of its rules.'

Council's differing interpretations of the legality of such measures are considered in view of selected legislative proposals. Finally, the principle of enumerated powers is discussed. This discussion takes into consideration the EU notion of institutional balance.

3. Why Stronger Powers?

In several ways, the procedural structure of the general EU infringement procedure resembles the private regulatory mode of governance-labelled responsive regulation.[10] Responsive regulation emphasizes optimal self-regulation, yet it assumes that a total lack of control and enforcement will result in the exploitation of a given set of rules. Thus, the theory has final resort to coercion. The idea is illustrated by a pyramid composed of escalating enforcement strategies and sanctions intended to anticipate compliance. Actual coercion is only seen as a last resort. The underlying logic of this model is that the mere awareness of a regulator's willingness to intensify pressure keeps most regulatory activity at the base of the pyramid.[11] Perhaps the most striking structural similarity between the general EU infringement procedure on the one hand and responsive regulation on the other, is the principle of optimized self-governance in the shadow of cooperation, negotiation, and bargaining. Similarly, the bilateral dialogue between the member state and the Commission during the administrative phase of Article 258 TFEU emphasizes problem-solving before coercion. The same applies to the Commission's supplementary methods of enforcement discussed in chapter two, including EU Pilot. Responsive regulation has a number of advantages in terms of proportionality and legitimacy. Significantly, the governance mode ensures a high degree of inclusiveness and enables the monitored party to engage in problem-solving dialogue. At the same time, the primary responsibility for implementation is decentralized. This is also the case in the EU generally.[12] Even so, Gunningham and Johnstone have undertaken a critical discussion of responsive

[10] Tallberg too has pointed out the structural similarities, however, without contemplating in detail the merits of such a comparison in J Tallberg, *European Governance and Supranational Institutions—Making States Comply* (Routledge, 2003), 7.

[11] The concluding chapter discusses responsive regulation in more detail.

[12] See Art 4(3) TEU and Art 291(1) TFEU.

regulation.[13] They argue that the bottom-up, pyramidal approach is intrinsically inflexible. Moreover, the authors contend, it fails to address situations where compliance tools such as advice and persuasion do not work. Rigidly confining initial enforcement measures to those of friendly advice and warnings undermines the integrity of the pyramid. Gunningham and Johnstone do not reject the enforcement pyramid entirely. Rather, they propose a 'litmus test of the duty holder's attitude'.[14] The aim is to evaluate whether the pyramidal approach constitutes an appropriate response in the concrete case of defiance. A targeted approach, ie, taking measures nearer the apex of the pyramid, should be applied to actors that appear unresponsive to encouragement.

In the EU context there are, figuratively speaking, examples of alternative points of entry in the enforcement pyramid. These have been decided on a sectoral basis and constitute policy areas where the interest in prompt remedy has been prioritized. These cases suspend the general principle that recourse to the Court of Justice should constitute a measure of last resort.[15] Thus, by way of derogation from the procedure laid down in Articles 258 and 260 TFEU, Article 108(2) TFEU, Article 114(9) TFEU, and Article 348 TFEU empower the Commission to bring a matter directly before the Court of Justice. In addition to these procedural 'shortcuts', the Commission has explicit power to make findings on the compatibility of state aid with the internal market and on misuse of state aid.

In the first of the two cases which will be examined in this chapter, the Commission argues that 'Community control and enforcement system for fisheries should be reinforced' in order to 'ensure effective implementation of the Common Fisheries Policy'.[16] Implementation and enforcement are distinct notions and the preamble must be taken to mean that, in the eyes of the Commission, strong enforcement powers can sustain national implementation and enforcement. Within the internal market the Commission proposed an ad hoc mechanism, maintaining that Articles 258 and 260 TFEU 'are not capable of ensuring that such breaches are remedied

[13] N Gunningham and R Johnstone, *Regulating Workplace Safety: Systems and Sanction* (Oxford University Press, 1999), 114–40 and 126–8.

[14] N Gunningham and R Johnstone, *Regulating Workplace Safety: Systems and Sanction* (Oxford University Press, 1999), 126.

[15] Compare case 20/59 *Italy v High Authority* [1960] ECR 325.

[16] Proposal for a Council Regulation on the Conservation and Sustainable Exploitation of Fisheries Resources under the Common Fisheries Policy, COM/2002/185 final, Art 23(4), and, generally, recital 15 of the preamble.

in due time'.[17] Thus, the Commission has motivated its pleas for strengthened powers in secondary legislation with arguments pertaining to effectiveness and timeliness.

4. Sources of Institutional Power

According to Article 5(1) and (2), TEU:

> the limits of Union competences are governed by the principle of conferral... Under the principle of conferral, the Union shall act only within the limits of the competences conferred upon it by the member states in the Treaties to attain the objectives set out therein. Competences not conferred upon the Union in the Treaties remain with the Member States.

The doctrine of conferred competences is a general principle of international public law.[18] It signifies a delimitation of the European Union's aggregate 'legal capacity'.[19] Moreover, it entails that the constituent states alone can create new EU competences (*Kompetenz-Kompetenz*).[20]

According to Article 13(2) TEU the EU institutions cannot act beyond the powers attributed to them in the founding Treaties. Thus, '[e]ach institution shall act within the limits of the powers conferred on it in the Treaties, and in conformity with the procedures, conditions and objectives set out in them'.[21] According to this principle of attributed powers, the institutions' respective powers are thus inter-delineated. That is to say, only the constituent states may further empower them through amendments of the basic constitutive Treaties. Hence, no institution can (i) affect another institution's ability to exercise its treaty-based powers;[22] (ii) broaden its own treaty powers; or (iii) delegate powers it does not itself possess. The specific

[17] Proposal for a Council Regulation (EC) on Certain Obstacles to Trade, COM/97/619, recital 3 of the preamble.

[18] C Sasse, 'The Common Market: Between International and Municipal Law' (1965–66) *The Yale Law Journal* 75, 695–753; B de Witte and G de Búrca, 'The Delimitation of Powers Between the EU and its Member States' in A Arnull and D Wincott (eds.), *Accountability and Legitimacy in the European Union* (Oxford University Press, 2002), 201; and J Klabbers, *An Introduction to International Institutional Law* (Cambridge University Press, 2002), 63–7.

[19] Compare case 6/64 *Costa v ENEL* [1964] ECR 585.

[20] Compare case 6/64 *Costa v ENEL* [1964] ECR 585.

[21] C-403/05 *Parliament v Commission* [2007] ECR I-9045, para 49, and the case law cited.

[22] See, eg, C-202/88 *France v Commission* [1991] ECR I-1223, para 26.

competences of the EU together with the powers of the institutions are stipulated throughout the Treaty on European Union and the Treaty on the Functioning of the European Union.[23]

In comparison with Intergovernmental Conferences (IGCs), the Commission's bargaining position changes profoundly under the general EU legislative process. Significantly, Union legislative acts may only be adopted on the basis of a Commission proposal, except where the Treaties provide otherwise.[24] This enables the Commission to leave significant policy imprints on EU law and to pursue stronger powers. More generally, the legislative phase provides an opportunity for the Commission, the Council, and also the European Parliament to pursue stronger institutional powers.

4.1 *The Court of Justice*

In comparison with the general infringement procedure under the ECSC Treaty, the functions and powers of the institutions involved under Articles 258 and 260 TFEU have changed in a number of ways. Importantly, whereas the High Authority was obligated to pursue infringements under the ECSC, the Commission enjoys full discretion in this respect. This enables the Commission to search for compromises and solutions with political elements. Concurrent with this politicization of the Commission's role and function according to Articles 258 and 260 TFEU, the Court of Justice has become the sole genuine guarantee of equality before the law.

The horizontal division of powers between the Commission and the Court is central to the understanding of the Commission's enforcement powers and the limits to its powers. It follows from Article 19(1) TEU that the Court of Justice 'shall ensure that in the interpretation and application of the Treaties the law is observed'. The powers attributed to the Court of Justice under the general infringement procedure are stipulated in Articles 258 and 260 TFEU. Whereas Article 258 TFEU merely stipulates that unresolved proceedings may be referred to it, further specification of the Court's powers can be inferred from jurisprudence. Of particular interest are the joined cases 142/80 and 143/80 *Essevi and Salengo*, which explicitly

[23] See generally A Dashwood, 'The Relationship between the Member States and the European Union/European Community' (2004) *Common Market Law Review* 41, 355–81.

[24] Article 17(2) TEU. The power of initiative has important implications for the legislator. Notably, decision-making presupposes that the Commission has put forward a proposal. Moreover, the finally adopted law is based upon the proposal and room for deviation is retained by the legislative procedures. See to that effect, Arts 289, 293, and 294 TFEU.

address the question and allow the scope of these powers to be understood in more detail. In the ruling, the Court of Justice clarifies that under the general infringement procedure 'the rights and duties of Member States may be determined and their conduct appraised only by a judgment of the Court'.[25]

Under Article 260(2) TFEU the Court of Justice has sole jurisdiction to award, in the light of the circumstances, financial penalties on states that fail to comply with a ruling of the Court.[26] The authority of the Court of Justice thus encompasses powers of binding interpretation, the power to establish infringements, and power to sanction member states.

4.2 *The scope of the Commission's powers*

Although the Commission merely possesses those powers stipulated in the Treaties, the exact scope is left open for interpretation. In the cases C-188 to 190/80 *France, Italy, UK, and Ireland v Commission*, the Court of Justice held that 'the limits of the powers conferred on the Commission by a specific provision of the treaty are to be inferred not from a general principle, but from an interpretation of the particular wording of the provision in question, analysed in the light of its purpose and its place in the scheme of the treaty'.[27] In the same judgment, the Court explicitly rejected the existence of an intrinsic division of powers and responsibilities between the institutions according to which, for example, only the Council has original law-making powers and the Commission 'only powers of surveillance and implementation'.[28] In the joined cases 188 to 190/80 the Court of Justice went on to state in a more general fashion, that '[u]nder the system governing Community powers, the powers of the institutions and the conditions on their exercise derive from various specific provisions of the Treaty, and the differences between those provisions ... are not always based on consistent criteria'.[29]

[25] Joined cases 142/80 and 143/80 *Essevi and Salengo* [1980] ECR I-1413, para 18; and more recently in C-191/95 *Commission v Germany* [1998] ECR I-5449, para 45. See also case T-258/06 *Germany v Commission* [2010] ECR II-2027.

[26] C-304/02 *Commission v France* [2005] ECR I-6263. According to Art 260(3) TFEU the Court of Justice may impose sanctions 'not exceeding the amount specified by the Commission'.

[27] Cases 188 to 190/80 *France, Italy, UK, and Ireland v Commission* [1982] ECR 2545, para 6.

[28] Cases 188 to 190/80 *France, Italy, UK, and Ireland v Commission* [1982] ECR 2545, para 4.

[29] C-242/87 *Commission v Council* [1989] ECR-1425, para 13.

Since no clear-cut delimitation can be made, it may be contemplated whether the Commission has 'inherent' enforcement powers. The question is whether a broad interpretation of the Commission's role as guardian encompasses institutional powers of enforcement beyond those explicitly established in the EU Treaties. Article 17(1) TEU stipulates that the Commission 'shall ensure the application of the Treaties, and of measures adopted by the institutions pursuant to them'. The provision constitutes a legal starting point when considering the extent of the Commission's powers of supervision, both in itself and in conjunction with Article 4(3) TEU.

Article 4(3) TEU establishes a legal obligation of cooperation in good faith. It contains a duty to take any appropriate measure, general or particular, to ensure fulfilment of the obligations arising out of the Treaties or resulting from the acts of the institutions of the Union. The Commission has promoted a broad understanding of the combined effect of its general institutional tasks as stipulated in ex Article 211 EC (Article 17 TEU) and the fidelity clause to provide it with powers to establish precautionary measures on its own initiative.[30] In response to a member state's failure to adopt adjustments of intervention prices for cereals as foreseen in Council Regulation 2727/75, the Commission issued Decision 85/309. In doing so it relied on a provision which merely stated that the 'marketing year for all products listed in Article 1 shall begin on 1 August and end on 31 July of the following year'. Thus no powers were conferred on the Commission by the Council to undertake implementation of intervention prices. According to Usher, the underpinning justification for the intervention by the Commission was that 'failure of Member States in Council to fix the prices in due time constituted a breach of their duties under art. 5 [Article 4(3) TEU] and that the Commission's duty under art. 155 [Article 17 TEU] was to ensure the application of the common organization of the market in cereals'.[31] The Commission action in that case takes the form of norm-setting, which clearly presupposed Council delegation of powers in accordance with ex Article 202 EC.[32] However, the Commission must

[30] See the preamble to Commission Decision 85/309. See also comments in chapter seven; and JA Usher, *EC Institutions and Legislation* (Longman, 1998), 47–9.

[31] JA Usher, *EC Institutions and Legislation* (Longman, 1998), 49.

[32] Ex Art 202 EC has been replaced, in substance, by Art 16(1) TEU and by Arts 290 and 291 TFEU.

have relied upon the perceived failure to act in accordance with the Treaty, when it inferred powers to act from ex Article 211 EC (Article 17(1) TEU).

It is clear that the Commission cannot charge the member states individually for failure to act in the Council. This is due to the fact that the Council in principle acts as an institution. The failure lies with the Council as such if it fails to act and thereby infringes TFEU.[33] Although the situation regarding cereal prices discussed above concerned implementation, it is notable that the Commission took ex Article 211 EC (Article 17(1) TEU) to be constitutive, ie, to provide a basis for further derived powers and thereby enabling it to act. In the following three years the Commission continued this practice. Neither the Council nor the individual governments made any objections. Had the practice however been contested, it could arguably have been challengeable owing to the Commission's lack of power to act under the Treaty.[34] Notably, Article 211 EC (Article 17(1) TEU) merely constitutes a factual enumeration of the Commission's institutional tasks. Likewise, it does not provide authority to establish infringements or to make compliance prescriptions.[35] This conclusion finds support in the specific procedures in the areas of state aid and competition as well as those concerning budgetary deficits. It has now been confirmed by the Court of Justice. In the case C-171/05 P *Piau v Commission*, which is only available in French, the Court of Justice thus states:[36]

> 51 Conformément à l'article 5 CE, la Communauté agit dans les limites des compétences qui lui sont conférées et des objectifs qui lui sont assignés par le traité.
>
> 52 S'agissant de la Commission, elle agit dans les limites des compétences qui lui sont conférées par le traité ou par le Conseil de l'Union européenne, conformément à l'article 211, quatrième tiret, CE.

[33] Article 265 TFEU (ex Art 232 EC).

[34] Earlier practice in breach of the Treaties cannot create a precedent binding on the institutions. Compare C-133/06 *Parliament v Council* [2008] ECR I-3189, para 60.

[35] RH Lauwaars, *Lawfulness and Legal Force of Community Decisions: Some Considerations on the Binding Decisions Which the Council and the Commission Can Take by Virtue of the Treaty Establishing the European Economic Community* (AW Sijthoff, 1973), 58, fn 12; S Galera, 'The EU's first pillar—Constitutional basis' in S Galera (ed.), *Judicial review: a comparative analysis inside the European legal system* (Council of Europe, 2010), 222, with reference to C-171/05 P *Piau v Commission* [2006] ECR I-37. See, in particular, paras 52–3.

[36] C-171/05 P *Piau v Commission* [2006] ECR I-37. See, in particular, paras 52–3. For a summary of the judgment in English, see point 2.2.2.5 on Rules concerning the organization of ancillary activities (agent licensing) in Commission Staff Working Document '*The EU and Sport: Background and Context*' accompanying document to the White Paper on Sport, SEC/2007/935 final.

53 Lorsque la Commission estime qu'un État membre a manqué à l'une des obligations qui lui incombent en vertu du traité, elle peut introduire le recours en manquement visé à l'article 226 CE, ou un recours plus spécifique, tel celui prévu à l'article 88, paragraphe 2, CE, ou encore adopter, à l'attention des États membres des directives ou des décisions conformément à l'article 86, paragraphe 3, CE.... [37]

Article 4(3) (ex Article 10 EC) does not alter the fact that:

[i]n principle, the Commission ... can thus only make decisions by virtue of special powers provided for in the individual provisions in the Treaty.[38]

A related question concerns the scope of Article 258 TFEU. Specifically, the question remains whether a teleological interpretation can be taken to mean that the Commission has powers beyond those explicitly established in the infringement procedure. This question can be posed in terms of auxiliary powers. Notably, early jurisprudence has established that 'where an Article of the EEC Treaty ... confers a specific task on the Commission it must be accepted ... that it confers on the Commission necessarily and per se the powers which are indispensable in order to carry out that task'.[39] The reasoning resembles, or indeed qualifies as an expression of, the doctrine of implied powers. This concerns situations 'where the Treaty gives one of the institutions, typically the Commission, a specific job to do, and the institution considers it needs a certain kind of power for this purpose, which has not been specifically provided for'.[40]

Clearly, the principle of attributed powers is more than just a negative limitation of the institution's functional space. Notably, it also implicitly

[37] Freely translated it reads: 'In accordance with Article 5 EC, the Community shall act within the limits of the powers conferred upon it and the objectives assigned to it by the Treaty. 52 As regards the Commission, it acts within the limits of the powers conferred by the Treaty or by the Council of the European Union, in accordance with Article 211(4) EC. 53 Where the Commission considers that a Member State has breached any of its obligations under the Treaty, it may bring infringement proceedings under Article 226 EC [Article 258 TFEU], or use a more specific action, such as that provided in Article 88(2) EC [Article 108(2) TFEU], or address directives or decisions to Member States pursuant to Article 86(3) EC [Article 106(3) TFEU].'

[38] RH Lauwaars, *Lawfulness and Legal Force of Community Decisions: Some Considerations on the Binding Decisions Which the Council and the Commission Can Take by Virtue of the Treaty Establishing the European Economic Community* (AW Sijthoff, 1973), 58–9, fn 12. The author is not concerned specifically with the Commission's enforcement powers.

[39] Joined cases 281, 283, 284, 285, and 287/85 *Germany v Commission* [1987] ECR 3203, para 28.

[40] A Dashwood, Inaugural lecture at Cambridge University, 13 November 1995, on 'The Limits of European Community Powers' (1996) *European Law Review* 113–28. Dashwood notes that the Court of Justice has applied a narrow interpretation of implied powers.

attributes to the institutions the power necessary for them to perform their treaty obligations. The early case law mentioned above concerned a member state communication and consultation procedure on migration policies set up by the Commission; the Court of Justice did however stress that the judgment merely concerned powers of a procedural character relating to the commencement of member state consultations.[41] Hence the division of power between the Commission and the Court of Justice under Articles 17 and 19 TFEU respectively was not upset.

Already, in 1980, the Court of Justice ruled on the Commission's powers under the general infringement procedure stating that 'the Commission is not empowered to determine conclusively, by opinions formulated pursuant to Article 169 of the EC Treaty [now Article 258 TFEU] or by other statements of its attitude under that procedure, the rights and duties of a Member State, or to give it guarantees concerning the compatibility of a given line of conduct with the Treaty'.[42] The Court of Justice has interpreted the scope of Article 4(3) TEU in a somewhat narrow manner in relation to the infringement procedure. Specifically, the Commission cannot lay down positive member obligations to report, for instance, on implementation merely by reference to that clause.[43]

In conclusion, the Commission's general enforcement powers do not include powers to undertake authoritative interpretation or to prescribe member state behaviour.

4.3 *The Council's power of delegation*

The section above argued that the Commission only possesses those institutional powers of enforcement specifically stipulated in the EU Treaties. Given that the Commission's remedies against non-compliance

[41] Joined cases 281, 283, 284, 285, and 287/85 *Germany v Commission* [1987] ECR 3203, paras 28, 34, and 30.

[42] T-258/06 *Germany v Commission* [2010] not yet published in the ECR; C-393/98 *Ministério Público and António Gomes Valente v Fazenda Pública* [2001] ECR I-1327, para 18; joined cases 142/80 and 143/80 *Essevi and Salengo* [1980] ECR 1413, para 16.

[43] The Commission cannot request that a state reports to it on the implementation and enforcement of EU law. Explicit reference to such obligations is frequently inserted in secondary legislation. The transposition measures are available at www.eur-lex.eu. As the Commission rightly cautions on the web-pages that display transposition measures, '[t]he fact that there is a reference to national implementing measures does not necessarily mean that these measures are either comprehensive or in conformity'. The special enforcement procedure stipulated in Art 260(3) TFEU concerning failure to notify transposition measures is examined in more detail in chapter three.

are narrowly construed and that Article 17(1) TEU is non-constitutive, the Council's powers to establish additional enforcement instruments in secondary legislation should be contemplated. This question will be examined in view of the Council's powers of delegation established in ex Article 202 EC, ie, prior to the Lisbon Treaty amendments. The reason is that the case studies also predate the Lisbon Treaty. Ex Article 202 EC has been repealed and replaced, in substance, by Article 16(1) TEU and by Articles 290 and 291 TFEU. After the analysis concerned with ex Article 202 EC, the conclusions will be discussed in view of the amendment.

Under the third indent of ex Article 202 EC, the Council shall confer implementation powers on the Commission in order to ensure that the objectives set out in the EC Treaty are attained in accordance with its provisions. The Council may impose certain requirements in respect of the exercise of those powers. It may also reserve the right, in specific cases, to exercise directly implementing powers itself. The question concerning the scope of the Council's powers to establish additional enforcement instruments in secondary legislation cannot be discussed in isolation of ex Article 211 EC (Article 17(1) TEU) concerning the Commission's tasks and functions. The cases C-9/95, C-23/95, and C-156/95 *Belgium and Germany v Commission*[44] are illustrative by analogy. The cases concerned the powers conferred upon the Commission under Article 16(3) of Regulation No 404/93 on the common organization of the market in bananas to adapt under comitology the tariff quota during a marketing year on reason of necessity. Here the Court of Justice ruled that the 'powers . . . conferred . . . do not . . . go beyond those which may be given it under the fourth indent of Article 155 of the Treaty'.[45] Thus, the limits to delegation are determined both with reference to the Council's and Commission's institutional powers and tasks.

The Council's own powers are imperative for its ability to delegate further, or to confer powers, and it is thus necessary to examine the scope of the Council's powers before it can be established whether it can strengthen the Commission's enforcement powers in secondary legislation. As Lasok and Lasok put it, '[t]he Council cannot create new powers by

[44] Joined cases C-9/95, C-23/95, and C-156/95 *Belgium and Germany v Commission* [1997] ECR I-645.

[45] Joined cases C-9/95, C-23/95, and C-156/95 *Belgium and Germany v Commission* [1997] ECR I-645, para 35. The fourth indent of ex Art 211 EC reads:

'In order to ensure the proper functioning and development of the common market, the Commission shall:

. . . exercise the powers conferred on it by the Council for the implementation of the rules laid down by the latter.'

delegation but will merely authorize the Commission to act within the scope of its own competence and according to its directions'.[46]

The Council merely possesses those powers of enforcement specifically stipulated in the EC Treaty (now the TFEU), and notably the powers which rest with the EcoFin Council under the Stability and Growth Pact.[47] It is soon clear, however, that it has no general powers of enforcement as an institution. Notably, the Treaty on the Functioning of the European Union does not attribute any role to the Council under Articles 258 and 260 TFEU.[48] Thus, in conclusion, the Council is not empowered to lay down ad hoc enforcement procedures in general.

The Lisbon Treaty repeals ex Article 202 EC and replaces it, in substance, by Article 16(1) TEU and by Articles 290 and 291 TFEU. The amended system distinguishes between *delegated acts* (Article 290 TFEU) and *implementing acts* (Article 291 TFEU).[49] The two categories can be thought of as legislative-type and executive-type of powers respectively. Delegated acts are of general application and established with a view to supplement or amend certain non-essential elements of the delegating legislative act. Article 291(2) TFEU concerning implementing acts reads: 'Where uniform conditions for implementing legally binding Union acts are needed, those acts shall confer implementing powers on the Commission.' Implementing acts will normally, however, not solely be general acts.[50] Article 291(1) TFEU specifies that the EU executive power rests primarily with the member states.[51] Yet, when needed, executive-type powers can thus be conferred on the Commission.[52] This implies a type

[46] KPE Lasok and D Lasok, *Law and Institutions of the European Union* (7th edn, Reed Elsevier, 2001), 241.

[47] Article 126 TFEU. The Council can delegate such enforcement powers to the Commission. This is the case, eg, in Regulation (EU) No 1173/2011 of the European Parliament and of the Council of 16 November 2011 on the effective enforcement of budgetary surveillance in the euro area [2011] OJ L 306/1–7.

[48] The individual members of the Council naturally have the option of initiating direct infringement procedures in accordance with Art 259 TFEU.

[49] For an analysis, see R Schütze, '"Delegated" Legislation in the (new) European Union: A Constitutional Analysis' (2011) *The Modern Law Review* 74, 661–93.

[50] P Craig, 'Delegated Acts, Implementing acts and the new Comitology Regulation' (2011) *European Law Review* 36:5, 671–87, 672.

[51] See also Art 4(3) TEU.

[52] The Lisbon Treaty fundamentally changes the former comitology-method of controlling the Commission's exercise of implementing powers. See also Regulation (EU) No 182/2011 of the European Parliament and the Council of 16 February 2011 laying down the rules and general principles concerning mechanisms for control by Member States of the Commission's exercise of

of executive subsidiarity.[53] Both provisions confirm the conferred nature of these powers onto the Commission and in that sense, there is no change to Articles 202 and 211 EC. Thus, the argument that the 'EU legislator' cannot establish ad hoc enforcement procedures extends to the legal framework post-Lisbon.

The flexibility clause in Article 352 TFEU deserves mention when discussing the Council's powers. Under specific conditions, it provides the Council with residual powers to take measures, should they 'prove necessary, within the framework of the policies defined in the Treaties, to attain one of the objectives set out in the Treaties, and the Treaties have not provided the necessary powers'.[54] The clause enables the Council to take measures which it is not specifically authorized to adopt under the Treaties. The provision has been subject to much debate in some member states, not least due to the perceived risk of misuse and that it may encroach the principle of conferral.[55] It is readily apparent that the provision should not be understood as a carte blanche for the Council, which has to observe the general requirements that action shall be 'necessary'. Moreover, it cannot proceed beyond the objectives established in the Treaties. This is in addition to the generally applicable subsidiarity principle. The criteria of necessity is taken by some to mean that 'where powers are present but inadequate' the Council may act under the provision.[56] It may consequently be considered whether the Council can establish Commission executive powers to make concrete compliance decisions. This discussion poses an isolated question within the wider discussion of the scope of legislative power, namely one relating to the 'form of intervention', rather than the question of 'material competence' most often addressed in literature. Schütze captures the two-fold nature of the provision by asking how and

implementing powers, (2011) OJ L 55/13, which repeals Council Decision 1999/468/EC of 28 June 1999 laying down the procedures for the exercise of implementing powers conferred on the Commission [1999] OJ L 184/23.

[53] R Schütze, '"Delegated" Legislation in the (new) European Union: A Constitutional Analysis' (2011) *The Modern Law Review* 74:5, 661–93,

[54] This provision implies a unanimous vote of the Council and the consent of the European Parliament.

[55] Final Report of Working Group V ('*Complementary Competencies*') of the European Convention, CONV 375/02. See also R Schütze, *From Dual to Cooperative Federalism—The Changing Structure of European Law* (Oxford University Press, 2009), 136–8.

[56] RH Lauwaars, *Lawfulness and Legal Force of Community Decisions: Some Considerations on the Binding Decisions Which the Council and the Commission Can Take by Virtue of the Treaty Establishing the European Economic Community* (AW Sijthoff, 1973), 86.

whether there is competence.[57] The query in this chapter concerns the question of whether the legislator can choose freely among the instruments listed in Article 288 TFEU, if deemed necessary by the legislator, but where an instrument has not been explicitly provided for in the Treaty.

The Court of Justice has established that 'provisions whose effect would, in substance, be to amend the Treaty'[58] cannot be adopted within the scope of Article 352 TFEU. The Court's Opinion concerned the lawfulness of employing the flexibility clause as a legal basis for the (then) Community to accede to the European Convention on Human Rights. Hence, it was a question of the Community's 'external constitutional limits'.[59] This should naturally be kept in mind when thinking more generally about Article 352 TFEU and its scope. It is, however, interesting to note that the European Convention Working Group in its report on the flexibility clause suggested that this matter should be established as a general criteria of the clause.[60] It cannot be ruled out that it already is a precondition. In the wording of the Court in Opinion 2/94, by analogy, the limits of Article 352 TFEU entail that the rules governing the institutions cannot be altered in such way as to have 'fundamental institutional implications for the Community and for the member states' and thus be of 'constitutional significance'.[61] Some additional guidance may be inferred from the Opinion in the *Massey-Ferguson* case to this fairly vague test. Although the Court of Justice applied a broad interpretation of Article 352 TFEU and consequently of the Court of Justice's discretionary powers, it noted that the application of the provision was lawful, inter alia, in view of the fact that the institutional balance had not been affected.[62] The jurisprudence does not directly address the question of ad hoc enforcement powers. However, it touches upon an identical concern, namely that of the institutional organization of the EU and its constitutional structure.

[57] R Schütze, 'Organized Change towards an "Ever Closer Union": Article 308 EC and the Limits to the Community's Legislative Competence' (2003) *Yearbook of European Law* 22, 79–115, 98, fn 87. See same for a comprehensive analysis of Art 352 TFEU.

[58] Opinion 2/94 *Accession by the Community to the European Convention for the Protection of Human Rights and Fundamental Freedoms* [1996] ECR I-1759, para 30.

[59] R Schütze, 'Organized Change towards an "Ever Closer Union": Article 308 EC and the Limits to the Community's Legislative Competence' (2003) *Yearbook of European Law* 22, 79–115, 95.

[60] European Convention Working Group, Final Report of WG V, CONV 375/1/02 REV1, can be found at http://register.consilium.eu.int/.

[61] Opinion 2/94 [1996] ECR I-1759, para 35.

[62] C-8/73 *Massey-Ferguson* [1973] ECR 897, para 4.

The test articulated in Opinion 2/94 is somewhat circular and almost any use of Article 352 TFEU that deals with an institutional rather than substantive policy issue will have institutional (and even constitutional) implications that are significant. Otherwise, it would be unnecessary to invoke Article 352 TFEU in the first place. The establishment of agencies with binding powers, like the Food Safety Authority or European Agency for the Evaluation of Medicinal products (EMEA),[63] which were enacted under Article 352 TFEU, have institutional and constitutional implications. In Opinion 2/94, it is arguably the magnitude and also the symbolism of accession to the ECHR that led the Court of Justice to conclude that it required a treaty amendment. Yet, in this author's opinion, the flexibility clause does not provide legal basis for the EU legislator to establish Commission powers of enforcement in addition to those explicitly foreseen in the EU Treaties. At least this appears to be the correct conclusion where such tools would encroach upon the powers normally reserved to the Court of Justice. Otherwise, the interrelationship between the Commission and the judiciary would be altered and the institutional balance upset. The effect of such provisions 'would, in substance, be to amend the Treaty without following the procedure which it provides for that purpose'.[64] Consequently it would have institutional significance.

5. Doctrine and Practice

The previous section argued that there is no legal basis for the 'EU legislator' to establish ad hoc enforcement procedures in secondary legislation. According to the analysis, the institutional prerogatives of the Court of Justice can only be conferred upon the Commission through an amendment of the EU Treaties. This conclusion, based upon a doctrinal examination of the attribution of powers according to the former EC Treaty and the EU

[63] Council Regulation (EEC) No 2309/93 of 22 July 1993 laying down Community procedures for the authorization and supervision of medicinal products for human and veterinary use and establishing a European Agency for the Evaluation of Medicinal Products [1993] OJ L 214/1–21. The regulation is based on ex Art 308 EC (Art 352 TFEU) because the former EC Treaty did not explicitly provide a legal basis for the adoption of a centralized authorization procedure.

[64] Opinion 2/94 [1996] ECR I-1759 para 30.

Treaties, deviates from two previous analyses by Hækkerup[65] and Ibáñez.[66] The authors identify extra enforcement powers in secondary legislation which enable the Commission to establish infringements and to sanction member states. Additional and more specific analytical work is needed to complement these studies and to explain the basis of the apparent discord between the conclusion contained in this chapter and their work. The remainder of this chapter discusses the legal qualification of the instruments analysed by Hækkerup and Ibáñez. Next, it examines, in more detail, two selected Commission proposals, which foundered in the law-making phase because of insufficient legal basis in the EC Treaty. The aim is to provide a case study where the Council adheres to a strict doctrinal distinction between enforcement and implementing mechanisms, in accordance with the Treaty on the Functioning of the European Union.

5.1 *Establishing infringements*

Ibáñez examines infringements procedures 'created by secondary legislation, without a clear legal Treaty basis'.[67] Ibáñez distinguishes between procedures 'developed, within the framework of Article 169 EC Treaty [now Article 258 TFEU]' and 'completely separate procedures'. In the first category he places public procurement procedures. This type of preventive measure is examined in more detail in chapter five. Although they can effectually be employed for enforcement purposes, it is central to observe that they qualify as preventive measures.[68] Ibáñez' second group comprises transport regulations and, more specifically provisions establishing safeguard mechanisms.[69] As is the case for preventive measures, these mechanisms *de jure* qualify as implementation tools and should consequently be

[65] N Hækkerup, *Controls and Sanctions in the EU Law* (DJOEF Publishing, 2001) on the Common Fisheries Policy.

[66] AJG Ibáñez, 'Commission Tools for the Supervision and Enforcement of EC Law Other Than Article 169 EC Treaty—An Attempt at Systematization' *Jean Monnet Working Paper* 98.

[67] AJG Ibáñez, 'Commission Tools for the Supervision and Enforcement of EC Law Other Than Article 169 EC Treaty—An Attempt at Systematization' *Jean Monnet Working Paper* 98.

[68] C-328/96 *Commission v Austria* [1999] ECR I-7479, summary section. See also C-79/94 *Commission v Greece* [1995] ECR I-1071, summary section: 'The procedure by which . . . the Commission may—where it considers that a clear and manifest infringement of Community provisions in the field of public procurement has been committed—take up the matter with a Member State, constitutes a preventive measure which can neither derogate from nor replace the powers of the Commission under Article 169 of the Treaty', now Art 258 TFEU.

[69] Council Regulation No 2407/92 on the licensing of air carriers [1992] OJ L 240/1; Council Regulation No 2408/92 on access for Community air carriers to intra-Community air routes

considered as such. The final directive considered by the author relates to general product safety.[70] The measure therein is risk-contingent. It is not aimed at bringing about compliance and it correctly qualifies as an emergency measure. Thus, the examples may be, as Ibáñez maintains, 'a result of the particular bargaining, between the Commission and the Council, with the Treaty giving no indications, that these procedures were needed'.[71] However, they are not intended as tools of enforcement and, therefore, they may not be employed for such purpose. Notably, they do not upset the horizontal division of powers and tasks established in the Treaty.

5.1.1 The Common Fisheries Policy

The Common Fisheries Policy (CFP) makes up a policy area in which the Commission has obtained vigorous enforcement-like powers in secondary legislation. They are enforcement-like in that they do not serve actual enforcement purposes. Strictly speaking they qualify as implementation measures even though they empower the Commission to establish infringements. One such example is Article 25 of Regulation 2847/93 laying down a control system applicable to the CFP.[72] According to that provision, the Commission can 'establish' that a member state has failed to comply with technical controls enumerated in the Regulation. If the Commission establishes that a member state has not complied with the provisions it may make proposals to the Council for the adoption of appropriate general measures. This procedural rule is without prejudice to the general EU infringement procedure. Moreover, the establishment of an infringement is not tantamount to an authoritative interpretation. Hence, the general division of institutional powers is not affected. It is of course conceivable that the procedure may be used by the Commission as a way to exert political pressure on defaulting member states in the Council.

The CFP also stands as a policy area in which the Commission has tested the legal, and to some extent political, limits on a strengthening of its enforcement tools in secondary legislation. The Commission's supporting

[1992] OJ L 240/8-14; Council Regulation No 2409/92 on fares and rates for air services [1992] OJ L 240/15-17.

[70] Council Directive 92/59/EEC of 29 June 1992 on general product safety [1992] OJ L 228/24-32.

[71] AJG Ibáñez, 'Commission Tools for the Supervision and Enforcement of EC Law Other Than Article 169 EC Treaty—An Attempt at Systematization' *Jean Monnet Working Paper* 98.

[72] Council Regulation (EEC) No 2847/93 of 12 October 1993 establishing a control system applicable to the common fisheries policy [1993] OJ L 261/1-16.

reasoning is that its general tools against infringements are 'far too weak' and that the recommended procedural changes are necessary to enable effective enforcement.[73] In its proposal for a Council Regulation on the conservation and sustainable exploitation of fisheries resources under the CFP, the Commission launched a number of extensive measures. These included preventive measures. Such measures are intended to hinder exploitation of fish stocks or to put an end to corrosion. They do not aim at rule-enforcement, but serve different purposes, such as conservation of fisheries resources.[74] The proposal originally put forward recommended that the Commission should be empowered to establish violations of fishing quotas allocated to a member state.[75] To establish violations, ie, infringements, however is a general institutional prerogative of the Court of Justice.[76] When comparing the legislative proposal and the final text it is apparent that the final provision was aligned to the particular allocation of tasks and powers established by the EC Treaty. In the Regulation the word 'violation' was left out.[77] This illustrates that the authority to decide on infringements remains with the Court of Justice.[78]

5.1.2 The Single Market

The general EU infringement procedure's ability to respond 'rapidly and effectively' was raised prior to the Amsterdam IGC in 1997. The governments expressed concern that the procedure according to Article 258 TFEU had intrinsic shortcomings with regard to rectifying infringements.

[73] Proposal for a Council Regulation on the Conservation and Sustainable Exploitation of Fisheries Resources under the Common Fisheries Policy, COM/2002/185, preamble on Chapter V of the proposal.

[74] Compare C-359/92 *Germany v Council* [1994] ECR I-3681.

[75] Proposal for a Council Regulation on the Conservation and Sustainable Exploitation of Fisheries Resources under the Common Fisheries Policy, COM/2002/185, Art 23(4).

[76] C-393/98 *Ministério Público and António Gomes Valente v Fazenda Pública* [2001] ECR I-1327, para 18; and joined cases 142/80 and 143/80 *Essevi and Salengo* [1980] ECR 1413, para 16.

[77] Council Regulation (EC) No 2371/2002 of 20 December 2002 on the conservation and sustainable exploitation of fisheries resources under the Common Fisheries Policy [2002] OJ L 358/59-80, Art 23(4).

[78] Fisheries resources are finite and the distribution of the annual TACs takes place under tough bargaining. At the same time, monitoring is difficult. This is partly because the member states are protective of their control zones, whilst, with certain exceptions, fishermen have free access to all waters. As the rich case law demonstrates, some member states enforce the CFP rules leniently, to say the least. See, eg, Commission Communication, '*Reports from Member States on behaviours which seriously infringed the rules of the Common Fisheries Policy in 2006*', COM/2008/0670 final.

Moreover, they agreed that the matter was particularly critical in relation to the functioning of the internal market and the free movement of goods.[79] On the request of the European Council, the Commission took action to examine ways of 'effectively guaranteeing free movement of goods'.[80] The result was an Action Plan for the Single Market, in which the Commission set four so-called Strategic Targets aimed at cases of 'serious breach[es] of Community law which gravely affect the functioning of the Single Market'.[81] The Commission contended that it should be empowered to take urgent action against member states 'which fail in these obligations, using sanctions if necessary'.[82] The follow-up proposal contained a mechanism whereby the Commission could intervene in order to remove certain obstacles to trade. There was however no mention of sanctions in the proposal, which read:

Article 2

Where the Commission establishes the existence in a Member State of obstacles within the meaning of Article 1, it shall address a *decision* to the Member State directing it to take the necessary and proportionate measures to remove the said obstacles, within a period which it shall fix.

...

Article 4

1. Where a Member State to which a decision is addressed fails to comply with it within the prescribed period, the Commission shall immediately put it on notice to submit its observations within three days.
2. Where the obstacle continues after the expiry of the period of three days mentioned in paragraph 1, the Commission shall immediately issue a reasoned opinion calling on the Member State to comply with it within three days.

[79] *'Report from the Commission to the Council and the European Parliament on the Application of Regulation (EC) No 2679/98'*, COM/2001/160, 3. As will be explained in more detail shortly the topic of enforcement was fuelled by events later referred to as the *Spanish strawberries* case. For the Commission, the political frustrations with the case thus provided an opportunity to push for ad hoc enforcement powers.

[80] Luxembourg European Council, 12 and 13 December, 13 December 1997, Presidency Conclusions.

[81] *'Action Plan for the Single Market'*, Communication of the Commission to the European Council, CSE(97)1 final, 4 June 1997 (not published in the Official Journal).

[82] *'Action Plan for the Single Market'*, Communication of the Commission to the European Council, CSE(97)1 final, 4 June 1997 (not published in the Official Journal), 2.

3. Where, by the end of the period referred to in paragraph 2, the Member State has not complied with the reasoned opinion, the Commission may institute proceedings before the Court of Justice.[83] (Emphasis added.)

The question of legal basis was not explicitly mentioned at the time of the Luxembourg Summit, when the Council and the European Parliament were asked to examine the proposal.[84] The Council took a political stand in favour of the follow-up legislative proposal for a Council Regulation creating a mechanism which allowed the Commission to intervene in order to remove certain obstacles to trade. Moreover its members 'supported the idea in principle of giving the European Commission stronger powers to force governments to lift barriers to single market trade. However, some delegations expressed doubts about the proposal, questioning the legal basis for Internal Market Commissioner Mario Monti's attempts to speed up procedures to punish governments which fail to dismantle serious obstacles'.[85]

Clearly, the Council and the Commission's different interpretations concerning the question of legal basis are tangled with their respective interests as institutions. For the Commission, there would be an institutional advantage in optimizing its own powers vis-à-vis the member states and in lessening its procedural burdens under the general EU infringement procedure. The individual Council members' interest in restraining the supervisor's direct powers of enforcement against themselves is more complex because of the apparent competing interest in ensuring that other members live up to their obligations. One infamous infringement case in particular brought to light the seriousness of persistent non-compliance. The case concerned the attacks by French farmers against Spanish fruit-lorries and the supine reaction of the French authorities in taking appropriate and adequate measures. Eventually the Court of Justice qualified it as impediments to intra-state movement of goods.[86] The situation suggested that the trade barriers were rooted in political inertia or even genuine unwillingness to comply. This was at the time when the Amsterdam IGC invited the Commission to explore alternative ways to ensure the free

[83] Proposal for a Council Regulation (EC) creating a mechanism whereby the Commission can intervene in order to remove certain obstacles to trade COM/97/0619, 14.

[84] Conclusions of Luxembourg Summit 1997, Luxembourg European Council, 12 and 13 December 1997, Presidency Conclusions.

[85] European Voice, Vol 4, 7: 19 February 1998.

[86] C-265/95 *Commission v France* [1997] ECR I-6959 (the *Spanish strawberries* case).

movement of goods. In the UK, the Commission's proposal caused debate. The procedure was clearly considered a method to ensure more effective enforcement. However, the uncertainties about the legal and practical implications were regarded as serious. In his letter to the Select Committee on European Communities, the Minister for Trade and Competitiveness in Europe Lord Simon of Highbury thus remarked that 'the Government considers that it would be contrary to the institutional balance established by the Treaty for the Commission to be able to adjudicate on whether a Member State had breached its Treaty obligations under Articles 30–36'.[87] This viewpoint was shared by a majority of the Council members.[88] Nevertheless, the Minister of Trade contended, the French incident had demonstrated the need for effective enforcement measures. Consequently, the UK parliamentary scrutiny reserve should be lifted.[89]

In spite of principled political support, the proposed enforcement mechanism failed in its original form because its legal basis was considered inadequate. Thus, the Council ultimately held on to a strict understanding of the principle of attributed powers and, importantly, a narrow reading of its own legislative powers. The Commission was, not surprisingly, of a different understanding. During the inter-institutional discourse leading up to the final adoption of Council Regulation (EC) No 2679/98 of 7 December 1998 it insinuated that this was a grey area between law and politics. At least the Commission depicted the choice to be made by the Council and the European Parliament to be of a political nature as much as a question of legality. Thus, the Commission urged the institutions to give the proposal 'political consideration'.[90] It is puzzling that the UK chose to endorse the Commission's proposal in view of its legal concerns. This should perhaps be understood in a political rather than legal context. The proposal was to be decided upon by unanimity and any Council member with legal or politically rooted reservations could block it with simple reference to the question of legal basis. For the UK presidency there were weighty reasons in terms of reputation not to move forward with the

[87] Letter from Lord Simon of Highbury, Minister for Trade and Competitiveness in Europe, to Lord Tordoff, Chairman of the Committee, 16 March 1998.

[88] Letter from Lord Simon of Highbury, Minister for Trade and Competitiveness in Europe, to Lord Tordoff, Chairman of the Committee, 16 March 1998.

[89] Letter from Lord Simon of Highbury, Minister for Trade and Competitiveness in Europe, to Lord Tordoff, Chairman of the Committee, 15 May 1998.

[90] *'Action Plan for the Single Market'*, Communication of the Commission to the European Council, CSE(97)1 final, 4 June 1997 (not published in the Official Journal), 4.

document. Significantly, the Council Legal Service had deemed it to be unlawful.[91] In addition, there was a risk that the provision could be challenged before the Court of Justice.[92] The UK decision to lift its scrutiny reserve and endorse the provisional text might simply be a way to position itself as a pro-enforcement state.

The member state governments did not provide the required general treaty basis for the establishment of ad hoc enforcement procedures at the ensuing Nice IGC.[93] This is interesting in the light of the principled political support expressed by the Council members in certain policy areas. The Commission is thus left to buttress enforcement within its general institutional powers of enforcement and the quest for stronger procedural powers has been replaced by softer approaches in the Internal Market Strategy 2003–06. The Commission proposes a strengthening of enforcement 'through closer cooperation between the Commission and Member States, so that quick and effective solutions can be obtained without systematic recourse to infringement procedures'.[94] This development towards alternative, supplementary, and non-binding methods to manage compliance applies both to the internal market and more generally. Thus, as described in chapter two, the Commission promotes heterarchical cooperation between the Commission and national authorities with a view to ensure compliance and solve specific infringements (so-called 'partenariats'), it has established EU Pilot and SOLVIT and, as discussed in more

[91] See the Opinion of the Council's Legal Service of 4 February 1998, 5731/98 JUR 53, as referred to in *'Report from the Commission to the Council and the European Parliament on the Application of Regulation (EC) No 2679/98'*, COM/2001/160, fn 4.

[92] The Court of Justice has demonstrated that there are legal limits to the Council's political discretion and that it will not succumb to political pragmatism. This is illustrated well in a case where the governments faced a two-fold interest in retaining the position that criminal proceedings fall within the member states' exclusive competence whilst also having an interest in establishing certain criminal standards for the protection of the environment. The Council relied on the former EU Treaty title on Justice and Home Affairs (Title VI), even though the Council's legal service objected that the criminal procedures could only be properly adopted on the basis of the former Community Treaty. See opinion of the Council Legal Service, 5 March, 6793/01. In point 7 of the preamble of the Framework Decision, the Council stated that a 'majority considered that the proposal went beyond the powers attributed to the Community'. The preamble arguably amounts to an expression of political activism, namely an attempt to influence the Court's legal reasoning. However, the Court of Justice rejected this interpretation and annulled the Decision. See C-176/03 *Commission v Council* [2005] ECR I-7879.

[93] The Nice Treaty was adopted at the Nice Council in December 2000, signed on 26 February 2001, and entered into force on 1 February 2003.

[94] *'Internal Market: Commission presents ten-point plan for making Europe better off'*, IP/03/645, Brussels, 7 May 2003.

detail in chapter six, there are numerous expert groups dealing with member state implementation of directives. Similarly, the Lisbon Treaty provides a legal basis for member state peer-review within the area of freedom, security, and justice, without prejudice to the general EU infringement procedure.

5.2 *Sanctioning non-compliance*

In 1986, the Commission 'consider[ed] the possible introduction of sanctions' in the context of the internal market.[95] The White Paper on completing the internal market did not touch upon the question of legal basis. Thus, it is not immediately clear whether the Commission contemplated the possibility of a comprehensive treaty amendment or merely ad hoc procedures. A similar proposal was tabled in the late 90s, once more within the scope of the Single Market. However, the proposal was not included in the eventual proposal for a Council regulation.[96]

When thinking about the possibility of establishing sanctions in secondary legislation it should be recalled that member state sanctions only became a reality after the Maastricht amendment of the EC Treaty. Thus, there is no rooted tradition of coercion-type enforcement in the EU against infringements of EU law. To the contrary, compliance has traditionally rested on ideas of non-reciprocity. Moreover, enforcement primarily takes the form of friendly settlements. As discussed in chapter three, the sanctioning mechanism in Article 260 TFEU has been strengthened and made easier to employ. However, pecuniary sanctions as a means of coercion constitute a last option even after the Lisbon amendments. With the exception of Article 260(3) TFEU concerning notification of measures transposing a directive, sanctions are merely foreseen to bring about compliance with judgments of the Court of Justice. This is 'second order compliance', as opposed to compliance with standing law.[97] The Court of Justice has clarified that both lump sum and penalty payments are intended

[95] *'Completing the Internal Market: White Paper from the Commission to the European Council'* (Milan, 28–29 June 1985) COM/85/310, June 1985, para 154.

[96] Compare *'Action Plan for the Single Market'*, Communication of the Commission to the European Council, CSE(97)1 final, 4 June 1997 (not published in the Official Journal) with Proposal for a Council Regulation (EC) creating a mechanism whereby the Commission can intervene in order to remove certain obstacles to trade COM/97/0619.

[97] See generally R Fisher, *Improving Compliance with International Law* (University Press of Virginia, 1981) for this distinction.

to induce defaulting member states to comply.[98] There is a clear element of coercion. However, sanctions constitute forward-looking, or persuasive and deterrent, types of sanction. They do not have a penal aim as such.[99] Lump sum payments are based on the more abstract 'assessment of the effects on public and private interests ... in particular where the breach has persisted for a long period since the judgment which initially established it'.[100] However, the sanctioning instrument is not of a compensatory nature and the amount does not reflect any damage caused.[101] Power to enforce compliance with the Court of Justice's judgment could have rested with the Council in accordance with the common practice of international law. In that case, enforcement would thus have a stronger diplomatic or political character.[102] However, the founding fathers decided otherwise and the Court of Justice is the sole institution with the authority to award sanctions under Article 260 TFEU.

In the light of these more general comments, the first question to be considered here is whether the Treaty on the Functioning of the European Union authorizes the EU legislator to establish ad hoc sanctions in secondary legislation. Hækkerup argues that '[a]s far as the Community has authority to regulate for sanctions, which have shown to be quite extensive, the Community also has the authority to regulate for its own sanctions on Member States'.[103] This section examines Hækkerup's examples and 're-qualifies' them as measures that are not *de jure* enforcement measures. It proceeds to examine a Commission proposal from 2002 for a regulation and compares it with the final regulation adopted the same year. The aim of this case study is to exemplify the boundaries of the Commission's powers and also the powers of the Council with regard to establishing sanctions in secondary legislation.

[98] C-177/04 *Commission v France* [2006] ECR I-2461, para 59.

[99] See also chapter three. For a different analysis, see L Borzsák, *The Impact of Environmental Concerns on the Public Enforcement Mechanism under EU* (Wolters Kluwer, 2011), 182–7.

[100] C-304/02 *Commission v France* [2005] ECR I-6263, para 81.

[101] C-177/04 *Commission v France* [2006] ECR I-2461, para 60.

[102] Opinion of Advocate General Colomer in C-387/97 *Commission v Greece* [2000] ECR I-5047, point 38, uses the example of Art 54 of the Convention for the Protection of Human Rights and Fundamental Freedoms according to which the Committee of Ministers is responsible for enforcement of rulings by the European Court of Human Rights. According to the UN Charter Art 94, the Security Council may take action against a state that fails to comply with a ruling of the International Court of Justice.

[103] N Hækkerup, *Controls and Sanctions in the EU Law* (DJOEF Publishing, 2001), 234.

There are implementation measures which the Council legitimately can delegate and which may include the power to determine that behaviour constitutes an infringement. One such is Article 23(4) of the 2002 framework regulation on conservation and sustainable exploitation of fisheries resources under the CFP. It enables the Commission to undertake quota management and make deductions in future fishing opportunities.[104] This mechanism falls within the ambit of the Commission's authority in accordance with ex Article 211 EC after delegation according to ex Article 202 EC. Clearly, a peripheral, or derived, enforcement effect may occur, even if the measure is not aimed at enforcement objectives. However, employing implementing measures as enforcement tools would be challengeable because the Commission as an institution lacks such supervisory power. The doctrine of misuse of power, or *détournement du pouvoir*, is codified in Article 263 TFEU, which authorizes the Court of Justice of the European Union to review the legality of Commission acts.

The provisions dealt with in this section concern the member states' responsibility to adopt measures, to allocate the financial and human resources and to set up the administrative and technical infrastructure necessary to ensure effective control, inspection, and enforcement.[105] It is a sensitive matter to regulate because of the division of competences and responsibilities between the EU and the member states. Notably, fisheries resources are a common, or an EU, policy.[106] Thus, losses due to non-compliance are losses of an EU good. Still, the responsibility for enforcement rests with the individual member states. There are considerable differences in the quality of supervision and enforcement within the member states. Thus, the Commission devotes substantial enforcement resources on this.[107]

In comparison with other EU policy areas, fisheries resource management measures arguably do resemble sanctions to a comparably higher

[104] Council Regulation (EC) No 2371/2002, Art 23(4) states that 'When the Commission has established that a Member State has exceeded the fishing opportunities which have been allocated to it, the Commission shall operate deductions from future fishing opportunities of that Member State'.

[105] Proposal for a Council Regulation on the Conservation and Sustainable Exploitation of Fisheries Resources under the Common Fisheries Policy, COM/2002/185 final.

[106] It became so in 1983.

[107] In 2011, the Commission tabled a number of communications concerning a reform of the common fisheries policy. The communications are available at http://ec.europa.eu/fisheries/reform/index_en.htm.

degree.[108] This should be seen against the backdrop of the particular nature of the fisheries. Specifically, it is as a common resource, which is allocated to the members on a periodic basis. These types of instruments cannot be presumed to gain general application because the regulated matters are specific (conditionality of Structural Funds might constitute the one exception).[109] Similar to EU sanctions, the measures are also not based on liability considerations. However, EU sanctions and the Total Allowable Catches (TAC) deductions and allocations in the Regulation are neither identical nor comparable. The aim of the latter measures is to remedy a prejudice,[110] or a wrongfully used Community (now EU) resource. The CFP deductions or allocations concern 'an excess . . . wrongly received' and it serves a different objective from the functionally distinct types of sanctions established under the general EU infringement procedure. The common objective of lump sum and periodic penalty payments is to induce compliance with a judgment.[111] That is to say, the objective is to bring about compliance by means of deterrence and persuasion and this way putting sustained pressure on the member state. Hækkerup rightly qualifies the CFP procedure as administrative measures. However, the categorization becomes unclear because they are considered in the author's chapter on 'Sanctions imposed by the Community on national authorities'.[112]

Hækkerup's analysis is based on measures from the area of fisheries, and more specifically on Council Regulation 2241/87[113] and Council

[108] Management of other common policies includes, for example, commercial policy, common agricultural policy, and customs union.

[109] In his examination of Commission tools for the supervision and enforcement of EC law other than Art 226 EC (Art 258 TFEU), Ibáñez considers procedures relating to expenditures under the framework of the European Agricultural Guidance and Guarantee Fund. AJG Ibáñez, 'Commission Tools for the Supervision and Enforcement of EC Law Other Than Article 169 EC Treaty—An Attempt at Systematization' *Jean Monnet Working Paper* 98. The legislator establishes specific criteria, which a state must observe in order to benefit from the Community Structural Funds. Albeit reminiscent of sanctions, it is actually a matter of conditionality.

[110] Council Regulation No 2241/87 of 23 July 1987 Establishing Certain Control Measures for Fishing Activities [1987] OJ L 207/1-7, Art 11(4) EC.

[111] C-304/02 *Commission v France* [2005] ECR I-6263, para 80 in conjunction with para 84.

[112] N Hækkerup, *Controls and Sanctions in the EU Law* (DJOEF Publishing, 2001), 231. The section is entitled 'Community sanctions imposed on Member States on the basis of their administration of Community law in relation to those subject to the law of the Member States' (235).

[113] Council Regulation No 2241/87 of 23 July 1987 Establishing Certain Control Measures for Fishing Activities [1987] OJ L 207/1-7; and Council Regulation 3483/88 of 7 November 1988 amending Regulation No 2241/87 [1988] OJ L 306/2-4.

Regulation (EEC) No 3483/88 of 7 November 1988 amending Regulation (EEC) No 2241/87 establishing certain control measures for fishing activities. According to Article 11 of the aforementioned regulation, all catches of a stock or group of stocks subject to quota made by fishing vessels flying the flag of a member state or registered in a member state shall be charged against the quota applicable to that state for the stock or group of stocks in question, irrespective of the place of landing. The member state itself sets a date from which the catches shall be considered to be exhausted. From here on after the state shall temporarily prohibit transshipment and landing of the specified breed of fish. After being notified thereof, the Commission is to advise the state of the prospects of fishing being halted as a result of the TAC being exhausted. Vessels of the state must stop all types of handling of such catches after the date a stock quota is considered to have been exhausted. Where the Commission halts fishing because the TACs[114] of a species have been exhausted, the regulation establishes a procedure, which allows 'deductions from a quota, allocation or share of the member state which has over-fished, the quantities so deducted to be allocated appropriately to the Member States whose fishing activities were halted before their quotas were fished'.[115]

Hækkerup asserts that with the amendment in 1988, the 'issue of sanctions imposed on Member States . . . [becomes] clear'. The provision he addresses prescribes that in cases where a vessel lands or transships in another state than the one in which it is registered, the state of landing or transhipment shall either take action against the master of the vessel or alternatively transfer pursuit to the state of registration. If it fails to do so, the landing may be counted against that state's quota. The author maintains that

> [w]hile the quantity of fish would normally relate to the quota of the member state of registration, in this regulation it is deducted from the member state where fish is landed or transshipped. This is a true penalty which hits the member state where the fish are landed or transshipped if it does not take proceedings against the infringement of Community law, since the fishing industry of the Member State in question will have a reduced quota of fish.[116]

[114] Or other listed technical measures than TACs—see provision.

[115] Council Regulation (EEC) No 2241/87 of 23 July 1987 Establishing Certain Control Measures for Fishing Activities [1987] OJ L 207/1-7.

[116] N Hækkerup, *Controls and Sanctions in the EU Law* (DJOEF Publishing, 2001), 235–6.

The deduction is not strictly speaking a penalty. The option of subtracting from a state's quota is established with a view to 'ensure compliance with the regime of conservation and management of fishery resources'.[117] The mechanism essentially ensures that fishing beyond the overall TACs decided upon in Council and the quotas allocated to the individual member states can be adjusted for, when the country of landing or transshipment is different from the country of registration. Thus, it is not a measure established to coerce or discourage EU infringements, but a quota-management measure. Comparable management tools exist under the CFP framework regulation from 1993.[118]

The provision examined in the following section concerns cases where the country of landing and registration is the same. The overarching aim of conservation of common resources is apparent from the enumerated parameters which the Commission shall take into account when it operates deductions from the annual quota, allocation, or share of that member state. The relevant factors concern the degree of overfishing, cases of overfishing of the same stock in the previous year, and the biological status of the resources concerned.

The 2002 proposal for a Council framework regulation gave rise to a dispute over what, if any, sanctioning powers the Council can lawfully confer to the Commission. The Commission suggested that any loss to the common living aquatic resources resulting from a violation of the rules attributable to a member state should be made good by the member state. The reparation should take the form of a deduction in the quota allocated to the member state. Again, the prospect of quota deductions per se may have a dissuasive effect on states with lax enforcement practices. They do not, however, serve enforcement purposes. Instead they aim at managing Community own resources and constitute a lawful measure. However, the Commission went a step further by suggesting a compensation scheme according to which the Commission could establish the quota equivalent value in cases where a quota deduction was not possible. These would either be awarded to states which have suffered prejudice or to the Community's own resources.

[117] Council Regulation (EEC) No 3483/88 of 7 November 1988 amending Regulation (EEC) No 2241/87 Establishing Certain Control Measures for Fishing Activities [1988] OJ L 306/2-4, preamble.

[118] Council Regulation (EEC) No 2847/93 of 12 October 1993 Establishing a Control System Applicable to the Common Fisheries Policy [1993] OJ L 261/1-16.

There are several problems with the proposal. The first one concerns the Commission's powers to establish an infringement outside the scope of resource management. This has been dealt with in the previous section. The Commission further suggested that if no specific member state has suffered prejudice, the quota equivalent value should be an assigned revenue of the Community. The purpose of regulating the distribution of resources is thus no longer present. The measure instead operates as a sanctioning of non-compliance, ie, to punish past conduct. The section was left out of the finally adopted regulation.

The doctrinal distinction between implementation and enforcement has been explained in some degree of detail. It is clear that although certain implementing measures may resemble enforcement tools, they are only lawful where they serve implementing objectives which may include management measures. The Commission does not explicitly refer to this distinction in its 2002 proposal for a framework regulation, but simply refers to its institutional responsibility 'for evaluating and controlling implementation'.[119] There was no explicit reference to sanctions in the legislative proposal. This may be an attempt to direct the Council's attention away from the question of enforcement power. It may however also be an attempt to advocate an expansive notion of implementation and thus to introduce sanctions disguised as implementing measures through the backdoor. Despite the, in legal terms, important difference, the Commission links implementing and enforcement measures by emphasizing the functionality of implementation measures as tools to further compliance. Thus, the examined proposal for a framework regulation, the preventive measures and other implementation powers are placed under a chapter on Community control and enforcement.

5.2.1 Preliminary conclusions

This section considered two sanction-related questions. The first one was of a doctrinal nature. Specifically, it asked whether there is legal basis in the EC Treaty (and now the EU Treaties) to establish ad hoc sanctioning powers against member states. This question was answered in the negative. Neither a comparison with sanctions against individuals nor a dynamic or broad interpretation of the EC (now EU) Treaties supports a different

[119] Commission Communication to the Council and the European Parliament 'Towards uniform and effective implementation of the common fisheries policy', COM/2003/130. See also point 24 in the preamble of Council Regulation (EC) No 2371/2002 of 20 December 2002.

conclusion. Thus, it concluded, the 'EU legislator' cannot establish sanctions in addition to those foreseen under Article 260(2) and (3) TFEU and the *lex specialis* provisions in the EU Treaties. It then examined legislative provisions used in literature as examples of ad hoc member state sanctions. However, it was argued, they are not *de jure* sanctions. The analysis leading to these conclusions is similar to the analysis in the first part of this chapter. There it was argued that the 'EU legislator' cannot delegate power to the Commission to establish member state infringements. Moreover, the Commission has no inherent powers to do so. Quite the contrary, these powers are explicitly attributed to the Court of Justice. According to the analysis undertaken in the first part of this chapter, such institutional prerogatives can only be conferred upon the Commission through an amendment of the EU Treaties. Next, by examining legislative proposals tabled by the Commission and comparing them to the subsequently revised and adopted pieces of legislation, it was demonstrated that the Council (in the examined cases, at least) adheres to a similar, narrow interpretation. The Commission's endeavours to obtain additional powers thus require that the member state governments amend the EU Treaties.

The jurisprudence directly dealing with the delimitation of the institutional competences of the Commission and the Court of Justice under the general EU infringement procedure is sparse. However, it allows for more general conclusions. As discussed in chapter two, the Commission has the general prerogative of initiating and forwarding possible infringements. In doing so it must observe a number of guarantees set up to protect the member states' interests in securing a fair trial. These are requirements grounded in rule-of-law considerations. The delineation of the Commission's enforcement powers should be made against the Court of Justice's general powers (i) to undertake authoritative interpretation of EU law; (ii) to appraise member state conduct; and (iii) to decide on the actual imposition of sanctions.[120]

6. The Function of Constitutional Limits to Institutional Powers

The problem of ad hoc infringement procedures in secondary legislation essentially concerns the principle of attributed powers. The Commission

[120] According to Art 260(3) TFEU the Court of Justice may impose sanctions 'not exceeding the amount specified by the Commission'.

and the member states represented in the Council have different opinions on the matter. They also have conflicting interests. Thus, it is useful to analyse the above inter-institutional discourse in view of the EU institutional balance as a constitutional principle[121] and implicitly so, with the principle of attributed powers.

The doctrine of attributed powers constitutes a core premise of the EU institutional balance. The EU institutional balance was first established as a principle of the EC Treaty by the Court of Justice.[122] Subsequently the member states[123] and the Commission embraced it.[124] The doctrine of institutional balance should not be conceived of in traditional *trias politica* terminology. In its most common meaning, this signifies the impermeable separation of legislative, executive, and judicial governmental functions. This public law doctrine does not correspond to the institutional structure of the EU Treaties and the indistinct, cross-institutional division of traditional governmental functions and powers.[125] The High Authority's institutional powers under the ECSC Treaty are illustrative thereof in its grouping 'together powers which on a national level are divided between various authorities and are subject to special rules and distinct powers'.[126] The ECSC division allowed for a functional rather than organic division of powers.[127] This division mirrors Kelsen's objection against the classical conceptualization of governmental powers, namely that there are not 'three distinct coordinated functions' with clearly demarcated inter-boundaries.[128] Instead, Kelsen contends, thinking about law creation and

[121] See B de Witte, 'General Principles of European Community Law', Reports from a Conference in Malmö, 27–28 August 1999 in U Bernitz and J Nergelius (eds.), *Institutional Principles: A Special Category of General Principles of EC Law* (Kluwer Law International, 2001), 152, on the notion of principle and its legal implications.

[122] C-25/70 *Köster* [1970] ECR I-1161.

[123] Protocol on the application of the principles of subsidiarity and proportionality. Protocol annexed to the Treaty establishing the Treaty of Amsterdam.

[124] See, eg, Commission Communication *'Strengthening the Social Dimension of the Lisbon Strategy: Streamlining Open Coordination in the Field of Social Protection'*, COM/2003/261, point 2.3.

[125] Compare C-242/87 *Commission v Council* [1989] ECR-1425, para 13.

[126] Case 31/59 *Acciaieria di rescia v High Authority* [1960], ECR 71. See also VA Schmidt, 'Europeanization in Simple and Compound Polities, Institutions, Ideas, Discourse'. Paper presented to the American Political Science Association National Meetings in Chicago, (1–5 September 2004), 38, who uses the vivid idiom 'dynamic confusion of [horizontal] powers'.

[127] K Lenaerts, 'Some Reflections on the Separation of Powers in the European Union' (1991) *Common Market Law Review* 28, 11–35.

[128] H Kelsen, *General Theory of Law and State* (Harvard University Press, 1945), 269.

application as fundamental statal functions gives a more accurate conception of the functional junctures.[129]

Lenaerts and Verhoeven nevertheless invoke Montesquieu's division of powers as a constructive concept in two different senses. The first one concerns the horizontal division of powers between the EU wings of government. It serves as constitutional 'limits on governmental power, by dividing it and subjecting it to mutual forms of control', which again form a citizen safeguard.[130] In the second account, the institutions embody dispersed, constitutive forums and supranational executives. Ultimately, they form a deliberative Community.[131] This chapter deals with institutional balance in the former sense. However, it only does so at a level of abstraction which is concerned with the 'concentration of uncontrolled power in a single authority'.[132] Ultimately, it is concerned with the balance of powers between the EU and the member states.[133]

Clearly, the allocation of EU institutional powers has not been static over time due to the several Treaty revisions that have taken place. Thus, the notion of 'balance' cannot imply that there is a constant division of powers at the core of the principle.[134] It rather suggests a parity characterized by stabilization of powers through opposing and separating powers of varying size. Such a functional account resembles the principle of checks and balances.[135] It thus establishes a member state safeguard 'against

[129] For an explanation of Kelsen's 'functional dichotomy' see R Schütze, 'Sharpening the Separation of Powers Through a Hierarchy of Norms. Reflections on the Draft Treaty's Regime for Legislative and Executive Law-making' *EIPA Working Paper* 2005/W/01, 6.

[130] K Lenaerts and A Verhoeven, 'Institutional Balance as a Guarantee for Democracy in EU Governance' in C Joerges and R Dehousse (eds.), *Good Governance in Europe's Integrated Market* (Oxford University Press, 2002), 40–1.

[131] K Lenaerts and A Verhoeven, 'Institutional Balance as a Guarantee for Democracy in EU Governance' in C Joerges and R Dehousse (eds.), *Good Governance in Europe's Integrated Market* (Oxford University Press, 2002), 42–3.

[132] K Lenaerts, 'Some Reflections on the Separation of Powers in the European Union' (1991) *Common Market Law Review* 28, 11–35, 12.

[133] C Joerges and E Vos, 'Structures of Transnational Governance and Their Legitimacy' in JAE Vervaele (ed.), *Compliance and Enforcement of European Community law* (Kluwer Law International, 1999), 84.

[134] Not least a strict textual interpretation the Danish and Dutch language versions ('ligevægt' and 'evenwicht' respectively) may give rise to such understandings.

[135] Compare American constitutional thought which is permeated by this power-temper principle. See generally JM Henry, *Five-Branch Government: The Full Measure of Constitutional Checks and Balances* (University of Illinois Press, 1980).

any concentration of uncontrolled power in a single authority'.[136] The Commission's function as guardian constitutes a guarantee in the EU's general interests in compliance. However, the Commission's powers are restrained vis-à-vis those belonging to the Court of Justice. In constituting a safeguard against excessive concentrations of powers within one or more institutions,[137] the horizontal separation of powers also reflects the member states' self-interests in restraining the Commission's powers as a potential constraint on their national autonomy.[138]

The subject of the Commission's enforcement powers is of a political nature when it arises at IGCs. The introduction of sanctions under Article 260(2) TFEU illustrates well the functional interrelationship between the institutions, which is supposed to be secured by the institutional balance. Although the Commission is empowered to request the Court of Justice to impose a pecuniary penalty upon defaulting member states, it possesses no general sanctioning powers of its own.[139] The Court of Justice, by contrast, enjoys full discretion in deciding whether a fine should be awarded and the amount.[140] In this way, the member states have accomplished a legal and political endorsement of the commonly agreed objective of a high level of compliance. All the same, in the direct confrontation between member states and the EU,[141] the sanctioning mechanism is carefully set out

[136] Compare K Lenaerts, 'Some Reflections on the Separation of Powers in the European Union' (1991) *Common Market Law Review* 28, 11–35, 13. The author is concerned with the general function of checks and balances as a safeguard of the 'subjects of law'.

[137] Compare Pescatore as quoted and translated by RH Lauwaars, *Lawfulness and Legal Force of Community Decisions: Some Considerations on the Binding Decisions Which the Council and the Commission Can Take by Virtue of the Treaty Establishing the European Economic Community* (AW Sijthoff, 1973), 60.

[138] See Pescatore on Member State prudence and the potential reach of the institutions on many policy areas. P Pescatore, 'La Personnalité internationale de la Communauté' in *Les Relations Exterieures de la Communauté Unifiée* (Actes du 3ieme colloque sur la fusion des Communauté européennes, Liège, octobre 1967) (Université de Liège, 1969), 77–117. Compare U Di Fabio, 'Some Remarks on the Allocation of Competences between the European Union and its Member States' (2002) *Common Market Law Review* 39, 1289–301 on vertical separation of powers.

[139] Article 260(2) TFEU.

[140] The question whether the Court of Justice may impose both sanction types when only one has been requested by the Commission has now been clarified by C-304/02 *Commission v France* [2005] ECR I-6263. The Court of Justice went along with Advocate General Geelhoed's argument that although the Commission only requested periodic penalty payments, the Court of Justice may impose both sanction types.

[141] CWA Timmermans, 'Judicial Protection against Member States' in D Curtin and T Heukels (eds.), *Institutional Dynamics of European Integration. Essays in Honour of Henry*

between the Commission and the Court of Justice.[142] Their respective institutional powers are, therefore, only relatively strengthened. The actual distribution of institutional powers establishes legal constraints on the institutions' powers at the EU level. It is also a manifestation of political choices. Specifically, at the core of this political dimension is a statal interest in retaining both a particular division of powers as well as a limitation of the respective institutions' powers. Therefore, the specific question of the delineation of the Commission's powers versus those of the Court of Justice (and the question of the Council's powers of delegation) has bearings on the relationship between the individual states and the Commission and also between the member states and the EU more generally.

The notion of EU institutional balance may be considered to be a primarily political notion concerned with the constitutional framework of the EU. However, it is indisputably also a legal principle. In his systemization of the general principles of EU law, de Witte distinguishes between vertical and horizontal institutional principles. With regards to the latter de Witte notes that the Court of Justice does not generally suggest the institutional balance to be 'a legal norm with an independent content' other than in Case 70/88 dealing with the European Parliament's right of standing under ex Article 230 EC.[143] To this it may be added that in C-25/70 *Köster*, the Court of Justice explicitly establishes that the management committee procedure is compatible with the 'Community structure and the institutional balance as regards both the relationship between institutions and the exercise of their respective powers'.[144] The judgment is interesting because it establishes the legal relevance of the principle of institutional balance for the lawfulness of secondary legislation.[145] In relation to the question of enforcement there is no potential conflict with the European Parliament's ability to exercise its treaty-based powers, which was the matter in C-70/88 *European Parliament v Council*. However, the power to establish and/or

G. Schermers. Volume II (Martinus Nijhoff Publishers, 1994), 397: Art 258 TFEU 'is an instrument for settling conflicts... between the Community [now the EU], represented by the Commission, and a Member State'.

142 See also chapter three on Art 260(2) and (3) TFEU.

143 B de Witte, 'General Principles of European Community Law', Reports from a Conference in Malmö, 27–28 August 1999 in U Bernitz and J Nergelius (eds.), *Institutional Principles: A Special Category of General Principles of EC Law* (Kluwer Law International, 2001), 151. C-70/88 *European Parliament v Council* [1990] ECR I-2041.

144 Case 25/70 *Köster* [1970] ECR 1161, para 4.

145 See also C-133/06 *Parliament v Council* [2008] ECR I-3189, para 57.

sanction infringements would clearly impinge on the EU judiciary's institutional prerogatives and the consequence would effectively be an unauthorized treaty amendment.

The member states (in the Council) have shown some willingness to employ a broad understanding of EU competences, even to the extent of transgressing their formal legal competence in matters of vertical separation of powers.[146] By contrast, there is little jurisprudence which touches upon the question of horizontal powers.[147] In the run-up to the Amsterdam Treaty amendment, the Court of Justice issued a report in which it pointed out legal problems that could result from its lack of *ratione materia* under the second and third EU pillars concerning Common Foreign and Security Policy and Justice and Home Affairs respectively. 'It may be', the Court argued 'necessary to determine the limits of the powers of the Union vis-à-vis the member states, and of those of each the institutions of the Union'.[148] This implies recognition that the Court of Justice cannot and will not corroborate an incremental erosion of the institutional balance when it comes to the limits of the institutions' powers.

7. Conclusion

This chapter examined the limitations on the 'EU legislator' to establish ad hoc infringement procedures in secondary law and the constitutional implications thereof. It argued that the EU Treaties exhaustively list the array of tools and powers available to the Commission in its role as guardian of the Treaties, with the exception of soft-law measures voluntarily embraced by the member states.

The Commission justifies its proposals for stronger policy-specific and general enforcement powers in terms of enhancing the effectiveness of EU law. When examining the preambles and policy papers accompanying the proposals, effectiveness appeared to have two meanings. One concerned a qualitative quest for better implementation and enforcement of EU law. The other concerned timely implementation and enforcement. However,

[146] C-376/98 *Germany v European Parliament and Council* [2000] ECR I-08419 (advertising and sponsorship of tobacco products).

[147] Case 25/70 *Köster* [1970] ECR I-1161.

[148] *Report of the Court of Justice on Certain Aspects of the Application of the Treaty on European Union*, Luxembourg, May 1995 (published in the Court's 1995 Annual Report).

the suggestion that effectiveness can be enhanced by instituting Commission top-down, steering type of powers would fundamentally alter the dynamics of the general EU infringement procedure. It is arguably a protracted procedure. However, an account that sees enforcement as a semi-legal and semi-political process alters the standards of appraisal. The Commission's powers of enforcement according to Article 258 TFEU, and also the member state guarantees largely established through jurisprudence, serve a rule-of-law purpose. At the same time, they have entailed significant extra-legal importance for the member states and also for the Commission. Importantly, the step-by-step approach and the bilateral nature of the procedure enable the parties to engage in a problem-solving, interpretive dialogue. The political conditions underpinning this type of dialogue were discussed in chapter one. When applying a contextual understanding of the infringement procedure and the role of the Commission accordingly, it becomes apparent that effectiveness is a deceptive notion. Specifically, it tends to obscure the very central point that EU enforcement is a dialectical exercise in which the Commission and the Court of Justice help refine EU law.

The general EU infringement procedure was compared to the regulatory steering-mode responsive regulation. Both are inherently decentralized and only gradually can the supervisor increase pressure on defaulting supervisees. Similar to responsive regulation, the Commission lacks stronger and readily available enforcement powers when responsive, cooperative dialogue for some reason fails or when speedier responses are required.

The legal question of ad hoc infringement procedures was framed as a matter of institutional balance. It was argued that this question has broader implications not only for the horizontal, but also for the vertical division of EU powers. Notably, the Commission's current tools of enforcement mirror basic constitutional choices. To recap, the Commission's present general enforcement powers should be understood in the context of the irrefutably political relationship between the Commission and the member states and, ultimately, in the light of the relationship between the member states and the EU. Thus, even if the general EU infringement procedure is, in some respects, imperfect, a strengthening of the Commission's enforcement powers should be decided upon in primary law.

5

The Functional Overlap of Enforcement and Implementation Tools

1. Introduction[1]

Implementation concerns putting law into effect. Enforcement only becomes relevant in the phase succeeding implementation, if the question arises whether EU law has been implemented, applied, and enforced effectively. In this understanding the notions of implementation and enforcement are distinct and seemingly neither compatible nor interchangeable. The Court of Justice has, however, acknowledged that there are cases in which the Commission could have pursued a situation as an infringement case under Article 258 TFEU instead of making use of its implementation powers. In addition there is a range of mechanisms explicitly foreseen to prevent infringements.[2]

This chapter identifies implementation measures that display functional overlap with enforcement. The aim is to discuss their characteristics and compare them to genuine enforcement powers. The argument proceeds as follows: first, the notion of implementation in the context of EU law will be discussed in some detail. Then, selected measures will be grouped and examined under the headings (i) preventive measures, (ii) safeguard and

[1] This chapter is based on my article 'The Functional Overlap of Enforcement and Implementation Tools' published in 2007 in *Croatian Yearbook of European Law and Policy* 3.

[2] For an analysis of some of the tools also considered in this chapter, see AGJ Ibáñez, 'Commission Tools for the Supervision and Enforcement of EC Law Other Than Article 169 EC Treaty—An Attempt at Systematization' *Jean Monnet Working Paper* 98; and AJG Ibáñez, 'Exceptions to Article 226: Alternative Administrative Procedures and the Pursuit of Member States' (2000) *European Law Journal* 6:2, 148–76.

emergency measures, and (iii) conditionality.[3] The closing section discusses a number of issues regarding the application of implementation measures with the aim of securing member state compliance. These include the potential legal constraints on the Commission, such as the proportionality principle, but also political constraints. It is argued that although the Commission is largely at liberty to employ the examined measures with a functional aim of ensuring compliance, any perceived misuse may have ramifications on the Commission's future ability to obtain certain implementation powers.

2. The Notion of Implementation

The previous chapter argued that the principle of attributed powers prevents the 'EU legislator' from establishing binding ad hoc infringement procedures in secondary legislation. Thus, the Commission cannot be empowered to interpret EU law in an authoritative manner or to make a binding assessment of member state behaviour and its conformity with EU law. It would require a treaty amendment. The Commission can nevertheless make implementation decisions by virtue of specific delegation or on the basis of special powers provided for in individual treaty provisions. While some of these tools best qualify as *lex specialis* enforcement powers, such as the powers under the European competition policy, others again are implementation tools. This chapter discusses the notion of 'implementation powers' in more detail. Moreover, it identifies and categorizes implementation powers which, notwithstanding their legal characterization, may have implications for the comprehensive EU enforcement picture. A power will qualify as an extra-treaty enforcement power insofar (1a) it concerns an interpretive uncertainty and/or (1b) it implies an assessment of member state application of EU law (performance/lawfulness) and (2) the Commission is entitled to issue a binding dictate upon the member states to take action in a general or specific manner.

The EU Treaties represent a catalogue of primary norms that encompass the internal and external competences of the treaty-regime as well as the powers of the legislative, adjudicative, and executive branches of government. Within this framework of primary law, the 'EU legislator' is

[3] The enumeration of directives and regulations in this chapter is not exhaustive.

empowered to articulate substantive rules in secondary law. In addition, there are organizational, as well secondary, rules that establish the specifications required for putting the law into practice. Such secondary and tertiary, implementing, norms facilitate the 'putting into effect of legislation, decisions, or policies formulated and agreed by the EU's policy-making institutions'.[4] Secondary and tertiary norms are plentiful within the EU and unprecedented in any other international law-regime. In this chapter such norms are referred to as 'implementation'.

Prior to the Lisbon Treaty, powers to implement Community law rest at the level of the member state and as well as at the Community level and there was no definite logic of separation. Similarly, there was no automatic connection to the type of competence in question.[5] The Convention working group on the delimitation of competences between the EU and the member states nevertheless maintains that as a general rule 'competence to implement and apply legislation in accordance with their respective constitutional rules ... rests with the Member States ... The Community exercises such competence in a subsidiary capacity only'.[6] The interpretation is based on a combined reading of ex Article 10 EC (repealed and replaced, in substance, by Article 4(3) TEU), ex Article 202 EC (repealed and replaced, in substance, by Article 16(1) TEU and Articles 290 and 291 TFEU) and ex Article 211 EC (repealed and replaced, in substance, by Article 17(1) TEU).

To the extent that implementation took place at the supranational level, it followed from ex Article 202 EC, that the Council should delegate powers of implementation to the Commission. It could, however, reserve the right to exercise implementing powers in specific cases. Notwithstanding the wording of ex Article 202 EC, which clearly suggested an obligation to delegate, the Council effectively retained unfettered power to reserve the right of implementation. That is to say, a Council decision to reserve the powers to implement in a specific case would not be examined in substance by the Court of Justice. However, in terms of quantity, the

[4] M Cini, 'Implementation' in M Cini (ed.), *European Union Politics* (Oxford University Press, 2003), 349.

[5] European Convention, '*Delimitation of competence between the European Union and the Member States—Existing system, problems and avenues to be explored*' (Note) CONV 47/02, 15 May 2002.

[6] European Convention, '*Delimitation of competence between the European Union and the Member States—Existing system, problems and avenues to be explored*' (Note) CONV 47/02, 15 May 2002.

Commission far outweighed the Council in sheer volume.[7] Thus delegation was not just the rule in legal terms, but also in actual terms. When reserving powers to implement, the Council should demonstrate in depth the grounds for its choice[8] and explain its reasons for departing from the conventional procedure.[9] Therefore, with the exception of instances where the Commission was explicitly empowered by the EC Treaty, there had to be express delegation from the Council. The Commission's corresponding institutional powers to carry out implementation were stipulated in Article 211 EC. According to Schäfer et al '[t]he authorising norm . . . , the delegating norm . . . and the norm exercising powers contained in the enabling norm (implementing act) form a whole that contains the relevant law'.[10]

Then, as now, derived legal norms must be within the substantive scope of their enabling provision. The reason is that the EU institutions cannot act beyond their explicitly granted powers. This followed from the principle of attributed powers as well as from the wording of ex Article 249 EC (Article 288 TFEU), which listed (and still lists) a range of instruments available to the institutions in order to carry out their task and in accordance with the provisions of the EC Treaty (and now the EU Treaties). Bast notes that the wording of ex Article 249 EC articulates 'a strict hierarchy between (primary) Treaty law and (secondary) derived law'. Moreover, he continues, this hierarchy of norms is indeed a 'precondition that makes the principle of attributed powers work'.[11]

Employing a contextual and essentially pragmatic understanding of ex Article 211 EC, the Court of Justice has consistently held that the scope of implementation is to be interpreted in a fairly broad manner.[12] On

[7] G Haibach, 'Separation and Delegation of Legislative Powers: A Comparative Analysis' in M Andenas and A Türk (eds.), *Delegated Legislation and the Role of Committees in the EC* (Kluwer Law International, 2000).

[8] C-16/88 *Commission v Council* [1989] ECR 3457, para 10.

[9] C-257/01 *Commission v Council* [2005] ECR I-345, para 51.

[10] GF Schäfer, G Haibach, and A Türk, 'Subproject 3: Policy Implementation and Comitology Committees' (May 2000) *EIPA Working Paper* 39:4, 47. The working paper can be accessed at http://www.eipa.nl/Publications/Summaries/2000/chap_4.pdf.

[11] J Bast, 'On the Grammar of EU Law: Legal Instruments' *Jean Monnet Working Paper* 9/03, 17.

[12] Joined Cases C-37/02 and C-38/02 *Di Lenardo Adriano Srl/Dilexport Srl v Ministero del Commercio con l'Estero* (reference for preliminary ruling) [2004] ECR I-6911, para 53. The judgment in Case C-240/90 *Germany v Commission* [1992] ECR I-5383, para 36, states that ex Articles 202 and 211 EC 'distinguish between rules which, since they are essential to the subject-matter envisaged, must be reserved to the Council's power, and those which being merely of an implementing nature may be delegated to the Commission'.

condition that it does not lay down measures which conflict with the delegating act, the Commission can thus 'adopt all the measures which were necessary or appropriate for the implementation of the basic legislation'.[13] Whereas ex Articles 202 and 211 EC simply used the expression 'implementation' without specification, it is clear from jurisprudence that delegated implementation powers encompassed both powers 'to adopt generally applicable or individual measures within specific areas'.[14] The EC Treaty itself did not make a distinction between those types of power. It was precisely the lack of specification of the notion of implementation in the Treaty which led the Court of Justice to reject a narrow reading of its scope. Implementation can thus be thought of as covering both (i) legislative powers and (ii) executive powers. Delegation of legislation is a normative power that enables the Commission to establish general rules or procedures, for applying the rules laid down by the legislator.[15] The Commission emphasizes the merits of delegating legislative powers from the Council to the Commission, particularly in 'policy sectors with rapid technical changes'.[16] These rules are, as are Advocate General Darmon notes, 'of a general and impersonal nature'.[17] Executive powers enable the Commission to put EU law into operation either through the adoption of detailed provisions or individual decisions. The same Advocate General denotes the latter administrative implementation.[18]

Historically, the oversight mechanisms established in connection with delegation to the Commission have caused inter-institutional frictions between the European Parliament and the Council and lead to incremental involvement of the European Parliament.[19] Moreover, these tensions have been exacerbated by the fact that the distinction between legislative-type and executive-type of powers were somewhat opaque. This matter is well

[13] Joined cases C-9/95, C-23/95, and C-156/95 *Belgium and Germany v Commission* [1997] ECR I-645, para 37.

[14] C-16/88 *Commission v Council* [1989] ECR-3457, para 16, and, in particular, para 11.

[15] C-298/89 *Government of Gibraltar v Council* [1993] ECR I-3605.

[16] Commission 'Questions and Answers: An Institutional Architecture for the European Union (Peace, Freedom, Solidarity)' MEMO (2002) 285, 5 December 2002.

[17] Opinion of Advocate General Darmon in C-16/88 *Commission v Council* [1989] ECR II-3457, point 15.

[18] Opinion of Advocate General Darmon in C-16/88 *Commission v Council* [1989] ECR II-3457, point 15.

[19] Notably, Council Decision 2006/512/EC of 17 July 2006 amending Decision 1999/468/EC (2006) OJ L 200) introduced a new comitology procedure ('regulatory procedure with scrutiny'). Delegated acts (Art 290 TFEU) cover almost the same type of measures as those adopted so far under the 'regulatory procedure with scrutiny'.

beyond the scope of this chapter. Suffice to say the member state governments have attempted to establish a more coherent framework to regulate centralized implementation and the corresponding powers of scrutiny by the 'EU legislator' and the member states. As mentioned in chapter four, the Lisbon Treaty distinguishes between *delegated acts* (Article 290 TFEU) and *implementing acts* (Article 291 TFEU). Articles 290 and 291 TFEU provide legal basis for legislative-type and executive-type of powers, respectively. The distinction is important because the procedures are subject to different oversight mechanisms. The European Parliament and Council are responsible for scrutinizing delegated acts.[20] The Commission's exercise of implementing powers is controlled by the member states.[21] However, the distinction is far from trouble-free.[22] Delegated acts are of general application. Acts according to Article 291 TFEU can be of general application as well as individual measures. They are primarily of general application.[23] Article 291(1) TFEU specifies that the competence to implement lies with the member states. However, according to Article 291(2) TFEU, such powers can be conferred on the Commission where 'uniform conditions for implementing legally binding Union acts are needed'.

In terms of scope and effect, executive decision-making may have similarities with court rulings. Such powers can appear reminiscent of genuine enforcement tools in that they enable the Commission to make concrete decisions. However, as will be demonstrated in the following section, legislative-type powers (irrespective of how they qualify post-Lisbon) can likewise display functional overlap with enforcement measures,

[20] See Communication from the Commission to the European Parliament and the Council *'Implementation of Article 290 of the Treaty on the Functioning of the European Union'*, COM/2009/0673 final.

[21] See Regulation (EU) No 182/2011 of the European Parliament and the Council of 16 February 2011 laying down the rules and general principles concerning mechanisms for control by Member States of the Commission's exercise of implementing powers, (2011) OJ L 55/13, which repeals Decision 1999/468, as amended by Council Decision 2006/512/EC ('the Comitology Decision'). It replaces the old comitology decision as far as the consultation, management, and regulatory procedures are concerned.

[22] On the difficulties connected with the distinction, see P Craig, 'Delegated Acts, Implementing Acts and the New Comitology Regulation' (2011) *European Law Review* 36:5, 671–87, 672.

[23] P Craig, 'Delegated Acts, Implementing Acts and the New Comitology Regulation' (2011) *European Law Review* 36:5, 671–87, 672.

in particular when applied with the intention of achieving interpretive clarification of ambiguous legal obligations.

3. Selected Implementation Powers

3.1 *Preventive measures*

3.1.1 Services in the internal market

There are a number of different types of Commission powers established in secondary legislation with the purpose of anticipating non-compliance. Executive, decision-making powers have the most obvious resemblance. However, norm-setting, or legislative, powers may also substitute or supplement enforcement actions. Before analysing such Commission powers it is useful to think, more generally, about how legislative measures can be interchangeable with (or supplementary to) enforcement powers.

In 2004, the Commission tabled a proposal for a framework directive on services in the internal market. The proposal, eventually adopted as Directive 2006/123/EC on services in the internal market, contained a 'general legal framework applicable, subject to certain exceptions, to all economic activities involving services'.[24] This horizontal method was motivated by the perception that infringements within the internal market in services are frequently 'common to a large number of different activities and have many features in common'.[25] In the pre-legislative and legislative phases the Commission as well as the European Parliament raised the issue of non-compliance. The European Parliament stressed the need for 'a rigorous infringement policy vis-à-vis Member States which take measures incompatible with Articles 43 [right of establishment] and 49 [free movement of services] of the Treaty'.[26] The Commission, for its part, emphasized that obstacles to these provisions do persist and that it would be 'ineffective' and

[24] Commission Proposal for a Directive of the European Parliament and of the Council on services in the internal market, COM/2004/2 final/3, recital 3a of the preamble. The proposal was adopted as Directive 2006/123/EC of the European Parliament and of the Council of 12 December 2006 on services in the internal market [2006] OJ L376/36.

[25] Commission Proposal for a Directive of the European Parliament and of the Council on services in the internal market, COM/2004/2, recital 3a of the preamble.

[26] European Parliament, '*Resolution on the Commission Communication "An Internal Market Strategy for Services"*', (A5-310/2001) 4 October 2001.

'unmanageable' to address them individually under the general infringement procedure.[27]

Section three of the Commission proposal lists member state requirements that are either prohibited or subject to evaluation. Article 14 of the proposal (and of the Directive) concerns member state requirements that should be abolished. To illustrate the degree of detail, Article 14(3) contains a prohibition of

> ...restrictions on the freedom of a provider to choose between a principal or a secondary establishment, in particular an obligation on the provider to have his principal establishment in their territory, or restrictions on the freedom to choose between establishment in the form of an agency, branch or subsidiary.

Article 15 requires member states to examine whether specified domestic requirements are in conformity with conditions of non-discrimination, necessity, and proportionality. After drawing up a self-assessment, all member states derive a mutual evaluation report and declare if they plan on maintaining any requirements as well as their reasons therefor, in addition to requirements that have been suspended or amended. The procedure thus leaves room for peer-review while also facilitating the exchange of arguments based upon interpretation, legal principles, and precedent. The member states can only introduce new requirements if they comply with the conditions of non-discrimination, necessity, and proportionality mentioned above. As an additional requirement, any such domestic obligation shall result from new circumstances.[28] Then,

> [w]ithin a period of 3 months from the date of notification, the Commission shall examine the compatibility of any new requirements with Community law and, as the case may be, shall adopt a decision requesting the Member State in question to refrain from adopting them or to abolish them.[29]

Whereas decisions are binding in their entirety upon those to whom they are addressed, the Commission is merely empowered to 'request' the

[27] Commission Proposal for a Directive of the European Parliament and of the Council on services in the internal market, COM/2004/2, para 30.

[28] Commission Proposal for a Directive of the European Parliament and of the Council on services in the internal market, COM/2004/2, Art 15(5).

[29] Commission Proposal for a Directive of the European Parliament and of the Council on services in the internal market, COM/2004/2, Art 15(6). The proposal was adopted as Directive 2006/123/EC of the European Parliament and of the Council of 12 December 2006 on services in the internal market [2006] OJ L376/36. The provision is now Art 15(7); however, no substantive amendments have been made.

member state to 'refrain from' or 'abolish' a requirement. The wording avoids the constraints set by the EC Treaty (and now by the EU Treaties) against ad hoc infringement procedures.[30] At the same time, it ascertains and formalizes a Commission soft-law tool to address potential or existing infringements. Finally, Article 16 specifies a list of prohibited restrictions.

In the preamble of the proposal, the Commission explains that the proposal's list of prohibited requirements (Article 14), requirements to be evaluated (Article 15), and restrictions prohibited on the one hand, and ex Article 226 EC (Article 258 TFEU) on the other, have different aims:

> While the latter concern individual cases resulting from specific circumstances and measures in a particular Member State, the former are on the other hand aimed at ensuring, in a general and systematic fashion, that the legal systems correspond to the requirements of a genuine internal market in services in which, the freedom of establishment and free movement of services are facilitated.[31]

The proposal thus contains a mechanism that can deal with potential infringements of EU law by systematizing Commission scrutiny. Moreover, it enables self-assessment and multilateral peer-review of clearly spelled out obligations. Although the procedure attributes a central function to the Commission, it is fairly decentralized in the way it functions. In comparison with the general infringement procedure it displays apparent gains in terms of economies-of-scale, both when measured up to informally negotiated agreements reached during the administrative stage, and to rulings by the Court of Justice. Notably, the Court of Justice merely rules on specific infringement incidents. The approach seems apt for other policy areas where a substantial body of jurisprudence indicates that there are clusters of compliance failures that apply to a large number of member states. However, the method restricts the member states' autonomy when implementing the Directive. Thus it is only suitable when the member states' interest in ensuring compliance prevail over their interest in maximum room for manoeuvre in the implementation phase.

3.1.2 Draft technical regulations

Standardization makes up an instrument against barriers to free movement of goods and services and has long been hailed as a central measure for the

[30] See generally chapter four.

[31] Commission Proposal for a Directive of the European Parliament and of the Council on services in the internal market, COM/2004/2, preamble.

realization of the Single Market.[32] Currently, EU standardization is largely regulated by Directive 98/34[33] and a number of sector-specific regulations. Harmonization of technical standards and regulations are frequently accompanied by preventive clauses. Council Directive 83/189/EEC of 28 March 1983 laying down a procedure for the provision of information in the field of technical standards and regulations is illustrative of this.[34] In its Communication from 1993 on the handling of urgent situations in the context of implementation of EU rules, the Commission discusses the notion of technical harmonization measures and its institutional powers:[35]

> [T]he Commission must ensure that the directive has been properly implemented ... It acts under the competences conferred on it by Article 155 [repealed and replaced, in substance, by Article 17(1) TEU]. Safeguard clauses give the Commission powers of enquiry; these are, however, limited since they are not powers of investigation but involve consultation of the interested parties.... Once consultations are completed, the Commission must draw up a report as to whether the measure is justified.

According to the original Council Directive 83/189/EEC, the member states are obliged to announce to the Commission draft technical regulations and submit a justification for their introduction. The Commission informs the other member states and can further refer the draft to a Committee for its opinion. The member states and the Commission are given the chance to make remarks and the member state must take these

[32] Council Resolution of 7 May 1985 on a new approach to technical harmonisation and standards [1985] OJ C136/1; and Council Resolution of 28 October 1999 on the role of standardisation in Europe [2000] OJ C141/5.

[33] Directive 98/34 of the European Parliament and of the Council laying down a procedure for the provision of information in the fields of technical standards and regulations and of rules on information services [1998] OJ L204/37, amended by Directive 98/48 of the European Parliament and of the Council [1998] OJ L217, Arts 8 and 9. Directive 98/34/EC now applies to all industrial, agricultural, and fishery products as well as Information Society services. Commission '*The Operation of Directive 98/34/EC from 2002–2005*', COM/2007/125 final (Commission Staff Working Document).

[34] Council Directive 83/189/EEC of 28 March 1983 laying down a procedure for the provision of information in the field of technical standards and regulations [1983] OJ L109/8, as amended by Directive 88/182/EC [1988] OJ L81/75, Directive 94/10/EC [1994] OJ L100/30, and Directive 98/34/EC [1998] OJ L204/37. For a comprehensive analysis of Directive 83/189 and subsequent directives on compulsory notification of draft technical regulations, see S Weatherill, 'Compulsory Notification of Draft Technical Regulations: The Contribution of Directive 83/189 to the Management of the Internal Market' (1996) *Yearbook of European Law* 16:1, 129.

[35] Commission '*Communication on the handling of urgent situations in the context of implementation of Community rules: Follow-up to the Sutherland report*', COM/1993/430, 40.

into account in the subsequent preparation of the technical regulation. Upon member state or Commission requests, the final text must be provided to the supplicant. The member states shall suspend the draft for six months from the date of the notification if the Commission or another member state presents a comprehensive opinion within three months of that date. The Commission may decide to propose or adopt a directive in response to the notification. In that case, the standstill period is prolonged to 12 months.[36] The Directive enables the Commission to forewarn a member state of cases 'where draft technical regulations, if adopted, would run counter to EU law'.[37] Moreover, the Commission contends, it enables the other member states 'to play an important role in preventing the creation of new technical barriers to trade'.[38] The mechanism constitutes a key instrument in ensuring the proper functioning of the internal market. Specifically, it makes it possible for the Commission to 'to identify possible barriers to trade before they enter into force and thus to avoid the need to initiate many infringement procedures'.[39]

The obligation to notify the Commission of draft technical regulations is, however, no guarantee of compliance. Notably, the obligation itself requires monitoring. Thus the Commission initiated procedures under the general EU infringement procedure more than 100 times during the period between 1995 and 1998 in cases where the member states had failed to notify draft measures or to adopt them before the end of the standstill period.[40]

In a judgment from 1996, the Court ruled on Articles 8 and 9 of Directive 83/189/EEC, now Directive 98/34/EC, stating that individuals may rely on them before national courts. Significantly, the national courts shall refuse to apply a national technical regulation unless it has been notified in line with the Directive. Accordingly, a breach of the obligation to notify renders the technical regulations concerned inapplicable and consequently unenforceable against individuals.[41] The legal justification for this is based on the obligation to inform the Commission about draft legislation. The

[36] Council Directive 83/189/EEC, Arts 8 and 9.

[37] Council Directive 83/189/EEC.

[38] Commission '*Communication concerning the non-respect of certain provisions of Council Directive 83/189/EEC of 28 March 1983 laying down a procedure for the provision of information in the field of technical standards and regulations*' [1986] OJ C245/4.

[39] Commission '*Better monitoring of the application of Community law*', COM/2002/725.

[40] Commission '*The operation of Directive 98/34/EC from 1995 to 1998*', COM/2000/429.

[41] C-194/94 *CIA Security International* [1996] ECR I-2201, para 54 and summary.

obligation is, the Court of Justice ruled, unconditional and sufficiently precise in terms of content as to establish direct effect. Under Article 258 TFEU the Commission's acts or forbearance are without any legal significance to legal and private persons. Thus, in comparison with the general infringement procedure, this type of preventive measure is relatively more effective. According to the Commission, the procedure has a number of additional advantages in comparison with the general EU infringement procedure. These include the fact that:

- It allows new barriers to the internal market to be detected before they have any negative effects, thus avoiding long and costly infringement proceedings.
- It allows the detection of protectionist measures which might be drawn up by member states under exceptional circumstances, such as an economic and financial crisis.
- It allows member states to ascertain the degree of compatibility of notified drafts with European Union legislation.
- It allows an effective dialogue between Members States and the Commission when assessing notified drafts.
- It is a benchmarking tool allowing member states to draw on the ideas of their partners in order to solve common problems regarding technical regulations.
- It allows economic operators to make their voices heard and to adapt their activities in good time to future technical regulations. This right of scrutiny is used extensively by economic operators, helping the Commission and national authorities to detect any barriers to trade.
- It contributes to the application of the subsidiarity principle.
- It is a regulatory instrument which can be used to identify areas where harmonisation is necessary.
- It is an instrument for industrial policy.[42]

The advantages pointed out by the Commission pertain to effectiveness and ready availability. However, they also touch upon the fact that there are no means to verify compliance under general infringement procedure other than by judgment. Additional merits concern the involvement of stakeholders and member states. Finally, the Commission points out, the procedure helps identify need for further harmonization. The Commission thus links

[42] Report from the Commission, '*The Operation of Directive 98/34 in 2009 and 2010*', COM/2011/853 final.

the issue of national implementation with centralized enforcement and even further with the possibility of EU regulation.

3.1.3 Public procurement/pre-contractual review

As described in chapter two, the Commission has to observe a range of procedural steps under Article 258 TFEU and member state guarantees, including minimum time limits connected with the defence of the member state. Moreover, the burden of proof rests with the Commission. The general EU infringement procedure is in some ways protracted and, as van Rijn points out, it contains no legally enforceable remedies.[43] The general EU procedure is not employed as a tool against individual infringements, but rather as a means to manage priority cases. Against this backdrop, Directive 89/665/EEC on the application of review procedures to the award of public supply and public works contracts establishes a notification procedure according to which, the Commission can notify a member state if it considers a contract to be unlawful. In its original proposal for a directive, the Commission proposed a provision according to which the Commission could intervene in the domestic administrative or judicial procedures concerning public procurement.[44] The procedure was anticipated to strengthen enforcement by private litigants with a view to 'ensur [ing] the precedence of Community public interest and compliance with the Community rules applicable to the award of public supply and public works contracts'.[45] However, it was not ultimately adopted. Instead, the ensuing procedure for the award of public contracts authorizes the Commission to take interim measures. They aim at suspending the implementation of unlawful decisions when the Commission considers that a 'clear and manifest infringement has been committed during a contract award procedure'.[46] The decision must be taken prior to a contract being concluded.

[43] T van Rijn, 'Powers of the Commission' in D Curtin and T Heukels (eds.), *Institutional Dynamics of European Integration. Essays in Honour of Henry G. Schermers. Volume II* (Martinus Nijhoff Publishers, 1994), 413.

[44] Commission Proposal for a Council Directive coordinating the laws, regulations and administrative provisions relating to the application of Community rules on procedures for the award of public supply and public works contracts, COM/1987/134 (SYN 89).

[45] Commission Proposal for a Council Directive coordinating the laws, regulations and administrative provisions relating to the application of Community rules on procedures for the award of public supply and public works contracts, COM/1987/134 (SYN 89).

[46] Council Directive 89/665/EEC of 21 December 1989 on the coordination of the laws, regulations and administrative provisions relating to the application of review procedures to the award of public supply and public works contracts [1989] OJ L395/33, recital 9 of the preamble.

The Commission notifies the member state explaining its conclusion and the member state must reply within 21 days of receipt of notification, confirming that the infringement has been corrected or issue a reasoned submission as to why no correction has been made. As a last option, the member state may issue a notice to the effect that the contract award procedure has been suspended. If a member state opts for the second scenario because judicial review is already taking place, it must keep the Commission informed of the result thereof when possible. The aim of ensuring enforcement is indisputable. Thus the Council explicitly motivates its act by stating that

> the existing arrangements at both national and Community levels for ensuring their [Community Directives on public procurement] application are not always adequate to ensure compliance with the relevant Community provisions particularly at a stage when infringements can be corrected.[47]

At first, the measure appears to be a broadening of the Commission's general enforcement powers. However, the procedure is a preliminary measure. Its functional aim is to ensure compliance by institutionalizing effective and rapid remedies at the stage where infringements can still be rectified.[48] The Court of Justice has clarified the relationship between the procurement procedure and preventive measures vis-à-vis the general EU infringement procedure. It established that infringement proceedings according to Article 258 TFEU constitute the single tool available to the Commission against committed infringements. The special procurement procedure is 'a preliminary measure which can neither derogate from nor replace the powers of the Commission under Article 169 [258 TFEU]'.[49] Hence, the Court of Justice further notes, the Commission's general powers to bring a member state before the Court remains unfettered.[50]

In the White Paper on the Internal Market from 1985, the Commission listed preventive measures as one of the ways it intended to 'carry out its duties of enforcing the rules' and it continues to acclaim the instruments'

[47] Council Directive 89/665/EEC, preamble.

[48] C-433/93 *Commission v Germany* [1995] ECR I-2303, para 23.

[49] C-359/93 *Commission v Netherlands* [1995] ECR I-157, para 13; C-353/96 *Commission v Ireland* [1998] ECR I-8565, para 22, and Opinion of Advocate General Alber in that case, at point 18; Case C-328/96 *Commission v Austria* [1999] ECR I-7479, para 57; and C-79/94 *Commission v Greece* [1995] ECR I-1071, para 11.

[50] C-359/93 *Commission v Netherlands* [1995] ECR I-157.

merits in the broader context of ensuring compliance.[51] Preventive measures no doubt constitute a strong enforcement tool per se and also in conjunction with general EU infringement procedure. Thus, this enforcement power should be taken into account when making a comprehensive depiction of the EU enforcement picture. It should at the same time be noted that corrective measures are no longer applied. According to the Commission this is due to the fact that they 'suffer[ed] from several weaknesses (for instance the need for the Commission to make its decision before the contract is signed; and to show that the alleged infringement was "clear and manifest")'.[52]

There is now a range of sector-specific procurement procedures including one on entities operating in the water, energy, transport, and telecommunications sectors.[53] Measures to anticipate compliance such as consultation, notification, and also prior consent are exceptionally invasive. Thus, FL Kirgis remarks with reference to international law, 'to the extent that formal procedural structures for prior consultation may be desirable, they should be tailored to recurring, relatively well-defined, troublesome situations'.[54] The Directive was intended to provide more easily and directly employable tools to complement the general EU infringement procedure. At the same time, the (then) EC Council members have clearly not been willing to confer strong enough powers on the Commission. Rather, they have tied the procedure in with certain member state safeguards such as the condition that the Commission should demonstrate that an infringement is clear and manifest. However, by doing so, the instruments become

[51] Commission *'Completing the Internal Market'* COM/1985/310; EC Commission *'Internal Market: Commission Presents Ten-Point Plan for Making Europe Better Off'* IP (2003) 645, 7 May 2003; Commission Communication *'European Governance—A White Paper'*, COM/2001/428.

[52] Commission *'Impact Assessment Report: Remedies in the Field of Public Procurement'* (Commission Staff Working Document) SEC/2006/557 (Annex to Commission Proposal for a Directive of the European Parliament and of the Council amending Council Directives 89/665/EEC and 92/13/EEC CEE with regard to improving the effectiveness of review procedures concerning the award of public contracts COM/2006/195).

[53] Council Directive 92/13/EEC of 25 February 1992 coordinating the laws, regulations and administrative provisions relating to the application of Community rules on the procurement procedures of entities operating in the water, energy, transport and telecommunications sectors [1992] OJ L76/14.

[54] FL Kirgis, *Prior Consultation in International Law* (University Press of Virginia, 1983), 375. Cf, JG Merrills, *International Dispute Settlement* (2nd edn, Grotius Publications Ltd, 1991), 3–4. The author distinguishes between consultation, notification, and prior consent in international dispute settlement, the latter being 'an extremely important power'. Moreover, he recognizes that when 'closer regulation is needed more complex institutional arrangements may be appropriate'.

cumbersome to employ. The Commission is of the view that pre-contractual reviews can be made more effective. Notably, it has subsequently proposed a directive which, among other things, aims at ensuring respect for the right to effective remedy and to a fair trial for private and legal persons.[55]

Given the administrative resources of the Commission, it has been unable to achieve comprehensive supervision of all contracts granted in the member states under the public procurement Directives.[56] The Commission's attempt to decentralize supervision by strengthening citizens' remedies against infringements should be seen in that context.

3.2 *Safeguard and emergency measures*

Under the general EU infringement procedure, the Court of Justice appraises member state measures and their compatibility with EU law. It may be different when it comes to safeguard measures taken unilaterally by member states. There is no all-encompassing design for such safeguard clauses. However, the standard type comprises two correlated provisions. One authorizes the member state to take interim measures in derogation from a given harmonized requirement. The authorization is conditional on immediate notification of the Commission. The other allows the Commission to apply the measures at the EU level by means of a committee procedure. Sometimes, for instance, a member state will be required to withdraw a product from the market.[57]

[55] Commission Proposal for a Directive of the European Parliament and of the Council amending Council Directives 89/665/EEC and 92/13/EEC CEE with regard to improving the effectiveness of review procedures concerning the award of public contracts, COM/2006/195 final, recital 20 of the preamble. The proposal was adopted as Directive 2007/66/EC of the European Parliament and of the Council of 11 December 2007 amending Council Directives 89/665/EEC and 92/13/EEC with regard to improving the effectiveness of review procedures concerning the award of public contracts [2007] OJ L 335/31.

[56] Answer by Monti on behalf of the Commission (23 October 1997) to European Parliament Written Question No 2722/97 (Awarding of contracts for projects co-financed by the European Union) [1998] OJ C134/18.

[57] Opinion of Advocate General Jacobs in C-359/92 *Germany v Council* [1994] ECR I-3681, with reference to C-D Ehlermann, 'The Internal Market following the Single European Act' (1987) *Common Market Law Review* 24, 398–9. See, eg, Art 9 of Council Directive 92/59/EEC of 29 June 1992 on general product safety. The provision enables the Commission to adopt a decision requiring Member States to take measures whereby the placing of a specific consumer product on the market is restricted or that product is withdrawn from the market.

Maintenance of public order and the safeguarding of internal security fall within the member states' exclusive competences. This in turn affects the margin of discretion enjoyed by the member states.[58] To prevent member states from unilaterally introducing protectionist measures disguised as safeguard measures, the Commission has attained special powers of supervision. This right to monitor provisional measures includes powers to require modifications or changes of the measures.[59] Similar instruments are established concerning derogations from Common Market harmonization measures[60] and national security measures.[61]

According to Article 168 TFEU, a high level of human health protection shall be ensured in the implementation of all EU policies and activities. The European Parliament and the Council shall contribute to that objective through adopting measures in the veterinary and phytosanitary fields which have as their direct objective the protection of public health.[62] This is a field where overriding considerations may call for rapid action against non-compliance, in addition to the general interest in ensuring compliance. Thus, the food security rules have been strengthened significantly in favour of the Commission. For instance, the Commission has successfully proposed a range of emergency measures that would 'allow effective action to be taken and avoid artificial disparities in the treatment of food representing a serious risk to human health'.[63] In doing so, it maintained that severe food crises had revealed a need for crisis management procedures. Notably, a number of animal feed and food scares in the 1990s and, in particular, the Belgian crisis in 1999 concerning animal products contaminated with dioxin and polychlorinated biphenyls (PCBs) gave cause for concern. Under the 2002 regulation, the Commission, acting on its own-initiative or at the demand of a member state, can choose among a range of measures of varying intensity in accordance with the situation's seriousness. The most rigorous action is suspension of the placing on the market or use of

[58] C-265/95 *Commission v France* [1997] ECR I-6959, para 33.

[59] European Commission, Directorate General Internal Market (A Philipson), '*Guide to the Concept and Practical Application of Articles 28–30 EC*' (January 2001) 23.

[60] Article 114(4)–(9) TFEU.

[61] Articles 346, 347, and 348 TFEU.

[62] Article 168(4)(b) TFEU.

[63] Commission Proposal for a Regulation of the European Parliament and of the Council laying down the general principles and requirements of food law, establishing the European Food Authority, and laying down procedures in matters of food, COM/2000/716, recital 56 of the preamble.

the food in question.[64] Such measure is no doubt of an intrusive nature. In particular, the member state is without influence on the Commission's decision. However, the powers conferred upon the Commission were carefully counterbalanced by a supplementary clause. It prescribes that the instrument chosen should be confirmed, amended, revoked, or extended within the framework of a regulatory committee.[65]

The Commission readily admits that such measures are interchangeable with Article 258 TFEU. Thus, in a later proposal for a regulation on Community safeguard measures concerning feed and food controls, the Commission reasons that the general EU infringement procedure

> ...offers a tool for the Commission to proceed against Member States that fail to implement Community law. Although this procedure is a powerful instrument, the time constraints imposed render it impractical where a failure to implement Community law requires prompt action to safeguard feed and food safety.[66]

In the particular case of dioxin contamination, the award of executive powers to the Commission has had considerable merits in terms of scaling down direct infringement actions. Thus, in 1999 alone, the dioxin crisis triggered 100 cases under the general EU infringement procedure.[67] Proceedings were opened against Belgium, which was held responsible for failing, for months, to inform the Commission of the contamination.[68] However the majority of cases concerned other member states, which

[64] Regulation No 178/2002 of the European Parliament and of the Council of 28 January 2002 laying down the general principles and requirements of food law, establishing the European Food Safety Authority and laying down procedures in matters of food safety [2002] OJ L31/1 Art 53. The Regulation has a legal basis in ex Arts 37, 95, 133, and 152(4)(b) EC.

[65] Article 5 of Council Decision 1999/468/EC of 28 June 1999 laying down the procedures for the exercise of implementing powers conferred on the Commission [1999] OJ L184/23. As mentioned in the introduction, Art 291 TFEU changes the Commission's exercise of powers of implementation. See, in that regard, Regulation (EU) No 182/2011 of the European Parliament and the Council of 16 February 2011 laying down the rules and general principles concerning mechanisms for control by Member States of the Commission's exercise of implementing powers [2011] OJ L 55/13. The Regulation repeals Decision 1999/468.

[66] Commission Proposal for a Regulation of the European Parliament and of the Council on official feed and food controls, COM/2003/52, recital 56 of the preamble.

[67] Commission *'17th annual report on monitoring the application of EU law'*, 2000/92 final.

[68] The notification obligation is stipulated in Council Directive 89/662/EEC of 11 December 1989 concerning veterinary checks in intra-Community trade with a view to the completion of the internal market [1989] OJ L395/13; and Council Directive 90/425/EEC of 26 June 1990 concerning veterinary and zootechnical checks applicable in intra-Community trade in certain live animals and products with a view to the completion of the internal market [1990] OJ L224/29.

imposed unlawful trade restrictions against Belgium in response to its apparent non-compliance.[69]

3.3 *Correction measures (conditionality)*

According to Article 317 TFEU, the Commission shall implement the EU budget

> on its own responsibility and within the limits of the appropriations, having regard to the principles of sound financial management. Member States shall cooperate with the Commission to ensure that the appropriations are used in accordance with the principles of sound financial management.

Prior to the Lisbon Treaty the Court of Justice confirmed that oversight through comitology arrangements does not infringe the Commission's power under Article 317 TFEU (ex Article 274 EC) to implement the budget on its own responsibility.[70] In a proposal for a Regulation on the financial rules applicable to the annual budget of the Union, the Commission suggests that it should be empowered to adopt delegated acts in accordance with Article 290 TFEU.[71] According to this legal basis the European Parliament and the Council may entrust delegated powers to the Commission only '... to supplement or amend certain non-essential elements of the [concerned] legislative act'.

Article 174(1) TFEU stipulates that the EU shall 'develop and pursue its actions leading to the strengthening of its economic, social and territorial cohesion'. The aim is to reduce 'disparities between the levels of development of the various regions and the backwardness of the least favoured regions'.[72] In the period 2007–13, the regional policies are allocated some 348 billion euros. 278 billion euros are assigned under the Structural Funds and 70 billion euros under the Cohesion Fund. Amounting to 35 per cent of

[69] For other examples of safeguard measures, see, eg, Directive 2009/142/EC of the European Parliament and of the Council of 30 November 2009 relating to appliances burning gaseous fuels [2009] OJ L 330/10–27; and Commission Staff Working Document *'Situation in Different Sectors'*—accompanying document to the Report from the Commission 27th Annual Report on Monitoring the Application of EU Law (2009), SEC/2010/1143 final, 43.

[70] Case C-16/88 *Commission v Council* [1989] ECR 3457, para 18.

[71] Commission Proposal for a Regulation on the financial rules applicable to the annual budget of the Union, COM/2010/815 final.

[72] Article 174(2) TFEU.

the Community budget, it is the second-largest item on the Community budget.[73]

The autonomous powers of the Commission have been used to forge the Commission's role in EU regional policy. Bausili thus notes that the Commission, particularly owing to its institutional autonomy, has been the driving force behind the current system where funding relies on EU criteria.[74] Moreover, this development has resulted in 'material expansion of competences, or to the development of new policy directions'.[75] This effectively reflects the fact that the Rome Treaty did not foresee the inception of Structural Funds. In its administrative function managing EU resources and in particular the Structural Funds, the Commission possesses implementing powers that bear some resemblance to actual enforcement powers. Significantly, the procedural arrangements include compliance assessments. The ensuing appraisals entail genuine consequences, such as the loss of privileges.

In relation to the common agricultural policy the Court of Justice has confirmed that the Commission has power to provide for penalties on a trader. This includes exclusions from subsidies and surcharges on amounts wrongly received and having to be repaid. Those penalties in fact come within the scope of implementing powers that the Council may delegate to the Commission. The mechanism is not a mere correction tool, but has an additional enforcement purpose.[76] It is different vis-à-vis member states. Correction may effectively appear interchangeable with the general EU infringement procedure from the member states' viewpoint. For instance, Greece maintained that a 'correction may be regarded as a penalty' in its interventions in case C-332/01.[77] However, whereas penalties serve the purpose of ensuring compliance in line with the literal meaning of the word, namely to punish or to deter unlawful conduct with a view to bring about compliance, conditionality is different in its purpose and method. It is a substantive and formal management principle and its modus operandi for

[73] See Europa.eu website, glossary entry for Structural Funds and Cohesion Fund. Can be found at http://europa.eu/legislation_summaries/glossary.

[74] AV Bausili, 'Rethinking the Methods of Dividing and Exercising Powers in the EU: Reforming Subsidiarity and National Parliaments' Jean *Monnet Working Paper* 2000/9.

[75] AV Bausili, 'Rethinking the Methods of Dividing and Exercising Powers in the EU: Reforming Subsidiarity and National Parliaments' *Jean Monnet Working Paper* 2000/9, 3.

[76] C-240/90 *Germany v Commission* [1992] ECR I-5383, para 29.

[77] C-332/01 *Greece v Commission* [2004] ECR I-7699. See also C-247/98 *Greece v Commission* [2001] ECR I-1, paras 13 and 14.

clearing accounts 'serve to determine that the financial burdens . . . are correctly apportioned between the Member States and the Community'.[78] The mechanism is foreseen to remedy unlawful expenditure and the correction is typically proportional to the scale of the infringement, ie, the unlawful receipt of aid.

Council Regulation 2988/95 on the protection of the European Communities' financial interests provides some guidance on the difference between penalties and administrative measures. In this regulation, the administrative measures are aimed at the 'withdrawal of . . . wrongly obtained advantage' either by (re)payment of the received amount or total or partial loss of prepaid security. Thus, there is a correlation between the unlawfully obtained amount and the size of the administrative fine. More exactly, the method of calculation entails that there is no sanctioning effect in the corrective measure.

The relationship between the Commission's actions as an executive branch of government managing Structural Funds and in its function as guardian according to Article 258 TFEU has been clarified by the Court of Justice. *De jure*, the procedures are not related and action undertaken under one is without relevance for the other. In C-325/94 P *An Taisce v Commission*, An Taisce, The National Trust for Ireland, and the World Wide Fund for Nature UK, brought a case against the Commission. It sought, first, annulment of the Commission's decision not to suspend or withdraw the allocation of Community Structural Funds for financing an interpretative centre for tourists in Mullaghmore, Ireland and, secondly, not to initiate infringement proceedings for failure to live up to Community environmental standards.[79] The applicants claimed that the Court of First Instance (now the General Court) should annul both decisions. However, as discussed in chapter two, the Commission enjoys wide discretion according to the general EU infringement procedure. The remaining question was whether such a decision implicitly meant that the Commission also decided, at that time, not to suspend or reduce Community funds. The Court of First Instance and, subsequently, the Court of Justice rejected this line

[78] C-247/98 *Hellenic Republic v Commission* [2001] ECR I-1, para 13.

[79] Council Directive 85/337/EEC of 27 June 1985 on the assessment of the effects of certain public and private projects on the environment [1985] OJ L175/40; and Council Directive 80/68/EEC of 17 December 1979 on the protection of groundwater against pollution caused by certain dangerous substances [1980] OJ L20/43.

of interpretation.[80] The Court of Justice ruled that the 'two procedures are independent of each other, serve different aims and are subject to different rules'.[81] Hence, a decision in the administrative phase of Article 258 TFEU is without prejudice to the Structural Funds. The Commission has subsequently decided that although politically and legally independent of each other 'there must be a degree of consistency between the two [procedures]', ie, between infringement proceedings and the procedure provided for by Article 24 of Regulation No 4253/88.[82] In practice this has come to mean that the Commission as a rule suspends grant payments when it issues a letter of formal notice. When a reasoned opinion is issued, the Commission will initiate a process to reduce or withdraw funding.[83] The Commission nonetheless emphasizes that the jurisprudence does not imply that the procedures are mutually exclusive. Therefore it retains full discretion under the procedures.[84] Decisions concerning structural funding are binding, subject to judicial scrutiny according to Article 263 TFEU.

As discussed in chapter one, the semi-political nature of the Commission's role under general EU infringement procedure is reflected, among other things, by the fact that the Commission College bears collective, political responsibility for its actions.[85] By contrast, when it comes to supervision of revenue and expenditure, decision-making power can be delegated to the relevant Commission Directorate-General.[86] Thus, it takes the form of an administrative decision. As result, the political dimension is significantly downplayed. This is in part because the Commission is obliged under Article 325(1) TFEU to retrieve unlawful payments, 'whether by error, irregularity or deliberate fraud'.[87] No doubt, it makes a

[80] T-461/93 *An Taisce v Commission* [1994] II-733, para 38; and C-325/94 P *An Taisce v Commission* [1996] ECR I-3727, para 37.

[81] T-461/93 *An Taisce v Commission* [1994] II-733, para 38; and C-325/94 P *An Taisce v Commission* [1996] ECR I-3727, summary.

[82] Commission '*16th annual report on monitoring the application of Community law*', COM/1999/301.

[83] Commission, '*17th annual report on monitoring the application of Community law*', 2000/92 final.

[84] Commission '*15th annual report on monitoring the application of Community law*' [1998] OJ C250.

[85] C-191/95 *Commission v Germany* [1998] ECR I-5449, para 34.

[86] Commission Decision 74/55/EEC of 22 January 1974 conferring powers to carry out measures of control in Member States in respect of Community revenue and expenditure [1974] OJ L34/28.

[87] Commission '*Implementation of the European Union's Budget*', MEMO (2005) 421, 14 November 2005.

difference that subsidies for the most are based on conditions that are fairly concrete. Even when the Commission enjoys some discretion in determining whether they have been met, this type of executive decision-making is fundamentally different from the discretionary choices made by the Commission under the general EU infringement procedure.

The semi-political trait of the general EU infringement procedure, apparent from the margin of discretion attributed to the Commission, does not necessarily apply to the legal framework of the Structural Funds. Instead, the Commission can be obliged to undertake financial correction where the conditions for funding have not been observed.[88] Moreover, whereas the general infringement procedure is of a neutral nature, corrections may rest on a culpability criterion.[89]

To recap, the 'EU legislator' and also the Commission may make member state entitlement to resources conditional. Strictly speaking, conditionality does not serve an enforcement purpose. Rather, applying the system is within the Commission's powers of implementation (in the general sense of implementation, ie, not necessarily according to Article 291 TFEU). Conditionality appears to substantiate some of the assumptions behind coercion and incentive-based enforcement theories. The funds are however established with a view to tackle structural problems and essentially constitute managerial instruments. The measures entail a high degree of compliance with the regulations on Structural Funds. However, there is reason not to overestimate the general significance of conditionality. The vast majority of EU infringement cases relate to compliance with obligations of a non-(re)distributive nature and the conditions for establishing conditionality are not present. It may also not be desirable in that it necessitates close supervision. The costs connected with supervision may thus outweigh the advantages in terms of compliance.

Another question is whether the funding system can be expected to have some extra-legal effect on the member states' perception of direct sanctions. A judgment according to Article 258 TFEU does not affect the member state negatively like suspension and reduction of structural assistance.

[88] C-332/01 *Greece v Commission* [2004] ECR I-7699, para 63.

[89] See, eg, Regulation No 1655/1999 laying down general rules for the granting of Community aid in the field of trans-European networks [1999] OJ L197/1: 'Except where the Member States and/or the implementing authority provide proof that they were not responsible for the irregularity, the Member State shall be liable in the alternative for reimbursement of any sums unduly paid.' In comparison, the Court of Justice has consistently held that a member state cannot plead internal circumstances under the general infringement procedure.

Lump sum and penalty payments according to Article 260 TFEU and reduction and suspension of Structural Funds also have different *ratio legis*. The purpose of EU sanctions is to bring about compliance. Reduction and suspension are management measures. They are supposed to remedy situations where EU funds have been distributed without the conditions for receiving them have been fulfilled. However, given Greece's perception that corrections have a penal nature,[90] conditionality may indirectly bring about an incremental normalization of sanction-type Commission powers. Moreover, as the Commission plays an active role in defining the substantive conditions for Structural Funds, it may effectively turn conditionality into a new means of enforcement. This is the case when funds are linked to compliance with otherwise materially unconnected EU policies. To illustrate, in 2010 the Commission aired the idea of suspending Structural Fund payments to euro-area countries that display excessive deficits and fail to take effective action to comply with a Council recommendation according to Article 126(8) TFEU. The Commission thus employs implementation powers with the aim of enforcing EU legislation against recalcitrant member states.[91]

4. Limitations on the Commission in Ensuring Compliance via Implementation

4.1 *Proportionality*

This chapter has examined a range of implementation powers that have characteristics in common with enforcement powers. However, they are not strictly speaking enforcement powers and the 'EU legislator' can legitimately confer them to the Commission. Significantly, the Commission can choose to employ such powers to bring about changes in the member states' behaviour with a view to anticipate or remedy alleged non-compliance. Specifically, the instruments can function as extra-Treaty enforcement

[90] C-332/01 *Greece v Commission* [2004] ECR I-7699.

[91] Answer given by Commissioner Rehn on behalf of the Commission to Written Question E-3580/2010, OJ C 138 E, 07/05/2011. See also answer given by Commissioner Rehn on behalf of the Commission to Written Question E-3581/2010, OJ C 138 E, 07/05/2011; and Commission Communication '*Enhancing Economic Policy Coordination for Stability, Growth and Jobs–Tools for Stronger EU Economic Governance*', COM/2010/367 final.

powers in that (1a) they concern an interpretive uncertainty and/or (1b) they imply an assessment of member state future or present application of EU law (performance/lawfulness) and (2) the Commission is entitled to issue a binding dictate upon the member states to take action in a general or specific manner. This section examines whether there are limits to how and when the Commission can employ implementation measures as an auxiliary means of ensuring member state compliance. The primary focus is on legal constraints. The subsequent section discusses how any perceived abuse of such measures may entail extra-legal consequences for the Commission.

Implementation concerns putting law into effect. Enforcement by contrast concerns the question whether a given law has been implemented and enforced correctly. Under this conceptualization, the two notions are distinct and seemingly neither compatible nor interchangeable. The Court of Justice has, however, acknowledged that the 'EU legislator' (then, the Council) can attribute implementation powers to the Commission to tackle compliance obstacles that could otherwise be pursued under Article 258 TFEU. The Court proceeded to test the particular rule according to the EU principle of proportionality, which prescribes that 'measures taken by the Community institutions should be appropriate to achieve the objective pursued without going beyond what is necessary to that end'. The principle requires that a measure, be it a regulation, a directive, a decision, or an opinion, does not exceed the limits of what is appropriate and necessary in order to attain the objectives pursued. Furthermore, when there is a choice between several appropriate measures, recourse must be to the least onerous possible, and the disadvantages caused must not be disproportionate to the aims pursued.[92] These conditions can be made subject to judicial review. However, given the inherent degree of political discretion such decisions display it is unclear to what extent the Court of Justice of the European Union is willing to engage in a substantive review. In C-359/92 *Germany v Council*,[93] the Court of Justice ruled on Article 9 of Council Directive 92/59EEC of 29 June 1992 on general product safety. This provision allows the Commission to adopt a decision requiring member states to take temporary measures, such as restricting or prohibiting the sale

[92] See joined cases C-96/03 and C-97/03 *Tempelman and van Schaijk* [2005] ECR I-1895, para 47; C-189/01 *Jippes and Others* [2001] ECR I-5689, para 81; joined cases C-27/00 and C-122/00 *Omega Air and Others* [2002] ECR I-2569, para 62; C-112/00 *Schmidberger* [2003] ECR I-5659, para 79; and C-220/01 *Lennox* [2003] ECR I-7091, para 76.

[93] C-359/92 *Germany v Council* [1994] ECR I-3681.

of products in certain situations. The Directive was intended to establish mechanisms to remedy emergency product safety situations in an urgent manner. At the same time, it allowed for 'the adoption of measures applicable throughout the Community in the form of a decision addressed to the member states'.[94] Decision-making power was delegated to the Commission in this respect. However, the Council members retained some decision-making powers through comitology, establishing a regulatory committee.[95] Germany disputed the legality of Article 9, which enabled the legislator to lay down measures relating to a specific product or class of products and, if necessary, individual measures concerning those products. One of Germany's pleas in law concerned the proportionality of conferring those powers on the Commission. Thus, it was the original act of delegation that was reviewed. The Commission could, Germany argued, pursue non-compliance under the general infringement procedure. The Court of Justice, however, found the procedure to pass the proportionality test given that Article 258 TFEU is declaratory and hence does not allow for specific prescriptions as to which measures the member state shall take. Moreover, the infringement procedure was portrayed as protracted in that the Commission would have to pursue many individual infringements for failure to comply with the Directive. Finally, the objectives of the Directive, namely to uphold consumer protection in the shortest possible time, would not be attainable otherwise.

4.2 *Use and misuse*

The Commission has failed to gain power to award interim measures within the area of public procurement.[96] Hence, it remains a sole competence of the Court of Justice. However, the requirement for applying interim

[94] Council Directive 92/59/EEC of 29 June 1992 on general product safety [1992] OJ L228/24, recital 24 of the preamble.

[95] According to this comitology-type, the Council was the final decision-maker in cases where the Commission measure was not in accordance with a committee opinion. Note Regulation (EU) No 182/2011 of the European Parliament and the Council of 16 February 2011 laying down the rules and general principles concerning mechanisms for control by Member States of the Commission's exercise of implementing powers, (2011) OJ L 55/13, which repeals Decision 1999/468.

[96] Commission Proposal for a Council Directive coordinating the laws, regulations and administrative provisions relating to the application of Community rules on procedures for the award of public supply and public works contracts, COM/1987/134 (SYN 89), Art 2.

measures renders it of little use as a general instrument.[97] Commission powers to take specific emergency measures with immediate effect are, by contrast, commonly established in secondary legislation.[98] These emergency measures serve a different purpose from infringement proceedings. It could be, for instance, to counteract deterioration of fish stocks and other common marine resources. Thus, they have no implications for the distribution of enforcement powers between the Commission and the Court of Justice, which was discussed in more detail in chapter four. The Commission's actual usage of emergency measures may nevertheless give rise to legality questions since this type of measure opens up for the introduction of disguised interim measures.

The CFP provides an example of the possible combined effect of enforcement and implementation powers. The EU has the internal power to take any measure for the conservation of the biological resources of the sea.[99] However, the member states are responsible for compliance within their territories. Member state failure to comply in this regard can only be pursued under the general infringement procedure.[100] In a press release concerning proceedings against Spain and UK, the Commission states that '[f]ollowing the CFP reform, the procedure combines the three-step infringement procedure with the possibility for the Commission to take preventive measures if non-compliance could lead to a serious threat to fish stocks'.[101] The Commission has wide discretion to decide on preventive

[97] See Art 279 TFEU. The Court of Justice grants relief when required 'in order to prevent serious and irreparable damage by the immediate application of the measure which is the subject of the main proceedings'. See C-296/93 R *France v Commission* [1993] ECR I-4181, para 18. Pecuniary damage is, in principle, not to be regarded as irreparable. See C-195/90 R *Commission v Germany* [1990] ECR I-3351, paras 38 and 40. By contrast, 'harm caused to the protection of the environment and to health is generally irreversible since, more often than not, damage to such interests cannot, by reason of its nature, be eliminated retroactively'. See the summary of the Order by the President of the Court of 2 October 2003 in C-320/03 R *Commission v Austria* [2003] ECR I-11665 (interlocutory proceedings). See also chapter two on the Commission's use of interim measures.

[98] See, eg, Council Regulation (EC) No 2371/2002 of 20 December 2002 on the conservation and sustainable exploitation of fisheries resources under the Common Fisheries Policy [2002] OJ L358/59, Art 7.

[99] Joined cases 3/76, 4/76, and 6/76 *Kramer and Others* [1976] ECR 1279; and C-25/94 *Commission v Council* [1996] ECR I-1469.

[100] See, eg, European Parliament Fisheries Committee *'Own-initiative report on the Commission report "Towards uniform and effective implementation of the Common Fisheries Policy"'* (A5–331/2003), 5, point G.

[101] Commission *'Fisheries: Commission opens infringement procedure against Spain and UK for failure to enforce certain fisheries rules'* (Press Release IP/03/1534), 11 November 2003.

measures. When used in combination with Article 258 TFEU, it effectively introduces a fourth element to the general infringement procedure, namely interim measures issued by the Commission. It is likewise a strong bargaining power *ex ante*. In cases against Spain and UK, the Commission sent letters of formal notice concerning a number of detected, or proclaimed, shortcomings in terms of fishing inspections and landing activity. Spain and the UK were awarded two months to respond to the letter of formal notice. The message was that '[i]n case of non-compliance [with the letter of formal notice], the Commission may take the necessary preventive measures to protect the threatened fish resources and issue a reasoned opinion to the member state concerned'.[102] Preventive measures can thus be used as a means to put pressure on the member states to comply with non-binding instruments, such as letters of notice.

This would not however amount to a misuse of powers or abuse of process under Article 263 TFEU. Misuse of powers, or manifest misuse of powers,[103] is sometimes referred to as *Détournement de Pouvoir*[104] or the German notion *Ermessensmibrauch*.[105] The Court of Justice has clarified with specific address to the (E)EC Treaty that a decision may amount to

[102] Commission *'Fisheries: Commission opens infringement procedure against Spain and UK for failure to enforce certain fisheries rules'* (Press Release IP/03/1534), 11 November 2003.

[103] Opinion of Advocate General Lenz in C-45/86 *Commission v Council* [1987] ECR I-1493, point 73.

[104] The notion, borrowed from French administrative law, signifies an administrative measure which 'though within the legal competence of the agent, is in reality done for another purpose than that which the law authorising it had in mind'. JW Garner, 'French Administrative Law' (1924) *Yale Law Journal* 33:6, 597–627, 597, 609. The French notion moreover has a subjective connotation: the 'misuse of powers is understood as relating to the defect by which an administrative measure is vitiated where an administrative authority has wilfully used its powers for a purpose other than that for which they were conferred upon it'. FA Schockweiler, 'La notion de détournement de pouvoir en droit communautaire' (1990) *Actualité juridique de droit administratif* 435, translated by Advocate General Biancarelli in his opinion in Case T-120/89 *Stahlwerke Peine-Salzgitter AG v Commission* [1991] ECR II-279, point 27.

[105] G Bebr, *Judicial Control of the European Communities* (Stevens, 1962), 98, fn 69. The concept prescribes that 'where an administrative authority is empowered to act in its own discretion, it must exercise that power of appraisal in accordance with the purpose for which it was granted and within the legally prescribed limits. That obligation is infringed where . . . the authority exceeds the limits of its power of appraisal or deviates from the purpose for which the power was granted to it'. FA Schockweiler, 'La notion de détournement de pouvoir en droit communautaire' (1990) *Actualité juridique de droit administratif* 6, 435, translated by Advocate General Biancarelli in his opinion in Case T-120/89 *Stahlwerke Peine-Salzgitter AG v Commission* [1991] ECR II-279.

a misuse of powers only if it appears, on the basis of objective, relevant and consistent factors, to have been taken with the exclusive purpose, or at any rate the main purpose, of achieving an end other than that stated or evading a procedure specifically prescribed by the Treaty for dealing with the circumstances of the case.[106]

The condition that misuse hinges upon proof that 'the exclusive purpose, or at any rate the main purpose, of achieving an end other than that stated' allows the Commission a substantial margin of discretion. Thus, a secondary interest in enforcement considerations would be lawful, provided that the principal purpose of the legal basis is present. For the most part there is natural coincidence between infringements and the circumstances which justify, for instance, emergency measures.[107] More generally, the extensive body of EU administrative law should be kept in mind, and the procedural constraints that this increasingly places on the Commission. Thus, the Court of Justice and the General Court shape decision-making here in important ways, through reason-giving examples, demands upon the integrity of the informational base for decision-making, and the nature of the relevant expertise called to bear on the decision-making process.[108]

Whilst the legal analysis of this chapter concludes that the discretion of the Commission is virtually unfettered when it comes to employing implementation powers against the member states, in the broader context of ensuring compliance, some extra-legal considerations deserve a mention. That is to say, the Commission's tactical yet lawful use of implementation powers may have repercussions in the legislative phase. The following example is taken from the field of animal nutrition. In 2000, the Commission tabled a proposal laying down principles governing the organization of official inspections in the field of animal nutrition and on undesirable substances and products in animal nutrition.[109] The proposal authorized the Commission to take 'interim protective measures concerning feedingstuffs and products used in animal nutrition produced within the EU in the

[106] C-310/04 *Spain v Council* [2006] ECR I-7285, para 69.

[107] The burden of proving that the Commission has indeed pursued an aim other than those it invokes rests on the Member State. Joined cases C-296/93 and C-307/93 *France and Ireland v Commission* [1996] ECR I-795, para 38.

[108] I would like to thank Joanne Scott for pointing this out.

[109] Commission Proposal for a European Parliament and Council Directive amending Council Directive 95/53/EC fixing the principles governing the organisation of official inspections in the field of animal nutrition and Council Directive 1999/29/EC on undesirable substances and products in animal nutrition, COM/2000/162.

event of serious risks to public health, animal health or the environment'.[110] Article 15a, the proposed safeguard clause, read:

1. Where a problem, due to a product to be used in animal nutrition, *likely to pose a serious risk to human or animal health or to the environment* appears or spreads on the territory of the European Union, the Commission, on its own initiative or at the request of a member state, shall immediately, depending on the seriousness of the situation:

- suspend the putting into circulation within the Community and exports to third countries from all or part of the member state(s) concerned and/or
- lay down special conditions for the putting into circulation in the Community and/or exports to third countries of products from all or part of the member state(s) concerned.

2. The Commission shall notify the Council and member states of any decision adopted in accordance with paragraph 1. *Except in emergencies*, the Commission shall consult the member states before taking the measures referred to in paragraph 1.
3. Any member state may, within thirty days of such notification, refer the Commission's decision to the Council. *The Council, acting by a qualified majority, may take a different decision* within thirty days. (Emphasis added.)

In an address to the European Parliament, former Commissioner Byrne maintained that the possibility for the Commission to respond quickly in emergency cases and to react even before consulting member states constituted a landmark question with significant potential in terms of setting legislative precedent. It was, however, the perceived 'risk of abuse' of safeguard measures that had made the Council reluctant to go along with the proposal. According to the Commission, though, there was no evidence of such misuse of comparable instruments.[111] The point of misuse is interesting from a political viewpoint, in addition to the legal question of misuse of power, as dealt with above. In the specific context of safeguard measures and enforcement, the notion of misuse is ambiguous because the

[110] Commission Proposal for a European Parliament and Council Directive amending Council Directive 95/53/EC fixing the principles governing the organisation of official inspections in the field of animal nutrition and Council Directive 1999/29/EC on undesirable substances and products in animal nutrition, COM/2000/162, summary, point IV.

[111] European Parliament *'Animal nutrition inspections'* (Debate, 10 April 2000).

Commission may employ emergency measures whenever the substantive conditions are fulfilled. Thus, the Council's fear that the Commission abuses its powers is essentially a fear that the Commission will promote its preferences beyond those of the Council members'. It is not misuse *de lege*.

The proposed safeguard measures are only applicable in cases where a problem is likely to pose a serious risk and the Commission's special powers are thus conditional. There is, of course, a degree of uncertainty involved in making such an assessment. However, a comparison of the wording of the proposal and the final text shows that the Council has attempted to strike a balance between the interests of ensuring adequate action against foodstuff-contamination in emergency situations, while at the same time restraining the Commission's powers in that regard. Thus, the provision as subsequently adopted by the Council was altered on vital points concerning the Commission's decision-making authority.[112]

Article 15a

1. Where a problem due to a product to be used in animal nutrition, *likely to pose a serious risk to human health, animal health or to the environment*, appears in one or more Member States *and cannot be contained satisfactorily by means of the measures taken by the Member State(s) concerned* [reinforcement of the subsidiarity principle], the Commission, *acting in accordance with the procedure provided for in Article 23a* [The Commission shall adopt the measures envisaged if they are in accordance with the opinion of the Committee] on its own initiative or at the request of a Member State, shall immediately, depending on the seriousness of the situation adopt the following measures:

- suspend the putting into circulation within the Community, the use in animal nutrition or exports to third countries of products from all or part of the Member State(s) concerned or from one or more establishments situated in Community territory, or
- lay down special conditions for the putting into circulation in the Community, the use in animal nutrition or exports to third countries of

[112] Directive 2001/46/EC of the European Parliament and of the Council of 23 July 2001 amending Council Directive 95/53/EC fixing the principles governing the organisation of official inspections in the field of animal nutrition and Directives 70/524/EEC, 96/25/EC, and 1999/29/EC on animal nutrition [2001] OJ L 34/55.

products from all or part of the Member State(s) concerned or from one or more establishments situated in Community territory.

2. However, in emergencies, the Commission may provisionally adopt the measures referred to in paragraph 1 *after consulting the Member State(s)* concerned and informing the other Member States. It shall submit the matter to the Standing Committee for Feeding stuffs set up by Article 1 of Decision 70/372/EEC(10) *within ten working days* for its opinion, in accordance with the procedure laid down in Article 23a [The Commission shall adopt the measures envisaged if they are in accordance with the opinion of the Committee], with a view to the extension, amendment or repeal of those measures. (Emphasis added.)

Given that the Commission employs enforcement, implementation, and soft-law measures as interchangeable policy instruments, member states have reason to monitor the application of safeguard measures. Notably, they imply considerable independent powers on the side of the Commission in comparison with the general EU infringement procedure. Moreover, they have binding effect as opposed to soft-law measures. Tying in the Commission's powers in with scrutiny by the Council and European Parliament according to Article 290 TFEU or member state supervision according to Article 291 TFEU constitute useful methods to constrain the Commission's exercise of powers. Not least the member state oversight mechanism connected with implementing acts may prevent the Commission from applying additional enforcement pressure on individual member states, either in combination with or independent of the infringement procedure.[113]

A Commission proposal from 2003 for a regulation on official feed and food controls[114] illustrates the linkage between implementation measures

[113] The Commission's exercise of implementing acts is controlled by the member states. See Regulation (EU) No 182/2011 of the European Parliament and the Council of 16 February 2011 laying down the rules and general principles concerning mechanisms for control by Member States of the Commission's exercise of implementing powers (OJ 2011 L 55, p 13), which repeals Decision 1999/468, as amended by Council Decision 2006/512/EC ('the Comitology Decision'). The European Parliament plays a role according to Art 11 concerning right of scrutiny for the European Parliament and the Council. The European Parliament and Council scrutinize delegated acts. See Communication from the Commission to the European Parliament and the Council *'Implementation of Article 290 of the Treaty on the Functioning of the European Union'*, COM/2009/0673 final.

[114] Commission Proposal for a Regulation of the European Parliament and of the Council on official feed and food controls, COM/2003/52.

(in its general sense) and purposes concerning enforcement as well as the control the Council can establish when delegating power to the Commission. In the explanatory summary the Commission explains that the document

> ... contains *new tools for the Commission to enforce* the implementation of Community feed and food law by the Member States. Inspections and audits by the Commission's Food and Veterinary Office (FVO) shall be organised to verify the effectiveness of national control systems. *Additional tools for the Commission to enforce implementation of Community feed and food law by Member States must be made available.*[115] (Emphasis added.)

The regulation that was finally adopted contains a chapter explicitly dealing with enforcement of Community law and one of the sub-provisions establishes certain safeguard measures. It empowers the Commission to adopt measures against a member state that is non-compliant and has failed to remedy the situation upon the Commission's request within a deadline set by the Commission. The Commission shall demonstrate the existence of a 'serious failure in a member state's control systems', which 'may constitute a possible and widespread risk for human health, animal health or animal welfare'.[116] The list of measures available range from suspension of the placing on the market or use of the food in question, laying down special conditions for the food or feed in question, or interim measures. The Commission is assisted by a so-called Standing Committee on the Food Chain and Animal Health, then working according to the regulatory procedure. Under that procedure the Commission can only adopt a measure after committee approval by a qualified majority. Where the Commission fails to obtain approval, the Council can adopt it by qualified majority. If it fails to do so, the Commission can nevertheless adopt the measure as long as the Council does not block it by qualified majority.

4.3 *The interplay between implementation and enforcement*

Employing implementation measures with the aim of ensuring compliance raises the normative question of who shall decide on how to give EU law

[115] Commission Proposal for a Regulation of the European Parliament and of the Council on official feed and food controls, COM/2003/52, explanatory memorandum, point 5.

[116] Article 56 of Regulation (EC) No 882/2004 of the European Parliament and of the Council of 29 April 2004 on official controls performed to ensure the verification of compliance with feed and food law, animal health and animal welfare rules [2004] OJ L165/1.

effect. This is not least the case concerning the examined (i) preventive measures (ii) safeguard and emergency measures. Specifically, tackling compliance issues in this manner reduces the degree of autonomy and self-management member states would otherwise enjoy. This is one of the reasons why the member states insist on retaining political and legal oversight upon delegation to the Commission under Articles 290 and 291 TFEU (through the Council together with the European Parliament or acting as member states, respectively).

Delegating implementing powers (Article 291 TFEU) to the Commission and thus reintroducing the member states in the post-legislative phase through comitology changes the relative influence of the member states and the Commission. On the one hand the Commission is strengthened. On the other, comitology oversight constrains the Commission. The same holds true for delegated acts (Article 290 TFEU). Some argue that the Council and European Parliament '... now have the power to object to an individual Delegated Act on any grounds whatsoever'.[117] Similarly, the Council and European Parliament ultimately enjoy a right to revoke the delegation which has potential to become a strong bargaining tool.[118]

The next chapter maintains that the general EU infringement procedure can usefully be described in governance terms. The procedural framework fosters dialogue and semi-legal, semi-political political problem-solving. In this process, the Commission functions as an interpretative and political contestant and essentially as a facilitator of compliance. The method generates processes according to which the member states can refine the content of their legal obligations and discern how to meet them. The Commission's execution of power upon delegation and the attached oversight mechanisms also bring about political process, albeit within a clearly defined and outcome-relevant procedural framework. Policy implementation 'in the Community has to be understood as a mixture of majoritarian and deliberative elements which together form a peculiar European combination that can be conceived as a "political administration"'.[119] It may be contended that there is some resemblance between enforcement and implementation when characterized in the above manner. However, such a

[117] EIPA, 'Delegated & Implementing Acts—The New Comitology' (4th edn, *EIPA Essential Guide*, December 2011), 13.

[118] On a note, the Council and the European Parliament may have different opinions of how the Commission should manage its delegated powers.

[119] J Neyer, 'Limits of (the) Community: Compliance in the European Union—The Example of BSE', Paper presented at the 1999 ECPR Joint Sessions, Mannheim.

comparison blurs very central features of the respective processes. The Commission's absolute discretion under Article 258 TFEU does allow room for political considerations, in addition to the more technical, legal exchange of views. However, there is no procedurally recognized access to political recourse by, for instance, bringing up the matter in the Council, as there is to different degrees under the various comitology procedures.[120] It is not least the exclusion of the Council from the general EU infringement procedure which sets it apart from the infringement procedure under the former ECSC Treaty. Moreover, it constitutes a central element of the EU treaty-regime based on the rule of law. As Advocate General Mischo notes, it is 'indeed because each party sticks to its position, for whatever reason, that this stage of seeking a friendly settlement is followed by a contentious stage, during which both parties' positions are assessed by the Court in the light of the requirements of the rule of law'.[121]

To the extent that the Commission deals with non-compliance through implementation procedures, the potential consequences of reintroducing, so to speak, the 'EU legislator' and the member states merits further comment. Whereas inter-institutional rivalry between the Council and the Parliament over comitology has previously had a negative influence on the legislative process and made it more cumbersome, the general legislative climate may be improved post-Lisbon. In this way Mr Corbett, who negotiated on behalf of the European Parliament when the regulatory procedure with scrutiny was first introduced, noted that it will be an advantage for the Council to know that 'the Parliament will be more relaxed about delegating implementing powers in the first place, if we are given the right to object'.[122] However, some member states have been reluctant to

[120] See Council Decision 1999/468/EC of 28 June 1999 laying down the procedures for the exercise of implementing powers conferred on the Commission [1999] OJ L184/23, as amended by Council Decision 2006/512/EC of 17 July 2006 [2006] OJ L200/11.

[121] Opinion of Advocate General Mischo in Case C-1/00 *Commission v France* (British beef and veal) [2001] ECR I-9989, point 52. It is crucial to the ultimate authority of the Court of Justice that it is corroborated through Member State compliance with its judgments. Open non-compliance is seldom. For a persuasive explanatory approach, see, eg, D Beach, 'Why Governments Comply: An Integrative Compliance Model that Bridges the Gap between Instrumental and Normative Models of Compliance' (2005) *Journal of European Public Policy* 12:1, 113–42.

[122] Quoted in 'MEPs get new watchdog role on Commission's daily work' *EU Observer* (5 July 2006). The European Parliament previously used its budgetary authority to exert pressure on the negotiations. European Parliament, 'Report on Council Decision 1999/468/EC of 28 June 1999 laying down the procedures for the exercise of implementing powers conferred on the Commission' (A6–236/2006, 7 February 2006, 8).

empower the European Parliament in the implementation phase in politically contentious areas, in particular, when it comes to the question of genetically modified organisms (GMOs). For this reason, UK Minister of Europe, Mr Geoffrey Hoon remarks in an Explanatory Memorandum of 3 July, one 'Member State . . . was particularly concerned about sensitive areas such as GMO authorisations. These concerns have now been addressed by means of the statement in the Draft summary record of the Coreper meeting at Annex III of document 10125/1/06'.[123] It is possible that the European Parliament, and also the member states, will bring considerations to the table that would not be accepted by the Court of Justice during enforcement proceedings. The implications of the amended legal framework established under Articles 290 and 291 TFEU and partial introduction of the European Parliament in the implementation phase on certain safeguard procedures, and more generally, are currently unclear. However, there are policy areas in which the European Parliament is likely to be a proponent of consumer interests and also socio-economic considerations to a greater extent than the Council and certainly than the Commission. Shaffer and Pollack, for instance, argue that the 'EP has become a primary means for prompting the consideration of non-economic factors (environmental, societal, regional, and so forth) and has had increasing impact as its legislative powers have grown'.[124] To this, it can be added that non-economic concerns may now be backed by the European Parliament in the implementation phase. Thus whereas the European Parliament sometimes functions as a strategic ally of the Commission in enforcement matters, it may also prove to set hurdles when member state compliance is pursued through implementation measures.

In her examination of the prior authorization procedure adopted for the deliberate release into the environment of GMOs, Brosset demonstrates how procedures designed to handle different member state interpretations and ultimately to prevent and settle disputes among them, can be effectively 'obstructed by the collaboration itself, which far from eliminating divergent interpretations, has exacerbated them'.[125]

[123] As quoted in the 35th report of the Select Committee on European Scrutiny. Can be accessed at http://www.parliament.the-stationery-office.com/pa/cm200506/cmselect/cmeuleg/34-xxxv/3412.htm.

[124] C Gregory Shaffer and MA Pollack, 'Regulating Between National Fears and Global Disciplines: Agricultural Biotechnology in the EU' (2004) *Jean Monnet Working Paper* 10.

[125] E Brosset, 'The Prior Authorisation Procedure Adopted for the Deliberate Release into the Environment of Genetically Modified Organisms: The Complexities of Balancing Community and National Competences' (2004) *European Law Journal* 10:5, 555, 559.

Reintroducing the 'EU legislator' and the member states in connection with implementation thus raise questions pertaining to effectiveness.[126] The Commission's role under Article 258 TFEU and the unfettered discretion it enjoys is an important part of the story here. The Commission retains the option of initiating infringement proceedings at all time and can use that either as an isolated complementary procedure or as a means of pressure during implementation procedures. Thus, whilst implementation measures are lawful because they are anchored in considerations other than enforcement, they display potential to bolster the infringement procedure when employed in conjunction with it. This further attests to the interplay between enforcement and implementation.

5. Conclusion

Regardless of the lack of legal basis in the EU Treaties to establish infringement procedures on an ad hoc basis, there are apparent functional needs for ways of ensuring compliance in a more coordinated, inclusive, and at times rapid manner than the general EU infringement procedure is geared to. In response to that requirement there has been a proliferation of different types of implementation measures that display functional overlap with enforcement. This chapter demonstrated that various implementation powers can effectively be employed to prevent infringements of EU law, to end non-compliance, to exert enforcement pressure on member states, and as an alternative to interim measures. They have thus come to mark an incremental expansion into a domain otherwise dealt with bilaterally under the general EU infringement procedure. Moreover, acting as a strategic institutional actor, the Commission can pursue enforcement aims in multiple ways. By looking at the functional overlap between implementation and enforcement measures, this chapter advocates that the general EU infringement procedure can usefully be contextualized within the framework of a broader policy process. Indeed this gives a better understanding of the Commission's role in ensuring member state compliance than by looking at Article 258 TFEU as an isolated instrument.

The instruments and techniques examined take quite diverse forms and have different aims. The procedure established in the internal market

[126] It may also be argued that they bolster the legitimacy dimension.

enables self-assessment and multilateral peer-review and, although it attributes a central function to the Commission, it is fairly decentralized in its work-method. The procedure enables broad-spectrum and inclusive supervision with obligations that have proved difficult to enforce systematically under Article 258 TFEU. The Commission has obtained strong executive powers to supervise member states' draft technical regulations, and, significantly to propose or adopt generally applicable measures to forestall potential infringements. This type of mechanism can be applied to ensure that clearly specified types of future regulatory action are in conformity with EU law. However it is not a tool with potential to ensure member states compliance more broadly. The third type of preliminary measure examined concerns pre-contractual review of public supply and public works contracts as they exist in numerous sectors. Experience with procurement procedures suggests some shortcomings in broadening the Commission's executive powers generally with the aim of ensuring compliance. Unless the member states are willing to enlarge considerably the Commission and its resources, it is impracticable for it to monitor and enforce EU law in meticulous detail. It is noteworthy that the Commission, despite those strong powers attributed to it, attempts to enable more effective enforcement through strengthening private litigants' rights. Such decentralization would come to co-exist with the Commission's proactive, preliminary supervision as well as the actions it can take under Article 258 TFEU. However, it is clear that decentralizing enforcement gives the Commission more room of manoeuvre to focus on, for instance, policy-making and to facilitate softer forms of cooperation and spend less time on minute monitoring.

It is the circumstances surrounding safeguard and emergency measures that serve as their justification. Thus, there are situations that may have harmful or irreparable consequences and, for that reason, are best addressed in a highly centralized and swift manner. However, with exception of measures of very short duration, the Council seldom attributes absolute powers to the Commission in this regard. Finally, this chapter looked at the Commission's role in managing Structural Funds. Specific features of redistribution make it difficult to broaden experiences from this field. EU law does not rest on reciprocity and the premises for establishing conditionality are either not present or not desirable. Nevertheless, conditionality is an area in which the Commission plays a key role, resembling direct supervision.

The measures examined entail a loss of member state autonomy in the post-legislative phase and for that reason, the Council (historically) has insisted on retaining some degree of control when delegating powers to the Commission. Interestingly, the distributions of power under the amended comitology-regime and the oversight mechanisms attached to delegated acts beget a responsive dialogue between the Commission and the member states and increasingly so also the European Parliament. The resulting decision-making processes are multilateral; they facilitate mutual learning and broad-spectrum problem-solving, in addition to establishing binding obligations. When viewed as a whole, the measures do not form a coherent picture in the sense of a standardized or formalized procedure established with the purpose of supplementing the general EU infringement procedure. However, when conceptualizing the measures in terms of preventive measures, safeguard and emergency measures and conditionality, some common legal and functional traits stand out. Moreover, to the extent that the 'EU legislator' establishes oversight-mechanisms upon delegation, the comitology-regime (Article 291 TFEU) and oversight according to Article 290 TFEU naturally brings about some consistency. The lack of coherence partly reflects that the measures are tailored to the specific policy issue they address. Significantly, in contrast to the general infringement procedure established in primary law, they can be adapted relatively easily in the light of the experiences they generate. Thus, they come to constitute more flexible, broadly inclusive, discursive supplements to the Commission's powers under Article 258 TFEU.

6

The Emergence of Non-binding, Auxiliary Enforcement Procedures: Expert Management of Compliance with Directives

1. Introduction

Chapter five examined a range of binding implementation tools that display functional overlap with the general EU infringement procedure. This chapter is concerned with the emergence of non-binding, auxiliary enforcement procedures in the EU. It deals more specifically with groups of experts on implementation of directives. The Commission has established a number of groups of experts concerned with member state interpretation and application of EU law, including of directives.[1] Some groups are composed of member state representatives and others include non-state stakeholders. The expert group concerned with the Free Movement Directive[2] examined in this chapter is an example of the former. The Network of Legal Experts on the application of Community Law established in 1984 is an example of the latter. The network is composed of senior lawyers and/or academics, specialized in national legislation in the area of gender equality. It has a three-fold purpose:

[1] Directives frequently oblige member states to submit transposition data to the Commission.

[2] Directive 2004/38/EC of the European Parliament and of the Council of 29 April 2004 on the right of citizens of the Union and their family members to move and reside freely within the territory of the Member States amending Regulation (EEC) No 1612/68 and repealing Directives 64/221/EEC, 68/360/EEC, 72/194/EEC, 73/148/EEC, 75/34/EEC, 75/35/EEC, 90/364/EEC, 90/365/EEC, and 93/96/EEC (2004) OJ L 158/77–123.

> Facilitate the Commission to monitor the implementation of the *acquis communautaire* in the Member states with regard to legislation and case law on equal treatment between women and men. Assist the Commission in the preparation of European Court of Justice cases, in particular infringement procedures... Be a 'think-tank' for assisting the Commission to develop new strategies and ideas.[3]

Infringement proceedings according to the general EU infringement procedure are initiated against one member state and rely predominantly on bilateral, amicable settlements. The supplementary procedures examined in this chapter by contrast involve all the EU member states at the same time. The procedures are established on an ad hoc basis and cover a broad spectrum of EU policy areas, including temporary agency work, air safety, and law regulating the right of EU citizens to move and reside freely within the territory of the member states.[4]

This chapter is structured as follows: The first section discusses some of the limitations of the general EU infringement procedure and the merits of peer-review from an enforcement viewpoint. Against this background, it looks at implementation expert groups and more specifically at the expert group dealing with the Free Movement Directive. It proceeds to problematize the Commission's turn towards management of compliance through implementation expert groups, arguing that the method may obfuscate the fact that enforcement is also about contested norms. The final section examines Article 70 TFEU. This provision was introduced by the Lisbon Treaty and provides express legal basis for peer-review. Albeit not concerned with directives specifically, the provision addresses some of the general issues discussed in this chapter concerning peer-review.

[3] See bulletin posted at www.counsel.net by Network of Legal Experts on the application of Community Law on Equality between Women and Men on 11 December 2006. Another example concerns The Water Framework Directive and the Common Implementation Strategy (CIS). On CIS and other governance arrangements concerned with implementation of EU law and also directives, see CF Sabel and J Zeitlin, 'Learning from Difference: The New Architecture of Experimentalist Governance in the European Union' *EUROGOV* No C07-02.

[4] See, eg, Commission *'27th Annual report on monitoring the application of EU law'*, 5; and Commission Report on the application of Directive 2004/38/EC on the right of citizens of the Union and their family members to move and reside freely within the territory of the Member States, COM/2008/840 final. Implementation working groups are established in many and different policy areas. Often they are coupled with practical implementation reports. Commission Staff Working Document *'Situation in different sectors'*, SEC/2010/1143 final. See also Commission Communication *'Better Monitoring of the Application of Community Law'*, COM/2002/725, 6.

2. Management of Compliance with Directives Through Expert Groups

2.1 *Limitations of the general EU infringement procedure*

Chapter two appraised the general EU infringement procedure stipulated in Article 258 TFEU. The administrative phase of that procedure (where the vast majority of cases are settled) is bilateral and remains largely confidential. This confidentiality allows member states to engage in informal exchanges of view with the Commission and to discuss solutions to compliance problems. According to the Court of Justice there is a close link between this secrecy and the aim of the procedure, which is to reach an amicable agreement. The bilateral and confidential method has advantages in terms of solving concrete cases. In terms of effectiveness it also has drawbacks.[5] Notably, infringement cases do not become comprehensive learning opportunities for other member states. Likewise, the general EU infringement procedure cannot function as a method to examine comprehensively exactly how the member states interpret and implement specific provisions of EU law. Genuine compliance is complicated to establish and thus to monitor even when member states report national transposition measures to the Commission. Significantly, what constitutes correct interpretation and application of EU law is often contestable. Chapter one argued that enforcement of EU law, including directives, therefore requires policy decision-making, in addition to close scrutiny.

Because infringement proceedings are inherently case-specific they cannot deal with more systemic compliance hurdles. The work in implementation expert groups by contrast enables peer-review, peer-learning, and, not least, informal exchange of views between the Commission and the member states. It has a number of advantages in terms of effectiveness compared with the general EU infringement procedure. Both methods can bring about changes in member state behaviour. Expert groups, in addition, can tackle underlying compliance obstacles in a comprehensive manner and thus further general policy objectives.[6] The Commission thus

[5] This is in addition to legitimacy concerns from a citizen perspective.

[6] Compare K Raustiale and A Slaughter, 'International Law, International Relations and Compliance' in W Carlsnaes, T Risse, and BA Simmons (eds.), *Handbook of International Relations* (SAGE, 2002) on the notion of effectiveness.

holds that management of member state compliance through, for instance, meetings of national experts 'ensures efficiency in the application of the law, technical up-dating and ideas for further development of the law'.[7]

2.2 *The proliferation of expert groups on the implementation directives*

Directives are binding, as to the result to be achieved, but leave the choice of form and methods to the national authorities.[8] This entails that the member state shall adopt all the measures necessary to ensure that directives are fully effective, in accordance with the objective that the directives pursue. As pointed out by the Court of Justice, the types of obligation which directives impose on the member states vary significantly.[9] One of the strengths of directives is that they are implemented within the framework of the national legal systems. However, directives also pose a number of challenges for the member states. This holds true not least concerning the results to be achieved. Despite the advantages of directives in terms of flexibility and proportionality, directives thus also create potential legal uncertainty for the member states in the implementation phase.

The Commission has taken a range of initiatives targeting improved application of EU law in the member states.[10] These include 'preventive measures, including increased focus on implementation and enforcement issues in impact assessments, improved implementation planning on new legislation, creating implementation networks and assisting Member States with correlation tables'.[11] As part of this strategy the Commission endeavours to manage compliance with selected directives through expert groups.[12]

An example of this is the Capital Requirements Directive Transposition Group (CRDTG) set up by the Commission with a view to ensuring consistent implementation of the Capital Requirements Directive.[13]

[7] Commission Communication '*A Europe of Results—Applying Community Law*', COM/2007/502 final, 3.

[8] Article 288 TFEU.

[9] C-60/01 *Commission v France* [2002] ECR I-5679, paras 25–8.

[10] Commission Communication '*A Europe of Results—Applying Community Law*', COM/2007/502.

[11] Commission Communication '*Third strategic review of Better Regulation in the European Union*', COM/2009/15 final, para IV, 3.

[12] Commission '*27th Annual Report on Monitoring the Application of EU Law*', COM/2010/538.

[13] Commission Decision of 5 November 2003 establishing the European Banking Committee (OJ L 2004, L 3/36). Described in Commission Staff Working Document 'Situation in Different

The group is composed of member state representatives, business stakeholders, and the Committee of European Banking Supervisors. Among other things, it addresses the accuracy of member state transposition and whether provisions are adequately implemented, based in particular on the outcomes of CRDTG.[14] The Commission's Internal Market and Services Directorate General has established an interactive website called 'Your Questions on Legislation', where firms, trade associations, public organizations, and other stakeholders can submit questions relating to the single market.[15] Notably, the CRDTG's answers are made publicly available on the dedicated webpage. One advantage of this approach is of course that individuals have access to information and, encouraged by the answers, may want to challenge member states before domestic courts. Another advantage is that the Commission can make available guidance to the member states responsible for national implementation of the Directive.

The web-page explicitly states that the service does not cover the application of legislative acts by member states or their interpretation. As discussed in chapter four, this is a prerogative of the Court of Justice according to Article 19 TEU. Clearly, the arrangement formally complies with the principle of conferred powers, discussed in more detail in chapter five. However, the distinction between guidance and interpretation can be somewhat ambiguous.[16] This is illustrated by a response from the UK HM Treasury addressed to the Commission. In the response it notes that it is of the understanding that the expert group 'exists to provide interpretation of the Directive rather than formal guidance', and suggests that the Commission reflects further upon this option.[17]

Another type of expert group is composed exclusively of national officials representing the member states. In terms of composition, this type of group

Sectors' accompanying document to the Report from the Commission, 27th Annual Report on Monitoring the Application of EU Law, SEC/2010/1143 final, para 9.2.2.2, 280.

[14] 2006 Activity Report from the European Banking Committee. Can be accessed at http://ec.europa.eu/internal_market/bank/docs/ebc/ebc-activity-report_en.pdf.

[15] The webpage can be accessed at http://ec.europa.eu/yqol/index.cfm. More specifically, the questions and answers concern the Capital Requirements Directive, the Markets in Financial Instruments Directive, the Electronic Money Directive, and the Payment Services Directive.

[16] Article 13(2) TFEU.

[17] UK Response to the Commission on the Mortgage Funding Expert Group and Mortgage Industry and Consumers Expert Group Reports (February 2007). The response can be accessed at http://www.fsa.gov.uk/pubs/international/joint_response.pdf.

resembles the Council working groups. The notion of 'expert group', however, indicates that the work is less about policy-making and more about problem-solving. The member states are thus providing expertise on the application of EU law and as suggested by the rhetoric, the method is one of cooperation. An example of the latter type of expert group is the expert group on the implementation of the Services Directive set up by the Commission. In addition to the bilateral meetings between the Commission and the member states, the Expert Group discusses specific questions pertaining to the implementation of the Services Directive.[18] The purpose is two-fold, viz., to examine the member states' interpretation of the Directive and whether they are consistent and, in addition, to assemble member state accord for priorities for action.[19]

The ensuing section will examine the second type of group of experts composed solely of member state representatives. It focuses specifically on the group of experts concerned with implementation of the Free Movement Directive. The Directive lays down the right of free movement and residence within the territory of the Member States by Union citizens and their family members and their right of permanent residence. Moreover, it regulates the limits placed on those rights on grounds of public policy, public security, or public health.

2.3 *The Expert Group on the Implementation of the Free Movement Directive*

The Commission initiated infringement proceedings against 19 member states between June 2006 and February 2007 alone for failure to communicate transposition measures concerning the Free Movement Directive. At the same time, all member states failed to transpose the Directive effectively and correctly in its entirety. The Commission accounts for this in a 2008 report, which provides an overview of the transposition of the

[18] Commission Staff Working Document '*Situation in Different Sectors*' accompanying document to the Report from the Commission, 27th Annual Report on Monitoring the Application of EU Law, SEC/2010/1143 final, para 9.2.1.2 (Report on work done in 2009).

[19] Commission Staff Working Document '*Situation in Different Sectors*'—accompanying document to the Report from the Commission, 27th Annual Report on Monitoring the Application of EU Law, SEC/2010/1143 final. The group's work is explained on p 46 ff in Annex 1 to DG Internal Market and Services '*2007 Annual Activity Report*'. The annex can be accessed at http://ec.europa.eu/atwork/synthesis/aar/aar2007/doc/markt_annex1.pdf.

Directive and its day-to-day application by member states.[20] It also sets out the Commission's endeavours to develop supplementary methods to bring about member state compliance, including a group composed of member state representatives in charge of implementing the Directive. The aim of this group of experts is 'to identify difficulties and clarify issues of interpretation of the Directive'.[21]

The expert group discusses ways and best practices in implementing specific provisions of the Directive. The Commission sets the agenda; however, the member states can request that additional discussion points should be added. Thomson has established a link between the decision-making stage and the enforcement stage. Notably, his explanatory analysis indicates: 'states' policy preferences significantly affect the likelihood of transposition problems, and that this is conditioned by the behaviour of the Commission.'[22] Specifically, explicit Commission support for particular provisions translates into member state compliance. The explanation is that the Commission's mere support signals that the Commission will monitor compliance with the provisions and this prompts member states to comply. The member states access to bring up points for discussion in expert groups could be one way to ease this enforcement bias.

It happens that the Commission is asked for views on interpretation of some of the provisions. In those cases, the Commission normally gives its orientations on the basis of the jurisprudence and the past Commission Communications on the subject. The Commission does not however give any assurance of compliance. The expert group is also a forum where the member states can exchange practices among themselves, be informed about most recent jurisprudence in the field, and ask for clarifications. The Working Group does not discuss whether member states concretely comply. The Commission has at the same time launched a bilateral dialogue with the 27 member states on the transposition of the Directive. In 2011 this dialogue led a majority of the member states to amend or commit to amend their legislation and to 12 infringement procedures.

[20] Commission '*Report on the application of Directive 2004/38/EC on the right of citizens of the Union and their family members to move and reside freely within the territory of the Member States*', COM/2008/840 final.

[21] Commission '*Report on the application of Directive 2004/38/EC on the right of citizens of the Union and their family members to move and reside freely within the territory of the Member States*', COM/2008/840 final.

[22] Robert Thomson, 'Opposition through the back door in the transposition of EU directives' (2010) *European Union Politics* 11:4, 577–96, 577.

In these cases the Commission does not need the information from the expert group since it knows where member state legislation stands and has been taking measures already. There is no negotiation or discussion about such cases in the expert group.[23]

Not only has transposition and implementation of the Free Movement Directive proven complicated, it has also given rise to politically contentious questions, some of which the Commission in principle considers more apt for political rather than judicial resolution.[24] The polemics concerning France's expulsion of Roma EU citizens is instructive thereof.[25] In that case, the Commission put infringement proceedings on hold and allowed France an opportunity to demonstrate that it based expulsion orders on a specific, individual examination of each case.[26] This approach, whereby the Commission effectively circumvents the burden of proof, was politically tenable because of the particular circumstances of that case. According to Article 258 TFEU though, the Commission must prove the existence of an infringement.[27] Consequently, the Commission cannot generally suppose that member states will substantiate compliance at the Commission's request.

The Council supports the idea of reinforcing member state compliance with the Free Movement Directive through a group of experts. Thus, in 2008 it requested the Commission to provide 'guidelines for the interpretation of that Directive early in 2009 and to consider all other appropriate and necessary proposals and measures'.[28] In 2009 it further endorsed the Commission's initiative to issue guidelines with information on member state compliance with a view to 'facilitate effective application of

[23] Interview, Commission official (January 2012).

[24] The Commission, eg, called on Member States to set national strategies for Roma integration (IP/11/400, 5 April 2011).

[25] The decision by France to expel from its territory Roma EU citizens from Romania and Bulgaria prompted the Commission to initiate an exchange between the Commission and the French authorities on the transposition and application of EU law and the Free Movement Directive. Specifically, the Commission was of the opinion that France had not transposed the Free Movement Directive in national law in a manner that rendered those rights completely effective (letter from the Commission on file with the author).

[26] Letter from the Commission on file with the author.

[27] The member state in turn must contest substantively and in detail the information produced and the consequences thereof. See, eg, C-272/86 *Commission v Greece* [1988] ECR 4875, para 21.

[28] Press release 2908th meeting of the Council, Justice and Home Affairs, Brussels, 27 and 28 November 2008, 16325/1/08 REV 1 (Presse 344), 27–8.

the Directive'.[29] The broad support is important given that the method is non-binding. Significantly, it sustains the Expert Group's authority and legitimacy from a member state point of view.

The Commission's initiatives to ensure compliance in this area also gain support from the European Parliament.[30] In 2007, it thus called on the Commission to make a detailed member state compliance assessment of the Free Movement Directive.[31] Moreover, it endorsed the Commission proposal to draw up interpretative guidelines and also recommended that the Commission should monitor compliance with its guidelines. It furthermore proposed a range of specific methodologies to ensure member state implementation. This included a suggestion that the Commission should develop

> guidelines with common criteria in relation to the minimum amount regarded as 'sufficient resources' and to clarify on which basis Member States should take into account 'the personal situation of the person concerned' under Article 8(4) of Directive 2004/38/EC
>
> and
>
> develop in its guidelines a uniform interpretation mechanism of the normative categories of 'public policy', 'public security' and 'public health', and to clarify how taking account of considerations such as residence period, age, state of health, family and economic situation, social and cultural integration, and links with the country of origin, are relevant for the expulsion decision provided for in Article 28(1) of Directive 2004/38/EC.[32]

Following up on its recommendation that the Commission should monitor compliance with the guidelines, the European Parliament suggests that the Commission should go as far as setting a deadline for the implementation of the (non-binding) guidelines. After that deadline infringement proceedings would be brought.[33] The latter proposal thus suggests combining general interpretative guidance and infringement proceedings according to Article

[29] Press release, 2927th Council meeting, Justice and Home Affairs, Brussels, 26 and 27 February 2009, 6877/09 (Presse 51), 10.

[30] Resolution of the European Parliament of 2 April 2009 on the application of Directive 2004/38/EC (2008/2184(INI)).

[31] Resolution of the European Parliament of 15 November 2007 on the application of Directive 2004/38/EC (2008) OJ C 282 E/428.

[32] Resolution of the European Parliament of 15 November 2007 on the application of Directive 2004/38/EC (2008) OJ C 282 E/428.

[33] Resolution of the European Parliament of 15 November 2007 on the application of Directive 2004/38/EC (2008) OJ C 282 E/428.

258 TFEU. Finally the European Parliament proposed a mutual evaluation system essentially similar in method to the group of member state experts on implementation subsequently established by the Commission.

2.4 *The scope for objective evaluation vis-à-vis interpretation*

2.4.1 *Implications for the member states and the Commission*

In a 2007 Communication the Commission discusses the reasons behind the pending infringement files. It maintains that member states (i) may pay insufficient attention to the correct interpretation and application of the law; (ii) may be late with implementation work and the communication of national transposition measures; (iii) may encounter difficulties of interpretation and choice of procedural options; and/or (iv) may transpose a directive or interpret a regulation in a way that does not comply with the EU measure in question.[34] The group of experts can put pressure on defaulting member states in the first two types of situation. In the latter two types of situation there is also considerable scope for process. Peer-learning may relate to best practices, but it also raises questions concerning 'how' to implement directives correctly. This section considers what policy implications this has for the member states and their autonomy in implementing directives.

According to a member state official who participated in the Expert Group on the implementation of the Free Movement Directive, the Commission is responsive to member state expertise, interpretations, and needs. Sometimes the member states can affect the Commission's opinion on certain matters. Where the member states exert concerted political pressure on the Commission, the Commission 'understands the "signal"'. These characteristics are not necessarily that different from the interaction under the general EU infringement procedure. As discussed in chapter two, much EU law allows for flexibility when it comes to national implementation, application, and enforcement. Moreover, the Commission and the Court of Justice's powers according to Article 258 TFEU are inherently responsive towards the member states. The Commission merely possesses powers of investigation and the Court of Justice hands down declaratory judgments. Chapter one argued that these characteristics mirror the EU's general dependency on a dual source of authority. Moreover, it was argued,

[34] Commission Communication '*A Europe of Results—Applying Community Law*', COM/2007/502, 4.

although the EU is characterized by unprecedented autonomous powers, there are few examples of powers that can be employed without a high degree of appreciation of the member states either directly or indirectly, including in the enforcement phase.

The group of member state experts on the Free Movement Directive is supposed to identify difficulties and clarify issues of interpretation of the Directive.[35] Clearly, the expert group cannot produce binding clarification concerning the correct interpretation of the Directive.[36] The same applies to administrative networks between the Commission and member state administrations. Timmermans nevertheless cautions that administrative networks should not 'become a multilateral forum where possible infringements of Community law and problems of interpretation are negotiated between national administrations and the Commission'.[37] This type of concern seems even more acute in relation to the relatively formalized works of expert groups. Notably, they engage in interpretation concerning issues that, in principle, belong to the member states when they implement directives. The expert group on the Free Movement Directive deals with general problems of non-compliance and how member states transpose, implement, and enforce EU law. The processes thus seem prone to yield norm convergence. The method may also blur the fact that it is perfectly legitimate for a member state to insist on a certain interpretation up until the point when the Court of Justice has settled the question. Notably, negotiation in the EU is characterized by 'strong consensus norms'.[38] Moreover, the expert group engages in processes of communicating back and forth for the purpose of reaching a shared understanding on what constitutes correct interpretation of a given provision. This discourse is contained in an ongoing relationship (the Expert Group), which the member states by and large have an interest in maintaining. Thus,

[35] Commission *'Report on the application of Directive 2004/38/EC on the right of citizens of the Union and their family members to move and reside freely within the territory of the Member States'*, COM/2008/840 final.

[36] T-258/06 *Germany v Commission* [2010] not yet published in the ECR, para 45.

[37] CWA Timmermans, 'Judicial Protection against Member States' in D Curtin and T Heukels (eds.), *Institutional Dynamics of European Integration. Essays in Honour of Henry G. Schermers. Volume II* (Martinus Nijhoff Publishers, 1994), 406.

[38] O Elgström and C Jönsson, 'Negotiations in the EU: Bargaining or Problem-Solving?' (2000) *Journal of European Public Policy* 7:5, 684–704, 684.

there is a dual interest in the substance as well as the relationship.[39] This in turn makes hard (bargaining) positions less legitimate.[40]

For a number of reasons, such processes may have an impact on how member states interpret and consequently implement and apply EU law. First, they involve repetition, clarification, and gradual alignment, which in turn facilitate internalization. The extent to which the non-binding policy outcomes become internalized needs empirical substantiation. Preliminary interviews with member state and Commission officials confirm that member states adapt the way they interpret the Free Movement Directive in the light of the discussions in the Working Group. The second reason has to do with the interplay between the procedure and the general EU infringement procedure. Ibáñez provides an example thereof in relation to the Fiscal Policy Committee, which the Commission has used to address questions of interpretation on an ad hoc basis. According to Ibáñez, the Commission initiates proceedings against the minority of member states if the majority (even by one member state) support the Commission's interpretation. If all member states disagree with the Commission it 'very rarely' initiates infringement proceedings. Isolated member states usually adapt to the majority. Finally, Ibáñez notes, the Commission can use the results to sustain its arguments before the Court of Justice in infringement proceedings.[41]

The potential and actual combining of non-binding peer-review with the general EU infringement procedure makes the Commission's role in managing compliance through expert groups potentially much more vigorous than it appears at first sight. From a member state perspective, this touches upon broader questions of contestability in relation to the Commission's usage of non-binding, supplementary enforcement tools in combination with its general enforcement powers. The Commission's resulting powers have been tried in a case initiated by Germany against the Commission concerning public procurement.[42] The case concerned, among other things, a submission by the Commission that it would

[39] R Fisher and W Ury, *Getting to Yes: Negotiating an Agreement without Giving In* (Random House Business Books, 1981), 20.

[40] Compare O Elgström and C Jönsson, 'Negotiations in the EU: Bargaining or Problem-Solving?' (2000) *Journal of European Public Policy* 7:5, 684–704. The authors are not concerned with the examined expert group or expert groups on implementation generally.

[41] AJG Ibáñez, 'Exceptions to Article 226: Alternative Administrative Procedures and the Pursuit of Member States' (2000) *European Law Journal* 6:2, 148–76, 171.

[42] T-258/06 *Germany v Commission* [2010] not yet published in the ECR.

commence infringement proceedings in the event of non-compliance with a procedure laid down in a non-binding Commission Communication. Combining the measures in the Communication and the general EU infringement procedure in such a way, the General Court established, does not amount to binding effect. The result is based on several considerations. Notably, the risk of infringement proceedings is a mere consequence of fact and not a binding legal effect. In addition, the initiation of infringement proceedings pursuant to Article 258 TFEU does not constitute an act which has binding or compulsory effects. Finally, determining the rights and duties of member states and appraising their conduct is an exclusive prerogative of the Court of Justice. The judgment is (of course) doctrinally sound.[43] However, as Scott points out, like other new governance forms the Commission's approach 'give[s] rise to a form of complex normativity that combines European and national hard and soft law in a manner that presents a challenge for European administrative law'.[44] Scott makes a strong case why the Court of Justice of the European Union should 'exhibit greater openness to post-legislative guidance and be willing to subject it to judicial review'.[45]

Chapter four argued that the horizontal separation of institutional powers in the EU reflects the member states' self-interests in restraining the EU institutions' powers vis-à-vis their national autonomy. Thus, it constitutes a safeguard against excessive concentrations of powers within the EU institutions, including the Commission. This applies to the Commission generally and to the Commission in its role as guardian specifically. However, the idea that the EU institutional balance can work as a sort of checks and balances is challenged, if not legally then in actual fact, by the emergence of supplementary, non-binding enforcement tools. Still, this chapter demonstrated that the examined expert group dealing with compliance with the Free Movement Directive enjoys a high degree of support by the Council and indirectly by the member states. The interest in compliance notwithstanding, one reason for this support may be that the member states have some access to countervail the power and influence of the Commission. Clearly, combining expert group procedures with the

[43] T-258/06 *Germany v Commission* [2010] not yet published in the ECR, paras 150–3.

[44] J Scott, 'In Legal Limbo: Post-Legislative Guidance as a Challenge for European Administrative Law', (2011) *Common Market Law Review* 48:2, 329–56, 353.

[45] J Scott, 'In Legal Limbo: Post-Legislative Guidance as a Challenge for European Administrative Law', (2011) *Common Market Law Review* 48:2, 329–56, 353.

general EU infringement procedure provides the Commission with some bargaining power. However, there is also room for the member states to defend their individual and collective interests. Thus, similar to the administrative phase of the general EU infringement procedure, the process is responsive in nature.

2.4.2 Implications for the European Parliament

Management with compliance via expert groups on implementation poses additional questions concerning the rights and role of the European Parliament. Notably, to the extent the method is jurisgenerative, one consequence is that the European Parliament cannot exert its treaty-based influence as co-legislator (or according to Articles 290 and 291 TFEU concerning delegated and implementing acts). In relation to the Free Movement Directive, the European Parliament appears to be more concerned about compliance than the risk of norm development outside its own influence (and beyond judicial review). Notably, the European Parliament proposed that the Commission should combine interpretive communications with the general EU infringement procedure.[46] However, on other occasions the European Parliament has questioned the Commission's right to combine its non-binding tools with the general EU infringement procedure. Thus it intervened in the above mentioned case initiated by Germany against the Commission.[47]

2.4.3 Article 70 TFEU concerning peer-review within the AFSJ—general lessons

Whereas the expert groups examined in this chapter have emerged on an ad hoc basis without explicit legal basis in the EU Treaties, the Lisbon Treaty establishes a legal basis for peer-evaluation in relation to the area of freedom, security, and justice (AFSJ).[48] The European Convention

[46] Resolution of the European Parliament of 15 November 2007 on the application of Directive 2004/38/EC (2008) OJ C 282 E/428. In European Parliament Report on the Commission's 21st and 22nd Annual reports on monitoring the application of Community law (2003 and 2004) (A6–0089/2006 Final), explanatory statement at p 25 (section 2), the European Parliament 'welcomes the Commission's latest initiatives to assist Member States in the transposition and implementation of particularly complicated directives through guidelines and interpretative texts'.

[47] T-258/06 *Germany v Commission* [2010] not yet published in the ECR.

[48] According to Art 3(2) TEU, the Union shall offer its citizens an area of freedom, security, and justice without internal frontiers, in which the free movement of persons is ensured in conjunction with appropriate measures with respect to external border controls, asylum,

Group dealing with Freedom, Security, and Justice was presented with expert evidence that this particular policy area suffered from inadequate implementation in general and concerning Third Pillar matters in particular.[49] In order to find ways to improve member state implementation, the Group suggested that peer-review should be encouraged and stipulated directly in the Constitution. Different types of non-binding peer-review concerning national transposition measures and the implementation and enforcement of EU law had already emerged incrementally both concerning First and Third Pillar policy matters.[50] For instance, there was evidence that peer-review formed an effective tool ensuring compliance in relation to both combating organized crime and implementing the Schengen *acquis*.[51] Moreover, review arrangements were established as part of the preparatory framework facilitating the most recent enlargements.[52] The evaluation mechanism survived the ill-fated Constitution and is now stipulated in Article 70 TFEU. It reads:

> Without prejudice to Articles 258 . . . and 260 [the general EU infringement procedure], the Council may, on a proposal from the Commission, adopt measures laying down the arrangements whereby Member States, in collaboration with the Commission, conduct objective and impartial evaluation of the implementation of the Union policies referred to in this Title by Member States' authorities, in particular in order to facilitate full application of the principle of mutual recognition. The European Parliament and national Parliaments shall be informed of the content and results of the evaluation.

immigration, and the prevention and combating of crime. Prior to the Lisbon Treaty the Commission had powers to enforce Community law. However, the Lisbon Treaty abolishes the treaty pillar structure and broadens the scope of the Commission's powers of enforcement. After a transitional phase of five years after the Lisbon Treaty entered into force Art 258 TFEU will apply fully to the area of freedom, security, and justice. Article 10 in Protocol on Transitional Provisions, OJ C 306/163 of 17 December 2007.

[49] Working Group X: Freedom, Security and Justice, Final Report, CONV 426/02, Brussels 2 December 2002, 20. The report can be accessed at http://register.consilium.europa.eu.

[50] See generally, A Klip, E Versluis, and J Polak, 'Improving Mutual Trust amongst European Union Member States in the Areas of Police and Judicial Cooperation in Criminal Matters', 69–70. The text can be accessed at http://english.wodc.nl/.

[51] Working Group X: Freedom, Security and Justice, Final Report, CONV 426/02, Brussels 2 December 2002, 20.

[52] See, eg, 98/429/JHA: Joint Action of 29 June 1998 adopted by the Council on the basis of Article K.3 of the Treaty on European Union, establishing a mechanism for collective evaluation of the enactment, application and effective implementation by the applicant countries of the acquis of the European Union in the field of Justice and Home Affairs (1998) OJ L 191/8–9.

A number of traits emerge. Peer-review arrangements shall be without prejudice to the general EU infringement procedure. Thus, the procedures co-exist as independent mechanisms that both aim at monitoring adequate implementation of EU law by the member states. The language of Article 70 TFEU explicitly reaffirms the Commission's general responsibilities as guardian. Consequently there is still ultimate access to judicial recourse in concrete infringement cases. This is in line with Timmermans' warning concerning administrative networks between member state authorities and the Commission. Specifically, they should not generate 'a devolution from Community to Member States'.[53]

Another and interrelated element concerns the requirement that evaluation of implementation shall be 'objective and impartial'. To the extent peer-evaluation is concerned with implementation and compliance, it opens up for a non-confrontational type of enforcement discourse. However, as discussed above, peer-review may also blur the fact that much enforcement is essentially about contested norms. The requirement concerning objectivity and impartiality is difficult to operationalize. The wording of Article 70 TFEU nevertheless serves as a caution that the member states and the Commission shall refrain from negotiating or renegotiating EU law.

Whereas the Council could act on its own motion in earlier versions, the Lisbon Treaty empowers the Council to act 'on a proposal from the Commission'. This amendment reflects a proposal tabled by the Commission maintaining that it 'should play a more significant role in the . . . mechanism of evaluation'.[54] Not only does this amendment enable the Commission to frame and influence the content of peer-review, it also works to sustain an approach that is vested in the common interests of the EU and thereby ensure policy consistency.

The final clarification concerns the obligation to inform the European Parliament and national parliaments of the content and results of the evaluation. The Convention Working Group links the involvement of national parliaments to characteristics that are particular to the area of freedom, security, and justice. Notably, it holds, 'the work and the organisation of national police and the content of national criminal law

[53] CWA Timmermans, 'Judicial Protection against Member States' in D Curtin and T Heukels (eds.), *Institutional Dynamics of European Integration. Essays in Honour of Henry G. Schermers. Volume II* (Martinus Nijhoff Publishers, 1994), 406.

[54] Suggestion for amendment of Article 4 by Convention member Commissioner Hübner, part II. The proposal can be accessed at http://european-convention.eu.int/docs/treaty/pdf/847/4hubner.pdf.

are at the core of the competencies that define a state'.[55] It is likewise in accordance with the general objectives of making the works of the Council more transparent and involving the national parliaments.[56]

Chapter two argued that there are no mechanisms in place to ensure that the European Parliament can engage as a unitary and politically responsible institution in individual infringement cases initiated by the Commission under Article 258 TFEU. In addition, access to individual infringement case files would undermine secrecy, which is closely linked to the effectiveness of infringement proceedings. Informing the European Parliament of the content and results of evaluation would, by contrast, be one way to constructively engage the European Parliament in a dialogue about enforcement problems. In addition, the Commission links feedback of evaluation results with the decision-making processes.[57] This too warrants greater involvement of the European Parliament.

Commissioner Hübner proposed a further amendment of the text presented by the Praesidium. It included a penultimate sentence reading 'Evaluation mechanisms may in no way impair the independence of the judiciary'.[58] The proposal was aimed at ensuring 'that independence of the domestic judicial system is to be preserved'.[59] There is no such specification in the final provision. However, the advice applies more generally.

[55] Working Group X: Freedom, Security and Justice, Final Report, CONV 426/02, Brussels 2 December 2002, 22.

[56] Compare Final Report of Working Group IV on the Role of National Parliaments, CONV 353/02.

[57] See Commission Communication *'Evaluation of EU Policies on Freedom, Security and Justice'*, COM/2006/332 final; and O de Schutter, 'The Role of Evaluation in Experimentalist Governance: Learning by Monitoring in the Establishment of the Area of Freedom, Security, and Justice', in CF Sabel and J Zeitlin (eds.), *Experimentalist Governance in the European Union. Towards a New Architecture* (Oxford University Press, 2010), 281. The practice applies to other policy areas as well. The 'Expert Group on the Implementation of the Services Directive', eg, aims at ensuring 'a similar level of understanding by all the Member States of the work required and the priorities for action'. Commission Staff Working Document *'Situation in the Different Sectors'* accompanying document to the Report from the Commission 27th Annual Report on Monitoring the Application of EU Law (2009), SEC/2010/1143 final, section 9.2.1.2; and Commission Communication *'Third strategic review of Better Regulation in the European Union'*, COM/2009/15 final.

[58] The proposal can be accessed at http://european-convention.eu.int/docs/treaty/pdf/847/4hubner.pdf.

[59] The proposal can be accessed at http://european-convention.eu.int/docs/treaty/pdf/847/4hubner.pdf.

2.5 *The member states want directives* and *unity of application*

Historically, the member states have insisted on directives as their preferred regulatory tool and at the same time required unity of application. As a final point it may be considered whether this in part explains the turn towards management of directives through implementation expert groups. In 2001, a Commission working group advocated that regulations should be preferred to directives.[60] The Commission has since repeated this general viewpoint.[61] The principal difference between directives and regulations lies in their scope of application. Whereas regulations are binding in their entirety and directly applicable in all member states, directives leave it to the national authorities to choose the form and methods to achieve a result. The Commission's outlook is somewhat in opposition to the EU member states' standpoint expressed in the protocol on the application of the principles of subsidiarity and proportionality annexed to the Treaty of Amsterdam. According to the protocol 'directives should be preferred to regulations and framework directives to detailed measures'. Moreover, directives should 'leave as much scope for national decision as possible'.[62] Post-Lisbon, Article 296 TFEU reads: 'Where the Treaties do not specify the type of act to be adopted, the institutions shall select it on a case-by-case basis, in compliance with the applicable procedures and with the principle of proportionality'.[63] The Commission's contention was however not motivated by considerations of proportionality, but of enforceability.[64] High levels of compliance are, the working group contends, not merely

[60] Report of the Working Group *'Better regulation'* (Group 2c) May 2001 (White Paper on European Governance, Work Area no 2), *'Handling the Process of Producing and Implementing Community Rules'*, 6.

[61] Commission Communication *'A Europe of Results—Applying Community Law'*, COM/2007/502 final, section 1.1.

[62] Treaty of Amsterdam, Protocol annexed to the Treaty establishing the European Community, paras 6 and 7.

[63] The element that directives should be preferred to regulations is left out of Protocol no 2 annexed to the Lisbon Treaty and it does not appear explicitly from the Treaty text (OJ C 2010, 83/206). This former clarification was perhaps more of a political than legal nature and it is unclear whether the amendment has material content and thus legal bearings. For a discussion thereof see B de Witte, 'Legal Instruments and Law-Making in the Lisbon Treaty' in S Griller and J Ziller (eds.), *The Lisbon Treaty: EU Constitutionalism without a Constitutional Treaty?* (Springer, 2008), 96.

[64] Similar arguments have been advanced by legal scholars. See, eg, P Wennerås, *The Enforcement of EC Environmental Law* (Oxford University Press, 2007), 322.

a matter of enforcement design and powers, but should be seen as closely linked with the type of legislative instruments chosen. It further argued, in this regard, that strict adherence to the proportionality principle works against the interests of the business establishment. Specifically, it entails 'a less uniform and more complex legal framework'.[65] In arguing this way, the Commission establishes a link between its general, ie, cross-sectoral, argument that regulations often work in the interest of compliance and the interests of civil society. It is clear that succinct and immediately binding obligations are relatively easier to monitor. However, the choice between directives and regulations cannot be regarded as merely a technical matter of enforceability. It is also a policy choice. The characteristics of directives as a legislative tool which make them complicated to supervise might at the same time be their virtue and their very reason for existing. Then again, when discussing pros and cons of directives and regulations, the issues raised in this chapter should be factored in. Arguably, directives are increasingly managed by expert groups in a manner which render them somewhat comparable to regulations.

3. Conclusion

This chapter discussed the Commission's practice of establishing groups composed of member state experts on implementation. The groups are established on an ad hoc basis and their aim is to identify and clarify issues of interpretation of directives. The examined method has a number of advantages as a remedy against non-compliance and in terms of effectiveness. In particular, the Commission can manage compliance issues in a broadly inclusive and pre-emptive manner. Moreover, the Commission and the member states can identify underlying compliance problems that require further legislative (or soft-law) action and thus provide broader solutions.

Even so, management through expert groups has a number of policy implications that extend beyond merely securing compliance. Enforcement in the EU is often about contested norms. However, there is a risk that

[65] Report of the Working Group *'Better regulation'* (Group 2c) May 2001 (White Paper on European Governance, Work Area no 2), *'Handling the Process of Producing and Implementing Community Rules'*, 11.

expert management obfuscates this dimension. Consequently, although expert groups engage in non-binding interpretation, compliance management may bring about norm harmonization and a potential slippage of competence. A different scenario could be that evaluation brings about divergence and what Timmermans calls devolution from EU to member states. Either way, the Commission plays an important role. Notably, the Commission shall ensure that the processes are vested in the general interest of the EU. Thus, similar to Article 258 TFEU (see chapter two), the role of the Commission is semi-political and requires policy choices.

Clearly, the Commission has an advantage in that it can combine its general enforcement powers under Article 258 TFEU with supplementary, auxiliary tool such as expert groups. However, as the General Court has established in relation to interpretive communications, this is not a legal problem. Moreover, when it comes to expert groups, the active involvement of member states counterbalances the Commission's influence. Hence, the scope for accidental institutional empowerment is somewhat contained. Moreover, and similar to the administrative phase under Article 258 TFEU, the resultant dialogue is of a responsive nature.

The last part of this chapter looked at the evaluation mechanism stipulated in Article 70 TFEU concerning the area of freedom, security, and justice. Whereas the groups examined in this chapter have emerged incrementally and without an overarching procedural framework, the treaty-based procedure reflects more principled choices concerning the role and responsibilities of the Council, the Commission, the member states, and, in addition, the European Parliament and national parliaments. Notably, evaluation should be objective and impartial and the Commission should play a central role in this respect and more generally. Moreover, the European Parliament and national parliaments should be informed about the results.

7

The Commission's Enforcement Powers in Context

1. Introduction

This book aimed to provide a comprehensive analysis of the Commission's general role in supervising member state compliance with EU law. It started out by asking whether it is viable to establish stronger Commission powers of enforcement at this point in time. Against this backdrop, and as a means of exploring the role of the Commission, the chapters examined a number of different aspects pertaining to enforcement of EU law.

Chapters one, two, and three examined the Commission's function under the general EU infringement procedure stipulated in Articles 258 and 260 TFEU. Chapter one argued that the EU lacks independent self-sustained regime authority. Moreover, it argued, this is reflected in both substantive EU law and procedural law, including the general EU infringement procedure. More specifically, both the substantive law and procedural law are inherently flexible. Chapter two made the case that Article 258 TFEU can usefully be explained in terms of managerialism. Notably, the procedure presupposes that member states are in principle willing to comply. The resultant processes include interpretive guidance, argumentation, technical and legal exposition, persuasion, pressure through exposure, and juridical recourse.

Managerialism does not rely on sanctions. This has prompted scholarly criticism that the theory fails to appreciate the role of sanctions when there is considerable incentive for non-compliance. Notably, the general EU infringement procedure does comprise a sanctioning mechanism. Chapter three examined Article 260 TFEU concerning repetitive infringements.

It maintained that special characteristics of EU member state sanctions make them compatible with managerial enforcement. It moreover argued that the real significance of Article 260(2) TFEU is its capacity to bolster the iterative process of discourse and problem-solving between the Commission and a given member state in the period prior to actual judgment. Sanctions thus sustain the managerial approach. If such approach fails, the Commission can invoke sanctions without compromising basic considerations of legitimacy and effectiveness. Moreover, it can do so while retaining the member state in a constructive process of engagement leading to gradual compliance.

Chapter four examined the Commission's unsuccessful attempts to gain sharper enforcement powers through secondary legislation. It concluded that the Commission's present general enforcement powers touch upon the relationship between the member states and the EU. Thus, a strengthening of the Commission's enforcement powers should be decided upon in primary law. Chapter five then argued that notwithstanding the doctrinal distinction between enforcement and implementing measures, there are effective points of functional overlap between enforcement powers and certain types of implementing tools. The identified implementing tools are lawful in that they serve other aims and purposes than enforcement. Finally, chapter six discussed the Commission's role under various non-binding, ad hoc arrangements. This too, it was argued, is crucial to an understanding of compliance in the EU.

The first part of this chapter places the general EU infringement procedure (the enforcement stage) in the broader context of a comprehensive (negotiated) policy process. Moreover, it argues that the enforcement stage shares many features with earlier steps in the legislative process. These include flexibility and deliberation.

The second part of this chapter ties together the themes of the various chapters. It draws on responsive regulation theory and argues that implementation of EU law is primarily a member state responsibility. This is the case generally and also in the enforcement phase. Even when a member state fails to comply and the Commission initiates infringement proceedings, the member state plays a decidedly active role and retains responsibility for reinstalling compliance. Consequently, the member states have a high stake in the solutions to compliance problems.

2. Enforcement in the Broader Context of the EU Policy Process

The analyses and policy comments made throughout this book suggest that the general EU infringement procedure can usefully be described in the broader context of the EU policy process. First, enforcement is often about contested norms. Whether a member state complies inevitably requires interpretation of legislative acts, of the EU Treaties, and jurisprudence. Secondly, as discussed in chapter one, the Commission uses the general EU infringement procedure to pursue policy objectives. Moreover, actions in one policy stage can be employed as a lever in other policy stages. The 'Open Skies' agreements discussed in chapter one is illustrative thereof.[1] The works by Schmidt[2] and Steunenberg,[3] among others, investigate other important aspects of the linkages between the policy phases. Thirdly, the general EU infringement procedure and the Commission's enforcement powers are to various degrees interchangeable with (and complementary to) other non-enforcement tools in other policy phases. For instance, when breaches are common to a large number of different activities and have many features in common, the 'EU legislator' sometimes opts to manage compliance through detailed legislation. This happens on the initiative of the Commission. Such horizontal approach ensures compliance in a more general and systematic way than the general EU infringement procedure is capable of. Chapter five provided an example of this approach.[4] Chapter five furthermore examined implementation measures that display functional overlap with enforcement measures. Fourthly, as former Commissioner de Palacio points out, isolating a member state can be dangerous. Thus, member states should always be given a chance to find a compromise.[5] Likewise, the overall policy

[1] See also L Prete and B Smulders, 'The Coming of Age of Infringement Proceedings' (2010) *Common Market Law Review* 47:1, 9–61.

[2] SK Schmidt, 'Only an Agenda Setter? The European Commission's Power over the Council of Ministers' (2000) *European Union Politics* 1:1, 37–61, 38.

[3] Bernard Steunenberg, 'Implementation of EU Directives. Is Big Brother Watching? Commission Oversight of the National' (2010) *European Union Politics* 11:3, 359–80.

[4] Commission Proposal for a Directive of the European Parliament and of the Council on services in the internal market, COM/2004/2 final/3, recital 3a of the preamble. The proposal was adopted as Directive 2006/123/EC of the European Parliament and of the Council of 12 December 2006 on services in the internal market [2006] OJ L376/36.

[5] Interview with former Commissioner de Palacio, Florence, 21 April 2005.

process is vulnerable to deadlock conflicts between the Commission and a member state and ultimately, between the EU and a member state. Therefore, when exercising its powers of enforcement the Commission College balances competing interests, if need be, also across policy phases.

As discussed in chapters one, two, and three, the general EU infringement procedure is characterized by flexibility and deliberation. In this sense, the procedure shares important features with earlier steps in the legislative process and with jurisprudence from the Court of Justice. The dialogue between the Court of Justice and national courts was discussed in more detail in chapter one. According to Maduro, legitimacy and integrationist considerations have necessitated a jurisprudence of an essentially negotiated nature.[6] The dialogue taking place in the legislative phase (in the Council) and the EU implementation phase likewise rely on processes of law-governed dialogue. Clearly, the particular distribution of powers between the EU institutions and the member states matters for the outcome. However, any distribution of power inevitably necessitates some degree of dialogue.

When it comes to day-to-day negotiation in the EU, Elgström and Jönsson demonstrate that problem solving and bargaining types of negotiation take place in the various phases of the decision-making process, with the former being the dominant mode.[7] The authors argue that negotiation of a cooperative character prevails in the EU rather than conflictual or tough bargaining. They explain this by reason of the negotiations' 'permanence' and also the existence of 'strong consensus norms'.[8] However, they also observe some contextual variations and explain this with

[6] M Maduro, 'Contrapunctual Law: Europe's Constitutional Pluralism in Action' in N Walker (ed.), *Sovereignty in Transition* (Hart, 2003), 512. Alter examines what she calls a 'process of negotiation between the ECJ, national governments, and national courts, through which the relationship between European law and national law is continually defined, redefined and nuanced'. K Alter, *Establishing the Supremacy of European Law* (Oxford University Press, 2001). In this regard, see also K Alter, Memorandum, *The UK Parliament House of Lords*, Select Committee on European Union, 26 November 2003. The author is concerned with the constitutional dimension of supremacy claims by the Court of Justice on behalf of the EU. See also E Iankova and P Katzenstein, 'European Enlargement and Institutional Hypocrisy' in T Börzel and Rachel A Cichowski (eds.), *State of the European Union Volume 6: Law Politics and Society* (Oxford University Press, 2003), 277.

[7] O Elgström and C Jönsson, 'Negotiations in the EU: Bargaining or Problem-Solving?' (2000) *Journal of European Public Policy* 7:5, 684–704.

[8] O Elgström and C Jönsson, 'Negotiations in the EU: Bargaining or Problem-Solving?' (2000) *Journal of European Public Policy* 7:5, 684–704, 684. The authors explain that the prevalence of a strong *normative consensus* was first established with the common market.

classical negotiation theory variables. These include the degree of politicization,[9] the given stage in the decision-making process,[10] and the given policy type. Their analysis asserts that both types of negotiation take place and that this is perceived to be fully legitimate by the parties.

Considering the different policy phases in conjunction and thus taking a more holistic approach, the different phases constitute parts of a more encompassing governance process. The procedures are all politically agreed upon as acceptable. Moreover, the processes are largely consensus orientated.[11] They allow for a high degree of repetition, clarification, and gradual alignment. Arguing characterizes the negotiation; however, bargaining also takes place. The Commission takes a central role in all phases and generally it acts in a subtler and much more nuanced fashion than a formal description of its tasks and powers would suggest. Thus, it retains an important extra-legal function as facilitator.

3. Rethinking Articles 258 and 260 TFEU

3.1 *Article 88 ECSC and Articles 258 and 260 TFEU—different treaty contexts*

The Commission enjoys broad powers of discretion under the general EU infringement procedure. However, the method with a pre-litigation and contentious stage is long-drawn-out.[12] Moreover, the TFEU does not provide the Commission with remedies to address infringements more rapidly. This is symptomatic of the Commission's particular function as a mere prosecutor. Chapter one described the High Authority's relatively stronger powers according to Article 88 ECSC. Notably, it could establish member state infringements. The member state in turn could challenge the decision before the Court of Justice within a deadline. The Commission has

[9] O Elgström and C Jönsson, 'Negotiations in the EU: Bargaining or Problem-Solving?' (2000) *Journal of European Public Policy* 7:5, 684–704, 691.

[10] O Elgström and C Jönsson, 'Negotiations in the EU: Bargaining or Problem-Solving?' (2000) *Journal of European Public Policy* 7:5, 684–704, 692.

[11] F Hayes-Renshaw, W van Aken, and H Wallace, 'When and Why the Council of Ministers of the EU Votes Explicitly' *EUI Working Paper* 2005/25. The authors are concerned with EC law-making.

[12] C-359/92 *Germany v Council* [1994] I-3681.

proposed that it should be granted similar powers.[13] The Working Party on the Future of the European Communities' Court System has also proposed an amendment along the lines of Article 88 ECSC. However, it noted, 'it is clear that the Court of Justice would retain its powers under Article 228(2) [260(2) TFEU]'.[14]

The member state governments are unlikely to agree to such amendment. The procedural differences between the procedures established under the ECSC Treaty and the (E)EC Treaty (and the Commission's relatively weaker enforcement powers) should be seen in the light of the treaty regimes' different scope and nature. The ECSC is a 'traité-loi' and thus establishes a catalogue of detailed rules. The treaty competences and powers under the ECSC regime are thus defined rather narrowly.[15] By contrast, the EEC and the EU build on framework treaties with law-making capacity (a 'traité-cadre', sometimes referred to as a 'traité de procédure'). In the words of Advocate General Jacobs, this type of treaty 'merely provides a skeleton. The task of putting flesh on the bones falls to the Community legislature and to the Court of Justice'.[16] In addition, although initially in name only, the EEC Treaty introduced majority voting to be effective from 1966. These elements altered the nature of the member states' substantive compliance obligations considerably. Significantly, they removed the individual member states' final veto against potentially far-reaching policy developments.

3.2 *Process-based enforcement*

Despite the differences between Articles 258 TFEU and 88 ECSC, they both have judicial recourse as a means of last resort ('ultima ratio'). The pre-judicial method however has changed. Due to the Commission's relatively weaker powers under Article 258 TFEU it appears a facilitator above all. At the same time, its discretion regarding whether to initiate and forward infringement proceedings allows room for less legalistic

[13] Commission Communication on the institutional architecture '*For the European Union: peace, freedom, solidarity*', COM/2002/728, para 1.3.5.

[14] Report by the Working Party on the Future of the European Communities' Court System, 19 January 2000 (Due Report), 20. The report can be accessed at http://ec.europa.eu/dgs/legal_service/pdf/due_en.pdf.

[15] G Bebr, *Judicial Control of the European Communities* (Stevens & Sons Limited, 1962) with reference to Art 17 TEU.

[16] Opinion of Advocate General Jacobs in C-10/89 *SA CNL-SUCAL NV v HAG GF AG* [1990] ECR I-03711, point 10.

approaches to non-compliance. This method emphasizes the parties' problem-solving capacity. In the EU, the responsibility of giving effect to EU law rests primarily with the member states.[17] Thus, the Commission's investigatory powers are combined with a significant degree of member state autonomy concerning *how* to implement, apply, and enforce EU law. The resultant division of competence and the procedural features of Article 258 TFEU display characteristics often ascribed to governance steering-modes. Some of these characteristics are in italics (the references are not concerned specifically with enforcement of EU law):

The Commission negotiates compliance solutions with member states bilaterally and offer legal and technical assistance. In addition to the interpretive deliberation, the parties engage in fact-finding and assessment. Both formally and informally the general infringement procedure depends to a large degree on an 'iterative process of deliberation and knowledge-creation'.[18] The Commission's discretion throughout the infringement procedure allows it to *experiment* with alternative or complementary methods of bringing about compliance. Twinning projects between new-comers and 'older' member states have facilitated learning processes. This is one development, which is part of a more general move towards enabling, facilitating, and multilateral methods used to obtain better compliance rates. These practices have by and large come about on the initiative of the Commission. They include package meetings, technical guidance, interpretive communications, SOLVIT and EU Pilot (discussed in chapter two), peer-review, and expert groups on the implementation of directives (discussed in chapter six).

When comparing the general EU infringement procedure with governance modes, the most general and significant characteristics are the scope for *process* and the procedural framework, which allows for 'rule-structured influence on actor behaviour'.[19] The administrative phase of Article 258 TFEU is characterized by secrecy. Thus, it emphasizes the importance of *enabling action*. This is significant to the day-to-day problem-solving capacity of the EU. More concretely, the general EU infringement

[17] See, eg, the answer given by Commissioner Fischler on behalf of the Commission to European Parliament Written Question P-1052/2000; and Arts 4 TEU and 292 TFEU.

[18] Gráinne de Búrca, 'The Constitutional Challenge of New Governance in the European Union' (2003) *European Law Review* 28:6, 814–39, 823 ff.

[19] GF Schuppert, 'Governance im Spiegel der Wissenschaftsdisziplin' in GF Schuppert (ed.), *Governance-Forschung. Vergewisserung über Stand und Entwicklungslinien* (Nomos, 2005), 371–469. Translated from German.

procedure bears resemblance to responsive regulation, which is a private regulatory mode of governance.

3.3 *Articles 258 and 260 TFEU as an enforcement pyramid*

Responsive regulation takes self-organization as its starting point. However, it also has a control mechanism. Regulatees have maximal regulatory freedom, as long as their activities are executed in a manner that does not jeopardize established objectives. Compliance is foreseen to happen primarily through regulatory flexibility and cooperation; still there is eventual resort to coercion. Notably, the method assumes that a total lack of control and enforcement will result in abuse. As mentioned in chapter four, the idea is illustrated by a pyramid composed of escalating enforcement strategies. Sanctions are supposed to anticipate compliance. However, actual coercion is only seen as a means of last resort. The mere awareness of the regulator's willingness to escalate constitutes a tool to retain most activity at the base of the pyramid. For the explanatory comparison to make sense, it is useful to think about regulation in a broad sense. Parker and Braithwaite's description, for instance, extends beyond enforcement and implementation. Thus, they remark, 'much regulation is accomplished without recourse to rules of any kind. It is secured by organizing incentives to steer business behaviour, by moral suasion and by shaming. On this broadest view, regulation means influencing the flow of events'.[20] Curtin argues that regulation in this sense is closer to governance than to government.[21]

The Commission's limited powers compel it to negotiate with member states rather than confronting them with rigid demands on how to implement, apply, and enforce EU law. This point overlaps with a central assumption underpinning responsive regulation. Notably, it assumes that regulatees faced with only one deterrence option are more likely to be in opposition.[22] Responsive regulation furthermore presupposes that an approach founded on punishment risks undermining a cooperative position, when it is motivated by a sense of responsibility.[23]

[20] C Parker and J Braithwaite, 'Regulation' in P Cane and M Tushnet (eds.), *The Oxford Handbook of Legal Studies* (Oxford University Press, 2003), 119.

[21] D Curtin, 'Mind the Gap: the Evolving EU Executive and the Constitution' in W Devroe and D Droshout (eds.), *Third Walter van Gerven Lecture* (Europa Law Publishing, 2004), 11.

[22] I Ayres and J Braithwaite, *Responsive Regulation: Transcending the Deregulation Debate* (Oxford University Press, 1992), 37.

[23] I Ayres and J Braithwaite, *Responsive Regulation: Transcending the Deregulation Debate* (Oxford University Press, 1992), 19.

The methodology is suitable to deal with the inherent flexibility of most EU law, which was discussed in chapter one. Notably, it was argued, this flexibility is a consequence of the political relationship between the EU and the member states and it goes beyond legal ambiguity. Such politically rooted flexibility is not optimally enforced in a command-based manner. By contrast, the Commission's general powers of enforcement correspond to this procedural and institutional flexibility. The general EU infringement procedure enables it to act in response to various degrees of conflict and to engage in a responsive process towards compliance.

In its structure, the governance-mode of responsive regulation resembles some of the enforcement theories mentioned in chapter one, including the 'gradual turning the screw' variant of coercive diplomacy;[24] Brunée's theory of a 'persuasive continuum';[25] Audretsch's 'enforcement ladder';[26] and the combinations of managerial and enforcement types of interaction discussed by Tallberg.[27] The logic of responsive regulation also displays some likeness to the remote, yet imperative instrumentality Hobbes ascribes to power. Thus, Kratochwil explains, Hobbes is 'more interested in the latent presence of the sovereign, mediated by the establishment of the common meanings of words, and appropriate beliefs . . . than in coercion and its instruments'.[28] Similarly, international compliance theories that are primarily based on normative juxtaposition do not necessarily refute the role of coercive processes as facilitators of normative convergence.[29]

In his study on compliance with judgments of the Court of Justice, Beach maintains that pecuniary sanctions play an insignificant role in relation to compliance with EU law. Moreover, it cannot account for the high degree of rule-following by the member state governments. Beach therefore

[24] See AL George, *Forceful Persuasion: Coercive Diplomacy as an Alternative to War* (United States Institute of Peace Press, 1991), 9.

[25] J Brunée, 'Fine Balance: Facilitation and Enforcement in the Design of a Compliance Regime for the Kyoto Protocol' (2000) *Tulane Environmental Law Journal* 13, 223–70.

[26] HAH Audretsch, *Supervision in European Community Law* (Elsevier Science Publishers BV, 1986).

[27] J Tallberg, *European Governance and Supranational Institutions—Making States Comply* (Routledge, 2003), 7. As mentioned in chapter four, Tallberg too has pointed out the structural similarities with responsive regulation.

[28] FV Kratochwil, *Rules, Norms, and Decisions: On the Conditions of Practical and Legal Reasoning in International Relations and Domestic Affairs* (Cambridge University Press, 1989), 114.

[29] B Simmons, 'Compliance with International Agreements' (1998) *Annual Review of Political Science* 75–93, 77.

bridges instrumental and normative models of compliance.[30] In 2009, the Commission initiated a record 99 cases against repetitive infringements. However, it only made two second referrals to the Court of Justice under Article 260 TFEU and in 2008 it made no referrals.[31] Wennerås notes in this regard that 'several aspects of the jurisprudence still suggest a lack of enthusiasm on the part of the Commission and the Court to make effective use of Article 260(2) TFEU'.[32]

The Commission is constrained in its choice of method when exercising its enforcement powers. Significantly, in order for sanctions to remain effective they need to be exercised in a politically legitimate manner. Thus, even if the infringement procedure is dynamic and allows for variations in approach and intensity, there are legal and normative limits on the Commission's ability to pursue coercive enforcement. What the Commission can do as guardian (and also during the law-making and in comitology phases) is to rely on substantive argumentation and provide assistance. Moreover, it can hold member states politically accountable to their obligation to cooperate sincerely. When this fails, chapter three argued, sanctions and in particular the *threat* of sanctions, sustain managerial processes of dialogue. Actual coercion constitutes a means of last resort. To answer the question posed in the introductory chapter: amending the Commission's general powers of enforcement along the lines of Article 88 ECSC is not tenable at this point in time. At least it would imply a fundamental change of the manner in which EU law is enforced and the role of the Commission.

Chapters two, five, and six examined a number of powers and procedures other than the general EU infringement procedure. Chapter five examined

[30] D Beach, 'Why Governments Comply: An Integrative Compliance Model that Bridges the Gap between Instrumental and Normative Models of Compliance' (2005) *Journal of European Public Policy* 12:1, 1–30. Beach develops an 'integrative compliance model' and explains 'cases of governmental compliance that neither purely instrumentalist nor purely normative models are able to do'. In his conclusions, the author notes that work still remains to be done on 'detailing the conditions for the relative strength of normative and instrumental factors'.

[31] Commission, '*27th Annual Report on Monitoring the Application of EU Law*', COM 2010/538, 3. As discussed in chapter two, both political scientists and lawyers link non-compliance and repetitive infringements to capacity problems. The Commission likewise emphasized this dimension during the Maastricht IGS, thus questioning the effectiveness of sanctions. However, as mentioned in chapter three, Commission has later argued that sanctions have a more general dissuasive effect and thus ability to increase the general efficacy of the general EU infringement procedure.

[32] P Wennerås, 'Sanctions against Member States under Article 260 TFEU: Alive, but Not Kicking?' (2012) *Common Market Law review* 49, 145–76, 145.

a range of norm-setting and executive implementation powers attributed to the Commission. They do not *de jure* constitute enforcement powers. However, it was argued, they display functional overlap with enforcement powers. The Commission's powers managing EU resources, including the Structural Funds, resemble the High Authority's powers under Article 88 ECSC. Notably, the Commission makes binding compliance assessments. In addition, if a member state fails to comply with the conditions for funding this will usually entail loss of privileges. However, the majority of the types of powers discussed in chapter five are typically subject to oversight by the 'EU legislator' or the member states.[33] Thus, to varying degrees they too imply collective discussions, whilst it falls to the Commission to negotiate in the general interest of the EU. Chapter two discussed Commission initiatives to resolve non-compliance in practical ways, including in particular EU Pilot. Chapter six discussed the emergence of non-binding peer-review procedures likewise established by the Commission to facilitate correct member states implementation. These different types of lower-level institutional practice dealing with compliance retain activity at the bottom of the enforcement pyramid, figuratively speaking. This is in accordance with Article 4 TEU and the principle of proportionality. Thus, as opposed to Article 88 ECSC, they are consonant with the flexible and deliberative tradition of enforcement in the EU and the central role attributed to the member states in this regard.

[33] Articles 290 and 291 TFEU.

BIBLIOGRAPHY

Abbott, Kenneth W, Keohane, Robert O, Moravcsik, Andrew, Slaughter, Anne-Marie, and Snidal, Duncan, 'The Concept of Legalization' (2000) *International Organization* 54:3, 401–19

Alter, Karen, 'Who are the "Masters of the Treaty?": European Governments and the European Court of Justice' (1998) *International Organization* 52:1, 121–47

——, *Establishing the Supremacy of European Law* (Oxford: Oxford University Press, 2001)

——, Memorandum to the UK Parliament House of Lords, Select Committee on European Union, 26 November 2003

Amphoux, Jean, 'Recours en constatation des manquements des États, les traités CEE et Euratom' (1969) *Droit des Communautés Européennes*, 1042–88

Andersen, Stine, 'The Functional Overlap of Enforcement and Implementation Tools' (2007) *Croatian Yearbook of European Law and Policy* 3

——, 'Procedural Overview and Substantive Comments on Articles 226 and 228 EC' (2008) *Yearbook of European Law* 27

Audretsch, HAH, *Supervision in European Community Law* (Amsterdam: Elsevier Science Publishers BV, 1986)

Ayres, Ian, and Braithwaite, John, *Responsive Regulation: Transcending the Deregulation Debate* (Oxford: Oxford University Press, 1992)

Barav, Ami, 'Failure of Member States to Fulfil their Obligations under Community Law' (1975) *Common Market Law Review* 12, 369–83

Bausili, BV, 'Rethinking the Methods of Dividing and Exercising Powers in the EU: Reforming Subsidiarity and National Parliaments' *Jean Monnet Working Paper* 2000/9

Beach, Derek, 'Why Governments Comply: An Integrative Compliance Model that Bridges the Gap between Instrumental and Normative Models of Compliance' (2005) *Journal of European Public Policy* 12:1, 1–30

Bebr, Gerhard, *Judicial Control of the European Communities* (London: Stevens & Sons Limited, 1962)

Biering, Peter, 'Has the Court of Justice Ever Taken Integration Too Far?' in Koch, H, Hagel-Sørensen, K, Haltern, U, and Weiler, JHH (eds.), *Europe: The New Legal Realism: Essays in Honour of Hjalte Rasmussen* (3rd edn, Copenhagen: Djøf, 2011)

Borzsák, Levente, 'Punishing Member States or Influencing their Behaviour or Iudex (non) Calculat?' (2001) *Journal of European Law* 13, 235–62

——, *The Impact of Environmental Concerns on the Public Enforcement Mechanism under EU* (Alphen aan den Rijn: Wolters Kluwer, 2011)

Börzel, Tanja, 'Non-compliance in the European Union: Pathology or Statistical Artefact?' (2001) *Journal of European Public Policy* 8:5, 803–24

——, 'Guarding the Treaty. The Compliance Strategies of the Commission' in Börzel, Tanja A and Cichowski, Rachel A (eds.), *State of the European Union Volume 6: Law Politics and Society* (Oxford: Oxford University Press, 2003)

——, Hofmann, Tobias, and Panke, Diana, 'Caving in or sitting it out? Longitudinal patterns of non-compliance in the European Union' (2011) *Journal of European Public Policy* 1, 1–8

——,—— and ——, and Sprungk, Carina, 'Obstinate and Inefficient: Why Member States Do Not Comply with European Law' (2010) *Comparative Political Studies* 43:11, 1363–90

Bradford, William C, 'In the Minds of Men: A Theory of Compliance with the Laws of War' *ExpressO Preprint Series Working Paper* 2004/290

——, 'International Legal Compliance: Surveying the Discipline' *ExpressO Preprint Series Working Paper* 2004/331

Braithwaite, John, *Restorative and Responsive Justice for the Whole of Law*, Presentation to the Quinnipiac-Yale Dispute Resolution Workshop, New Haven, 29 April 2002

Broberg, Morten and Fenger, Niels, *Preliminary References to the Court of Justice* (Oxford: Oxford University Press, 2010)

Brosset, Estelle, 'The Prior Authorisation Procedure Adopted for the Deliberate Release into the Environment of Genetically Modified Organisms: The Complexities of Balancing Community and National Competences' (2004) *European Law Journal* 10:5, 555–79

Brunée, Jutta, 'Fine Balance: Facilitation and Enforcement in the Design of a Compliance Regime for the Kyoto Protocol' (2000) *Tulane Environmental Law Journal* 13

de Búrca, Gráinne, 'Sovereignty and the Supremacy Doctrine' in Walker, Neil (ed.) *Sovereignty in Transition* (Oxford: Hart Publishing, 2003)

——, 'The Constitutional Challenge of New Governance in the European Union' (2003) *European Law Review* 28:6, 814–39

——, 'Beyond the Charter: How Enlargement has Enlarged the Human Rights Policy of the European Union' (2004) *Fordham International Law Journal* 27, 679–714

Bulterman, MK and Kuijer, M (eds.), *Compliance with Judgments of International Courts* (The Hague: Martinus Nijhoff Publishers, 1996)

Burley, Anne-Marie and Mattli, Walter, 'Europe before the Court: A Political theory of Legal Integration' (1993) *International Organization* 47:1, 41–76

Carter, Kim, 'New Crimes against Peace? The Application of International Humanitarian Law Compliance and Enforcement' in Canadian Council on International Law and The Markland Group (eds.), *Treaty Compliance: Some Concerns and Remedies* (London: Kluwer Law International, 1998)

Chayes, Abram and Chayes, Antonia Handler, *The New Sovereignty: Compliance with International Regulatory Agreements* (Cambridge, MA: Harvard University Press, 1995)

Checkel, Jeffrey T, 'Why Comply? Constructivism, Social Norms and the Study of International Institutions' *ARENA Working Paper* 99/24

——, 'Compliance and Conditionality' *ARENA Working Paper* 00/18

Cini, Michelle, 'Implementation' in Cini, M (ed.), *European Union Politics* (Oxford: Oxford University Press, 2003)

Conant, Lisa, *Justice Contained: Law and Politics in the European Union* (Ithaca: Cornell University Press, 2002)

Craig, Paul, 'Once Upon a Time in the West: Direct Effect and the Federalisation of EEC Law' (1992) *Oxford Journal of Legal Studies* 12, 453–79

——, 'The Role of the European Parliament under the Lisbon Treaty' in Griller, Stefan and Ziller, Jacques (eds.), *The Lisbon Treaty: EU Constitutionalism without a Constitutional Treaty?* (Vienna: Springer, 2008)

——, 'Delegated Acts, Implementing Acts and the New Comitology Regulation' (2011) *European Law Review* 36:5, 671–87

——and de Búrca, Gráinne, *EU Law, Text, Cases and Materials* (3rd edn, Oxford: Oxford University Press, 2003)

Curtin, Deirdre, 'Mind the Gap: the Evolving EU Executive and the Constitution' in Devroe, W and Droshout, D (eds.), *Third Walter van Gerven Lecture* (Groningen: Europa Law Publishing, 2004)

Dashwood, Alan, Inaugural lecture at Cambridge University, 13 November 1995, on 'The Limits of European Community Powers' (1996) *European Law Review* 21, 113–28

——, 'The Relationship between the Member States and the European Union/ European Community' (2004) *Common Market Law Review* 41, 355–81

——, and White, Robin 'Enforcement Actions under Articles 169 and 170 EEC' (1989) *European Law Review* 14, 388–412

Downs, George W, Rocke, David, and Barsoom, Peter N, 'Is the Good News about Compliance Good News for Cooperation?' (1996) *International Organization* 50, 379–406

——and Jones, Michael A, 'Reputation, Compliance and International Law' (2002) *Journal of Legal Studies* 31:1, 95–114

Drezner, Daniel W, 'The Hidden Hand of Economic Coercion' (2003) *International Organization* 57:3, 643–59

Ehlermann, C-D, 'The Internal Market following the Single European Act' (1987) *Common Market Law Review* 24

EIPA, *Delegated & Implementing Acts—The New Comitology* (4th edn, EIPA Essential Guide, 2011)

Elgström, Ole and Jönsson, Christer, 'Negotiations in the EU: Bargaining or Problem-Solving?' (2000) *Journal of European Public Policy* 7:5, 684–704

Evans, A, 'The Enforcement Procedure of Article 169 EC: Commission Discretion' (1979) *European Law Review* 4:6, 442–56

Fabio, Udo Di, 'Some Remarks on the Allocation of Competences between the European Union and its Member States' (2002) *Common Market Law Review* 39:6, 1289–301

Falkner, Gerda (ed.), *The EU's Decision Traps: Comparing Policies* (Oxford: Oxford University Press, 2011)

——,Treib, Oliver, Hartlapp, Miriam, and Leiber, Simone, *Complying with Europe: EU Harmonisation and Soft Law in the Member States* (Cambridge: Cambridge University Press, 2005)

——, Hartlapp, Miriam, Leiber, Simone, and Treib, Oliver, 'In Search of the Worlds of Compliance: Promises and Pitfalls of Quantitative Testing' *IHS Political Science Series* Paper No 113, July 2007

——and Treib, Oliver, 'Three Worlds of Compliance or Four? The EU-15 Compared to New Member States' (2008) *Journal of Common Market Studies* 46:2, 293–313

Fisher, Roger, *Improving Compliance with International Law* (Charlottesville: University Press of Virginia, 1981)

——and Ury, William, *Getting to Yes: Negotiating an Agreement without Giving In* (London: Random House Business Books, 1981)

Galera, Susana, 'The EU's first pillar—Constitutional basis' in Galera, Susana (ed.), *Judicial review: a comparative analysis inside the European legal system* (Council of Europe, 2010)

Garner, James W, 'French Administrative Law' (1924) *Yale Law Journal* 33, 597–627

Garrett, Geoffrey, 'Competition Policy' in Wallace, Helen and Wallace, William (eds.), *Policy-Making in the European Union* (Oxford: Oxford University Press, 2000)

George, Alexander L, *Forceful Persuasion: Coercive Diplomacy as an Alternative to War* (Washington DC: United States Institute of Peace Press, 1991)

van Gerven, Walter and Zuleeg, Manfred, 'Einführung in die Problemstellung' in van Gerven, Walter (ed.), *Remedies and Sanctions for the Enforcement of European Community Law* (Cologne: Bundesanzeiger Verlagsgesellschaft, 1996)

Granger, Marie Pierre, 'When Governments go to Luxembourg: the Influence of Governments on the Court of Justice' (2004) *European Law Review* 29, 3–31

Gunningham, Neil and Johnstone, Richard, *Regulating Workplace Safety: Systems and Sanction* (Oxford: Oxford University Press, 1999)

Gutman, K, 'The Evolution of the Action for Damages against the European Union and Its Place in the System of Judicial Protection' (2011) *Common Market Law Review* 48:3, 695–750

Haas, Peter M 'Compliance with EU Directives: Insights from International Relations and Comparative Politics' (1998) *Journal of European Policy* 5:1, 17–37

Hækkerup, Nick, *Controls and Sanctions in the EU Law* (Copenhagen: DJOEF Publishing, 2001)

Haibach, Georg, 'Separation and Delegation of Legislative Powers: A Comparative Analysis' in Andenas, Mads and Türk, Alexander (eds.), *Delegated Legislation and the Role of Committees in the EC* (London: Kluwer Law International, 2000)

Hartlapp, Miriam and Falkner, Gerda, 'Problems of Operationalization and Data in EU Compliance Research' (2009) *European Union Politics* 10:2, 281–304

Hartley, Trevor C, *Constitutional Problems of the European Union* (Oxford: Hart, 1999)

Hayes-Renshaw, Fiona, van Aken, Wim, and Wallace, Helen, 'When and Why the Council of Ministers of the EU Votes Explicitly' *EUI Working Paper* 2005/25

Hedemann-Robinson, Martin, *Enforcement of European Union Environmental Law: Legal Issues and Challenges* (London: Routledge-Cavendish, 2006)

——, 'Article 228(2) EC and the Enforcement of EC Environmental Law: A Case of Environmental Justice Delayed and Denied? An Analysis of Recent Legal Developments' (2006) *European Environmental Law Review* 15:11, 312–42

Helfer, Laurence, and Slaughter, Anne-Marie, 'Why States Create International Tribunals: A Response to Professors Posner and Yoo' (2005) *California Law Review* 93

House of Lords Select Committee, Session 2007–08, Tenth Report, printed 26 February 2008

Hufbauer, Gary and Schott, Jeffrey, *Economic Sanctions Reconsidered: History and Current Policy* (Washington DC: Institute for International Economics, 1990)

Ibáñez, Alberto J Gil, 'A Deeper Insight into Article 169' *Harvard Jean Monnet Working Paper* 11/98

——, 'Commission Tools For The Supervision and Enforcement Of EC Law Other Than Article 169 EC Treaty—An Attempt at Systematization' *Harvard Jean Monnet Working Paper* 12/98

——, *The Administrative Supervision and Enforcement of EC Law* (Oxford: Hart, 1999)

——, 'Exceptions to Article 226: Alternative Administrative Procedures and the Pursuit of Member States' (2000) *European Law Journal* 6:2, 148–76

Iankova, Elena and Katzenstein, P, 'European Enlargement and Institutional Hypocrisy' in Börzel, Tanja and Cichowski, Rachel (eds.), *State of the European Union Volume 6: Law Politics and Society* (Oxford: Oxford University Press, 2003)

Jensen, Christian B, 'Implementing Europe: A Question of Oversight' (2007) *European Union Politics* 8:4, 451–77

Joerges, Christian, 'Compliance Research in Legal Perspectives' in Zürn, Michael and Joerges, Christian (eds.), *Law and Governance in Postnational Europe, Compliance Beyond the Nation-State* (Cambridge: Cambridge University Press, 2004)

——and Neyer, Jürgen, 'From Intergovernmental Bargaining to Deliberative Political Processes: The Constitutionalisation of Comitology (1997) *European Law Journal* 3:3, 273–99

——and Vos, Ellen, 'Structures of Transnational Governance and Their Legitimacy' in Vervaele JAE (ed.), *Compliance and Enforcement of European Community Law* (The Hague: Kluwer Law International, 1999)

Jönsson, Christer, 'Diplomacy, Bargaining and Negotiation' in Carlsnaes, Walter, Risse, Thomas, and Simmons, Beth A (eds.), *Handbook of International Relations* (London: SAGE, 2002)

Kadelbach, Stefan, 'Administrative Law' in Joerges, Christian and Dehousse, Renaud (eds.), *Good Governance in Europe's Integrated Market* (Oxford: Oxford University Press, 2002)

Kapteyn, Paul Joan Gorge, Gormley, Laurence W, and van Themaat Verloren, Pieter, *Introduction to the Law of the European Communities after the Coming into Force of the Single European Act* (Deventer: Kluwer Law International, 1989)

Katzenstein, Peter, Keohane, Robert, and Krasner, Stephen, 'International Organization and the Study of World Politics' (1998) *International Organization* 52, 645–85

Keohane, Robert, Moravcsik, Andrew, and Slaughter, Anne-Marie, 'Legalized Dispute Resolution: Interstate and Transnational' (2000) *International Organization* 54, 457–88

Kilbey, Ian, 'Financial Penalties under Article 228(2)EC: Excessive Complexity?' (2007) *Common Market Law Review* 44, 743–59

——, 'The Interpretation of Article 260 TFEU (ex 228 EC)' (2010) *European Law Review* 35:3, 370–86

Kirgis, Frederic L *Prior Consultation in International Law* (Charlottesville, University Press of Virginia, 1983)

Klabbers, Jan, *An Introduction to International Institutional Law* (Cambridge: Cambridge University Press, 2002)

Koh, Harold, 'Why Do Nations Obey International Law? (1997) *Yale Law Journal* 106, 2599–659

Kratochwil, Friedrich V, *Rules, Norms, and Decisions: On the Conditions of Practical and Legal Reasoning in International Relations and Domestic Affairs* (Cambridge: Cambridge University Press, 1989)

Kunz, JL, 'Supra-National Organs' (Editorial Comments) (1952) *American Journal of International Law* 46:4, 690–8

Lasok, KPE and Lasok, D, *Law and Institutions of the European Union* (7th edn, London: Butterworth, 2001)

Lauwaars, RH, *Lawfulness and Legal Force of Community Decisions: Some Considerations on the Binding Decisions Which the Council and the Commission can Take by Virtue of the Treaty Establishing the European Economic Community* (Leiden: AW Sijthoff, 1973)

Lefevre, Silvere, 'Interpretative Communications and the Implementation of Community Law at National Level' (2004) *European Law Review* 29:6, 808–22

Levy, Mark A, Young, Oran O, and Zürn, Michael, 'The Study of International Regimes' (1995) *European Journal of International Relations* 1:3, 267–330

Lenaerts, Koen, 'Some Reflections on the Separation of Powers in the European Union' (1991) *Common Market Law Review* 28, 11–35

——, 'The Rule of Law and the Coherence of the Judicial System of the European Union' (2007) *Common Market Law Review* 44, 1636–59

——and Arts, Dirk, 'Action for Infringement of Community Law by a Member State' in Lenaerts, Koen, Arts, Dirk, and Bray, Robert (eds.), *Procedural Law of the European Union* (London: Sweet & Maxwell, 1999)

——and Verhoeven, Amaryllis, 'Institutional Balance as a Guarantee for Democracy in EU Governance' in Joerges, Christian and Dehousse, Renaud (eds.), *Good Governance in Europe's Integrated Market* (Oxford: Oxford University Press, 2002)

Levasseur, Alain A and Scott, Richard E, *The Law of the European Union—A New Constitutional Order* (Durham, NC: Carolina Academic Press, 2001)

Macrory, Richard, *Regulation, Enforcement and Governance in Environmental Law* (London: Cameron May Ltd, 2008)

Maduro, Miguel Poiares, 'Contrapunctual Law: Europe's Constitutional Pluralism in Action' in Walker, Neil (ed.), *Sovereignty in Transition* (Oxford: Hart Publishing, 2003)

Majone, Giandomenico, *Dilemmas of European Integration: The Ambiguities and Pitfalls of Integration by Stealth* (Oxford: Oxford University Press, 2005)

Mason, Henry L, *The European Coal and Steel Community: Experiment in Supranationalism* (The Hague: Martinus Nijhoff, 1955)

Mayntz, Renate, 'The State and Civil Society in Modern Governance', Paper presented at the VI Congreso Internacional del CLAD, 2002

McGowan, Francis, 'Competition Policy' in Wallace, Helen and Wallace, William (eds.), *Policy-Making in the European Union* (Oxford: Oxford University Press, 2000)

Mead, Philip, 'The Obligation to Apply European Law: Is Duke Dead?' (1991) *European Law Review* 16, 490–501

Mendrinou, Maria, 'Non-Compliance and the European Commission's Role in Integration' (1996) *Journal of European Public Policy* 3:1, 1–22

Merrills, JG, *International Dispute Settlement* (2nd edn, Grotius Publications Ltd, 1991)

Merry, Henry J, *Five-Branch Government: The Full Measure of Constitutional Checks and Balances* (Illinois: University of Illinois Press, 1980)

Müller, Harald, 'Arguing, Bargaining and All That: Communicative Action, Rationalist Theory and the Logic of Appropriateness in International Relations' (2004) *European Journal of International Relations* 10:3, 395–435

Munoz, Rodolphe, 'Judicial Remedies' in Glockler, G et al (eds.), *Guide to EU Policies* (London: Blackstone Press, 1998), 69–86

——, 'The Monitoring of the Application of Community Law: A Need to Improve the Current Tools and an Obligation to Innovate' (2006) *Yearbook of European Law* 25:1, 395–428

Parker, Christine and Braithwaite, John, 'Regulation' in Cane, Peter and Tushnet, Mark (eds.), *The Oxford Handbook of Legal Studies* (Oxford: Oxford University Press, 2003)

Pescatore, P, 'La Personnalité internationale de la Communauté' in *Les Relations Exterieures de la Communauté Unifiée* (Actes du 3ieme colloque sur la fusion des Communauté européennes, Liège, octobre 1967) (Université de Liège, 1969), 77–117

Pierson, Paul, 'The Path to European Integration: A Historical Institutionalist Analysis' (1996) *Comparative Political Studies* 29:2, 123–63

Pollack, Mark A, *The Engines of European Integration. Delegation, Agency, and Agenda Setting in the EU* (Oxford: Oxford University Press, 2003)

Prete, Luca and Smulders, Ben, 'The Coming of Age of Infringement Proceedings' (2010) *Common Market Law Review* 47:1, 9–61

Rasmussen, Hjalte, *Domstolen i EF* (Copenhagen, Juristforbundets Forlag, 1975)

——, *EU-Ret i Kontekst* (Gad Jura, 1995)

Raustiale, Kal and Slaughter, Anne-Marie, 'International Law, International Relations and Compliance' in Carlsnaes, Walter, Risse, Thomas, and Simmons, Beth A (eds.), *Handbook of International Relations* (London: SAGE, 2002)

Rawlings, Richard, 'Engaged Elites: Citizen Action and Institutional Attitudes' in Kilpatrick, Claire, Novitz, Tonia, and Skidmore, Paul (eds.), *Commission Enforcement, the Future of Remedies in Europe* (Oxford: Hart Publishing, 2000)

——and Harlow, Carol, 'Accountability and Law Enforcement: the Centralised EU Infringement Procedure' (2006) *European Law Review* 31, 447–75

Rijn, Thomas van, 'Powers of the Commission' in Curtin, D and Heukels, T (eds.), *Institutional Dynamics of European Integration. Essays in Honour of Henry G. Schermers. Volume II* (The Hague: Martinus Nijhoff Publishers, 1994)

Sabel, Charles F, and Zeitlin, Jonathan, 'Learning from Difference: The New Architecture of Experimentalist Governance in the European Union' Paper prepared for presentation at the ARENA seminar, Centre for European Studies, University of Oslo, 13 June 2006

Sasse, Christoph, 'The Common Market: Between International and Municipal Law' (1965–66) *The Yale Law Journal* 75, 695–753

Shaffer, CG, and Pollack, MA, 'Regulating Between National Fears and Global Disciplines: Agricultural Biotechnology in the EU' (2004) *Jean Monnet Working Paper* 10

Scharpf, Fritz W, 'The Joint Decision Trap: Lessons from German Federalism and European Integration' (1988) *Public Administration* 66, 239–78

Schlacke, Sabine, 'Centralization and Europeanization of Administrative Implementation: Product Safety Legislation' in Andenas, Mads and Türk, Alexander (eds.), *Delegated Legislation and the Role of Committees in the EC* (The Hague: Kluwer Law International, 2000)

Schmidt, Susanne K, 'Only an Agenda Setter? The European Commission's Power over the Council of Ministers' (2000) *European Union Politics* 1:1, 37–61

Schockweiler, F.A., 'La notion de détournement de pouvoir en droit communautaire' (1990) *Actualité juridique de droit administratif* 6

Schrauwen, Annette, 'Fishery, waste management and persistent and general failure to fulfill control obligations: The role of lump sums and penalty payments in enforcement actions under Community law' (2006) *Journal of Environmental Law* 18:2, 289–300

Schuppert, Gunnar Folke, 'Governance im Spiegel der Wissenschaftsdisziplin' in Schuppert, Gunnar Folke (ed.), *Governance-Forschung. Vergewisserung über Stand und Entwicklungslinien*, (Baden-Baden: Nomos, 2005), 371–469

Schutter, Olivier De, 'The Role of Evaluation in Experimentalist Governance: Learning by Monitoring in the Establishment of the Area of Freedom, Security, and Justice' in Sabel, CF and Zeitlin, J (eds.), *Experimentalist Governance in the European Union. Towards a New Architecture* (Oxford: Oxford University Press, 2010)

Schütze, Robert, 'Organized Change towards an "Ever Closer Union": Article 308 EC and the Limits to the Community's Legislative Competence' (2003) *Yearbook of European Law* 22, 79–115

——, 'Sharpening the Separation of Powers through a Hierarchy of Norms. Reflections on the Draft Treaty's regime for legislative and executive Law-making *EIPA Working Paper* 2005/W/01 (2005)

——, *From Dual to Cooperative Federalism—The Changing Structure of European Law* (Oxford: Oxford University Press, 2009)

——, '"Delegated" Legislation in the (new) European Union: A Constitutional Analysis' (2011) *The Modern Law Review* 74, 661–93

Schwebel, SM, 'Commentary in the European Communities' in Bulterman, MK and Kuijer, M (eds.), *Compliance with Judgments of International Courts* (The Hague: Martinus Nijhoff Publishers, 1996)

Scott, Joanne, Flexibility in the Implementation of EC Environmental Law (2000) *Yearbook of European Environmental Law* 1 (Oxford: Oxford University Press)

——, 'In Legal Limbo: Post-Legislative Guidance as a Challenge for European Administrative Law' (2011) *Common Market Law Review* 48:2, 329–56

Simmons, Beth, 'Compliance with International Agreements' (1998) *Annual Review of Political Science* 75–93

Slaughter, Anne-Marie, Sweet, Alec Stone, and Weiler, JHH (eds.), *The European Court and National Courts—Doctrine and Jurisprudence: Legal Change in its Social* Context (Oxford: Hart Publishing, 1998)

Smith, Melanie, 'Enforcement, Monitoring, Verification, Outsourcing: The Decline and Decline of the Infringement Process' (2008) *European Law Review* 33:6, 777–802

——, *Centralised Enforcement, Legitimacy and Good Governance in the EU* (London: Routledge Cavendish, 2009)

——, 'Inter-institutional Dialogue and the Establishment of Enforcement Norms: A Decade of Financial Penalties under Article 228 EC (now Article 260 TFEU)' (2010) *European Public Law* 16:4, 547–70

Snyder, Francis, 'The Effectiveness of European Community Law. Institutions, Processes, Tools and Techniques' (1993) *Modern Law Review* 56, 19–54

Steunenberg, Bernard, 'Implementation of EU directives. Is big brother watching? Commission oversight of the national' (2010) *European Union Politics* 11:3, 359–80

Sutherland, Peter *The Internal Market after 1992: Meeting the Challenge.* Report presented to the Commission by the High Level Group on the functioning of the Internal Market (1992) ('Sutherland Report')

Tallberg, Jonas, 'Supranational Influence in EU Enforcement: the ECJ and the Principle of State Liability' (2000) *Journal of European Public Policy* 7:1, 104–21

——, 'Paths to Compliance: Enforcement, Management, and the European Union' (2002) *International Organization* 56:3, 609–43

——, *European Governance and Supranational Institutions—Making states Comply* (London: Routledge, 2003)

——and Jönsson, Christer, 'Compliance and Post-Agreement Bargaining' (1998) *European Journal of International Relations* 4:4, 371–408

——and ——, 'Compliance Bargaining in the European Union', Paper prepared at ECSA's 2001 International Conference (Madison, Wisconsin, 31 May–2 June 2001)

Tesauro, Giuseppe, 'Remedies for Infringement of Community Law by Member States' in van Gerwen, Walter and Zuleeg, Manfred (eds.), *Sanktionen als Mittel zur Durchsetzung des Gemeinschaftsrechts* (Cologne: Bundesanzeiger, 1996)

Teske, Horst, 'Die Sanktion von Vertragsverstoessen im Gemeinschaftsrecht' (1992) *Europarecht* 3, 265–86

Theodossiou, Maria A, 'An Analysis of the recent response of the Community to non-compliance with Court of Justice judgments: Article 228(2) E.C.' (2002) *European Law Review* 27, 25–46

Thomson, Robert, 'Opposition through the Back Door in the Transposition of EU Directives' (2010) *European Union Politics* 11:4, 577–96

——, Torenvlied, René, and Arregui, Javier, 'The Paradox of Compliance: Infringements and Delays in Transposing European Union Directives' (2007) *British Journal of Political Science* 37: 4, 685–709

Timmermans, CWA, 'Judicial Protection against Member States' in Curtin, D and Heukels, T (eds.), *Institutional Dynamics of European Integration. Essays in Honour of Henry G. Schermers. Volume II* (The Hague: Martinus Nijhoff Publishers, 1994)

——, 'Commentary' in Bulterman, MK and Kuijer, M (eds.), *Compliance with Judgments of International Courts* (The Hague: Martinus Nijhoff Publishers, 1996)

——, 'The Infringement Procedure and Judicial Errors' in de Zwaan, Jaap W et al (eds.), *The European Union: An Ongoing Process of Integration* (The Hague: TMC Asser Press, 2004)

Tsebelis, George and Garrett, Geoffrey, 'The Institutional Foundations of Intergovernmentalism and Supranationalism in the European Union' (2001) *International Organization* 55:2, 357–90

Usher, John, *EC Institutions and Legislation* (London: Longman, 1998)

Walker, Neil (ed.), *Sovereignty in Transition* (Oxford: Hart Publishing, 2003)

Weatherill, Stephen, 'Compulsory Notification of Draft Technical Regulations: The Contribution of Directive 83/189 to the Management of the Internal Market' (1996) *Yearbook of European Law* 16:1

Weatherill, Stephen, *Law and Integration in the European Union* (Oxford: Oxford University Press, 1995)

——, 'Addressing Problems of International Implementation in EC Law' in Kilpatrick, Claire, Novitz, Tonia, and Skidmore, Paul (eds.), *The Future of Remedies in Europe* (Oxford: Hart Publishing, 2000)

Weiler, JHH, 'The Community System: the Dual Character of Supranationalism' (1981) *Yearbook of European Law* 1, 267–306

——, 'The Transformation of Europe' (1994) *The Yale Law Journal* 100, 2405–83

——and Haltern, UR 'The Autonomy of the Community Legal Order—Through the Looking Glass' (1996) *Harvard International Law Journal* 37:2, 411–48

Weintraub, Sidney (ed.), *Economic Coercion and US Foreign Policy: Implications of Case Studies from the Johnson Administration* (Boulder, CO: Westview Press, 1982)

Wennerås, Pål, 'A New Dawn for Commission Enforcement under Articles 226 and 228 EC: General and Persistent (GAP) Infringements, Lump Sums and Penalty Payments' (2006) *Common Market Law Review* 43:1, 31–62

——, *The Enforcement of EC Environmental Law* (Oxford: Oxford University Press, 2007)

——, 'Sanctions against Member States under Article 260 TFEU: Alive, but not Kicking?' (2012) *Common Market Law Review* 49, 145–76

de Witte, Bruno, 'General Principles of European Community Law, Reports from a Conference in Malmö', 27–28 August 1999 in Bernitz, Ulf and Nergelius, Joakim (eds.), *Institutional Principles: A Special Category of General Principles of EC Law* (The Hague: Kluwer Law International, 2001)

——, 'Rules of Change in International Law: How Special is the European Community?' in Barnhoorn, LANM and Wellens, KC (eds.), *Diversity in Secondary Rules and the Unity of International Rules* (The Hague: Martijn Nijhoff Publishers, 2005)

——and de Búrca, Gráinne, 'The Delimitation of Powers Between the EU and its Member States' in Arnull, Anthony and Wincott, Daniel (eds.), *Accountability and Legitimacy in the European Union* (Oxford: Oxford University Press, 2002)

Woll, Cornelia, 'Transatlantic Relations as a Catalyst to European Integration: European Commission Activism in International aviation' *AICGS Policy Paper* (Washington DC: AICGS, 2003)

Young, Oran, *Compliance and Public Authority: A Theory with International Implications* (Baltimore: Johns Hopkins University Press, 1979)

Ziller, Jacques, 'Separation of Powers in the European Union's Intertwined System of Government—A Treaty Based Analysis for the Use of Political Scientists and Constitutional Lawyers' (2008) *Il Politico*, Vol LXXIII, No 3, 133–79

Zürn, Michael, 'Introduction: Law and Compliance at Different Levels' in Zürn, Michael and Joerges, Christian (eds.), *Law and Governance in Postnational Europe, Compliance Beyond the Nation-State* (Cambridge: Cambridge University Press, 2004)

——and Wolf, Dieter, 'European Law and International Regimes: The Features of Law beyond the Nation State' (1999) *European Law Journal* 5:3, 272–92

INDEX

Printed and bound by CPI Group (UK) Ltd, Croydon, CR0 4YY